Radicalism and Cultural Dislocation in Ethiopia, 1960–1974

Rochester Studies in African History and the Diaspora

Toyin Falola, Senior Editor
The Frances Higginbotham Nalle Centennial Professor in History
University of Texas at Austin

(ISSN: 1092–5228)

A complete list of titles in the Rochester Studies in African History and the Diaspora, in order of publication, may be found at the end of this book.

Radicalism and Cultural Dislocation in Ethiopia, 1960–1974

MESSAY KEBEDE

UNIVERSITY OF ROCHESTER PRESS

First published 2008

University of Rochester Press
668 Mt. Hope Avenue, Rochester, NY 14620, USA
www.urpress.com
and Boydell & Brewer Limited
PO Box 9, Woodbridge, Suffolk IP12 3DF, UK
www.boydellandbrewer.com

ISBN-13: 978–1–58046–291–4
ISBN-10: 1–58046–291–X

ISSN: 1092–5228

Library of Congress Cataloging-in-Publication Data

Kebede, Messay.
  Radicalism and cultural dislocation in Ethiopia, 1960–1974 / Messay Kebede.
      p. cm. — (Rochester studies in African history and the diaspora, ISSN 1092-5228 ; v. 36)
  Includes bibliographical references and index.
  ISBN 978-1-58046-291-4 (hardcover : alk. paper)
  1. Radicalism—Ethiopia—History—20th century. 2. Students—Ethiopia—Political activity—History—20th century. 3. Intellectuals—Ethiopia—Political activity—History—20th century. 4. Elite (Social sciences)—Ethiopia—History—20th century. 5. Communism—Ethiopia. I. Title.
  HN789.Z9R35 2008
  303.48′4—dc22
                                    2008019955

A catalogue record for this title is available from the British Library.

This publication is printed on acid-free paper.
Printed in the United States of America.

Contents

Preface

This book reflects my ongoing effort to understand the causes of Ethiopia's failure to become a prosperous and stable modern nation. As such, it continues, amplifies, and further validates the theoretical premises developed in my earlier book, *Survival and Modernization—Ethiopia's Enigmatic Present: A Philosophical Discourse*. It does so by focusing on the essential product of Emperor Haile Selassie's modernizing scheme, to wit, Ethiopia's educated elite. A complete picture of Ethiopia's failure to modernize requires an assessment of the basic instrument that the imperial regime forged to implement its modernizing goal. Without dealing with the question of whether the educated elite was an appropriate agent of renovation, the fiasco of Ethiopian modernization cannot be adequately explicated.

What could provide a better proof of inappropriateness than the undeniably negative role played thus far by the Ethiopian educated elite? No explanation of the country's continuous political crises and economic stagnation since the Revolution of 1974 is possible without examining the decisive role of its Western-educated elite. Admittedly, students and intellectuals spearheaded the uprising against the imperial regime; they were also instrumental in the radicalization of the military junta, known as the Derg, which seized power and ruled the country for 17 years. Intellectuals also launched the ethnic movements that brought down the Derg. The present rulers of Ethiopia are remnants of the Ethiopian student movement of the 1960s and early 1970s. In short, what happened in Ethiopia since the early 1970s is largely the handiwork of Ethiopians educated in modern schools.

Both the educated elite's leadership of the social protests against Haile Selassie and its decisive impact on the radicalization of the Derg attest to its crucial role. Without the birth and spread of political radicalism among students and intellectuals, the main outcome of which was the consecration of socialism as the legitimizing ideology of state power to the exclusion of all other ideologies, the social protests would not have been persistent nor would a committee like the Derg have seen the light of day. The prestige of modern education, the standing of Marxism as the dominant ideology of the time, students' multifarious and energizing participation in the civilian unrests, their vigorous defense of socialism as the right solution to Ethiopia's problems, the reputation they had acquired during their long and solitary struggle against Haile Selassie, all these factors combined to confer on the Ethiopian student movement a hegemonic standing. This hegemony, in turn, boosted the popularity of socialist ideology among civilian and military personnel. A proof of this is that the Derg's initial reason for arresting Haile Selassie and abolishing the monarchy was the need to respond to the pressure of students and intellectuals.

This study draws on results that a multitude of scholars gathered from the study of student movements in general and the Ethiopian student movement in particular and makes use of theoretical works on revolutionism and the causes of revolution. More yet, it is the product of direct observation, given that it has a tangible autobiographical aspect. Indeed, during the period in question, I too was a member of the educated elite, having for many years fallen under the spell of Marxism. I have thus been not only an eyewitness but also an active participant. The fact of my having been a participant in the generational uprising affords me the prerogative of an inside look. Even when some of my findings result from critical study of the vast literature dealing with the radicalization of students and the causes of revolutions, which I have contrasted with specific studies of the Ethiopian Revolution, these findings were constantly measured against insights drawn from my personal experience as both witness and actor.

Other primary sources of this study are the discussions I have had and the interviews I have conducted with many participants and leaders of the student movement. At times, I have sent questionnaires to certain influential leaders who, with the exception of Kiflu Tadesse and the late Makonnen Bishaw, were reluctant to put in writing what they were willing to discuss orally. I have supplemented this dearth of recorded testimonies with a thorough study of student publications of the time. Through the cooperation of several individuals, I was able to get the most important issues of *Struggle*, the journal of the University Students' Union of Addis Ababa, and *Challenge*, the journal of the Ethiopian Students Union of North America, as well as other less important publications. These publications provide priceless testimonies of the growth of radicalization among students through the depreciation of reformism; they make palpable the insidious but mounting supplantation of the nationalist and religious ethos of Ethiopian students by Marxist-Leninist beliefs.

Acknowledgments

I would like to thank the many people who have helped with the execution of this study. Thus, many thanks go to Workineh Kelbessa, my longtime friend and colleague at Addis Ababa University, and Shiferaw Bekele, also a longtime colleague at Addis Ababa University, for their assistance in providing many important materials on the Ethiopian student movement; to Endreas Eshete, current president of Addis Ababa University, for personally authorizing the photocopying of student publications; to Fentahun Tiruneh, who as a reference librarian of the Africana section of the Library of Congress has graciously put at my disposal important documents and studies of the Ethiopian student movement; to the late Makonnen Bishaw, both for responding to my questionnaire and for granting extended interviews concerning his involvement in the student movement; to Tibebe Eshetu for engaging in long hours of discussions on the student movement and for providing precious information about materials available in the Ethiopian section of the Michigan State University Library. Likewise, I thank the people, too numerous to mention, with whom I had lengthy conversations on the student movement because they were either in positions of leadership or had shown themselves to be exceptional activists. My thanks also extend to my colleagues in the Philosophy Department of the University of Dayton—namely, Bill Marvin, Marilyn Fischer, Joseph Kunkel, Michael Payne, and Patricia Johnson—for their comments and suggestions after reading parts of the manuscript. Lastly, I express my thanks to the chair of the Department of Philosophy, William M. Richards, for providing financial assistance for the book's cover image.

Abbreviations

EPLF	Eritrean People's Liberation Front
EPRP	Ethiopian People's Revolutionary Party
ESUNA	Ethiopian Students Union in North America
EUTA	Ethiopian University Teachers' Association
HSIU	Haile Selassie I University
HAESA	Haimanote-Abew Ethiopian Students' Association
MEISON	Mela Ethiopia Socialist Neqenaqe (All-Ethiopia Socialist Movement)
NUES	National Union of Ethiopian Students
NUEUS	National Union of Ethiopian University Students
USUAA	University Students' Union of Addis Ababa

Note on Ethiopian Names

Since the custom in Ethiopia does not use a system of family names, the book identifies Ethiopians by their first name rather than their last name. The latter, which is the first name of the father, is not used to identify a person; it is simply an addition to the real name, namely, the given first name.

Introduction

In attempting both to unravel the root causes of the 1974 Ethiopian Revolution and to understand the incessant political instability and persistent economic inertia of the country since the revolutionary change took place, one cannot fail to recognize the decisive role of students and intellectuals. Such recognition invites reflection on the defining feature of these groups, that is, the formative impact of modern education on them. One cannot help but suspect that the nature of the Ethiopian system of education had a hand in the gestation of the lingering tribulations besieging Ethiopian society. Aspirations to stabilize and put the country to work are certainly less achievable in a social context dominated by an educated elite too prone to radical and polarizing views.

True, the reluctance of the imperial regime to make necessary reforms had already polarized the country and created the conditions of class and ethnic confrontations. No scholar can seriously underestimate the impact of repression and lack of reforms on the radicalization of students. The impatience generated by the long postponement of social progress certainly favored the adoption of radical positions. Still, the question remains whether structural conditions resulting from the lack of reforms fully account for the radicalization of the educated elite.

I see no better way to convey the gist of the present study than to call attention to a matter involving Randi Rønning Balsvik's book on the Ethiopian student movement. Originally a PhD dissertation with the title "Haile Selassie's Students—Rise of Social and Political Consciousness," this detailed and well-documented empirical study was later published by the African Studies Center of Michigan State University under the title *Haile Sellasie's Students: The Intellectual and Social Background to Revolution, 1952–1977.* What is worth mentioning is that the published version reproduced all the chapters of the dissertation except the one titled "Religious Sentiments," in which Balsvik lays out the quest of the young for new religious beliefs on account of their displeasure with the traditionalism and political conservatism of the Ethiopian church. She speaks of "the need and subsequent search for a faith which could provide a comprehensive meaning to life."[1] In addition to socioeconomic problems, says Balsvik, an atmosphere of spiritual malaise was perceptible among educated Ethiopians. Quite correctly, the dissertation connects the adoption of Marxism-Leninism by many educated Ethiopians with the spiritual need that arose from the cultural context of frustration over unreformed religious traditions.

The excising of a distinct chapter on religion in *Haile Sellassie's Students* signifies the reduction of the conversion of students to Marxist-Leninist ideology to economic and political demands. On top of impoverishing the approach, this lack leaves us wanting as to the reason political and economic discontent led to the espousal of the Marxist-Leninist philosophy of reality and social change. Nationalist indignation or commitment to liberal ideas could have as well motivated opposition to the imperial regime. Besides, Balsvik's hesitant approach is already evident in the title of the dissertation. What happened in Ethiopia went beyond "the rise of social political consciousness"; it was a commitment to the most dogmatic and extremist form of social change.

By "liberal ideas," I refer to a change focusing on the protection of individual rights achieved through such means as the rule of law, limitations on state power, freedom of expression and organization, and support to private enterprises through the expansion of the free market economy. To the extent that these means realize democratization, they contained many elements able to deal with the main ailment of imperial Ethiopia, namely, the protection of established privileges by means of exclusion. Indeed, as will be explained in various parts of this study, Haile Selassie initiated a form of modernization that protected the privileges of the old nobility by suppressing the political rights of producing classes and the modern educated elite. The remedy to this type of exclusion was none other than the democratization of political life and the organization of free elections resulting in the establishment of a representative government.

For instance, one major form of exclusion was the marginalization of Ethiopian Muslims even though they constitute, according to many estimates, half of the population of the country. In advocating the separation of church and state, liberalism shows the way of reversing the exclusion. Likewise, the hegemony of the Amhara ruling class over other ethnic groups was another form of widespread exclusion. Here, too, liberal principles— namely, the organization of free elections and the establishment of a representative government—suggest the way to achieve equality among the various ethnic groups. The equality would apply to minority ethnic groups, since the government cannot be representative without a provision protecting the rights of minorities.

Ethiopian students rejected the liberal solution, not because it was inappropriate, but because it contradicted their prior ideological commitment to radicalism. The rejection was essentially ideological; it was not the product of reflection on the merits or flaws of liberalism. The decisive concern was less about facts than about doctrinal consistency. Thus, one basic idea of this study is that doctrinal consistency has a force of its own. Accordingly, the students' commitment expressed something more than mere discontent over the economic and political performances of the imperial regime.

It is easily forgotten that not even V. I. Lenin was willing to reduce Marxist ideology to socioeconomic frustrations. The fact that he assigns three sources to Marxism—namely, "German philosophy, English political economy and French socialism"—testifies to his multipronged understanding.[2] Another proof is his insistence that workers could not by themselves develop revolutionary consciousness, that the latter "could only be brought to them from without," to wit, from doctrines that intellectuals belonging to the middle and upper classes elaborated.[3] Interestingly, referring to the particular case of Russia, which had only a nascent capitalism, Lenin writes: "The theoretical doctrine of Social-Democracy arose quite independently of the spontaneous growth of the labor movement; it arose as a natural and inevitable outcome of the development of ideas among the revolutionary Socialist intelligentsia."[4] However paradoxical this may seem, his explanation of the radicalization of the Russian intelligentsia gives primacy to the impact of ideas coming from developed capitalist countries, given that Russia's structural conditions were too immature to breed the advanced ideas of socialism.

The decisive involvement of intellectuals points to motives transcending economic demands. It implicates new spiritual needs springing from the development of science and philosophical doctrines. Marxism presupposes the context of the progress of science increasingly challenging traditional religious beliefs. That Marxism rests on a materialist philosophy means, of course, that it sides with science against religious beliefs. But more importantly, its commitment to social utopianism means that it recovers some aspects of the religious aspiration. Its particularity from ordinary materialism, and hence its wider attractiveness, emanates from the rescue of the religious promise of happiness. Speaking of religion Marx says: "Religious suffering is at the same time an expression of real suffering and a protest against real suffering. . . . The abolition of religion as the illusory happiness of the people is the demand for their real happiness."[5] Marx negates the religious promise of happiness in the world beyond but keeps the aspiration to happiness, nay, turns it into an earthly conquest. Revolutionism of the type promising earthly happiness cannot be disconnected from the transcendental vision fostered by a religion like Christianity.

This study firmly maintains that the detrimental structural legacies of Haile Selassie's long reign do not fully explain the drift of the country into the path of radicalization and confrontation, since reformist and less oppositional solutions were available. The venture into a revolutionary path is the direct product of the infatuation of Ethiopian students and intellectuals with Marxism-Leninism. Hence the assumption that the educational system may have caused cultural cracks into which radical ideas, which were then in vogue, were injected. The assumption perfectly agrees with the effect of an educational system pervaded with Eurocentric norms, as was modern education under Haile Selassie. Is not Eurocentrism a paradigmatic construct that views the world and its different cultures from the perspective asserting the preeminence of Western values, beliefs, and history? Inasmuch as Western preeminence demeans the characteristics of other cultures and decenters them through marginalization, its internalization by native elites causes a severe cultural dislocation, which in turn becomes a breeding ground for extremist beliefs.

In order to demonstrate the link between cultural dislocation and radicalization, the book analyzes the multifarious impact of Western education on Ethiopian youth. It shows how the internalization of Eurocentric concepts and its dissolving effect on traditional values and references produced a characteristic cultural crisis that fed on a rejectionist state of mind. It draws the infatuation with Marxism-Leninism from the negatory attitude, thereby exhibiting the concrete correspondence existing between the needs arising from the cultural crisis and the precepts of revolutionary doctrine. Going beyond a purely exogenous explanation, the analysis inquires into the Ethiopian legacy and establishes the existence of a messianic trend that responded favorably to Marxist utopianism. In other words, in light of the internalization of Eurocentrism that caused deep fractures, the inquiry harnesses the emergence of radicalism to the therapeutic, but alas illusory, promises of Marxism-Leninism.

I say "illusory" in order to dismiss in advance the charge of contradiction. The detection of a messianic trend in the traditional culture may provoke the objection that Marxism was not so much a dislocation as a form of continuity. Alienation converted Ethiopian students to Marxism because it either was opposed to or had affinity with the traditional culture. In the second case, to speak of cultural dislocation, as I do, would be nothing short of contradictory. It would have been contradictory if those who were culturally alienated simply contented themselves with cutting ties with the old culture. Just as nature abhors a vacuum, so too culture, as a repository of human identity, does not simply vanish. Under normal conditions, this survival ethos expresses itself through a work of reinterpretation and domestication intent on lessening the disruptive nature of borrowed items. Not so when seduction overrides reinterpretation because the alien culture echoes deep longings of the traditional culture.

What this attraction reveals is the fact of dislocation craving for a remedy. Unfortunately, the therapy can only be illusory for the simple reason that it does not overcome alienation. While reinterpretation domesticates, that is, integrates borrowed cultural elements, seduction further uproots since the alien culture emerges as a substitute for a scorned legacy. This form of change does not upgrade and enrich the cultural legacy; rather, the attempt to repress the traditional personality yields a confrontational mind-set in which feelings of guilt, contempt, and the vocation of redeemer constantly compete. Unlike reinterpretation, which opts for a more holistic integration or hybridization, the medicine that cultural desertion advocates only aggravates the initial pathological condition.

Culture designates the full realm of beliefs and behaviors that are learned and shared through the socialization process. To quote Edward B. Taylor, it is "that complex whole which includes knowledge, belief, art, morals, law, custom, and any other capabilities and habits acquired by man as a member of society."[6] As a learned and transmitted phenomenon, culture identifies the members of one category of people and distinguishes them from another. Systemness is another important characteristic of culture in that it is composed of interrelated elements realizing a unified, coherent whole. As a product of human learning, culture is not a static phenomenon, either. Changes can come from inside the culture or can flow from exogenous forces, such as environmental alterations or contacts with other cultures. Both the changing nature of culture and its systematic aspects offer various possibilities, one of which is the loss of self-directiveness under the influence of foreign cultural norms. A basic purpose of this study is to demonstrate that when culture goes haywire, it tends to succumb to radicalism.

The emphasis on the cultural dimension does not mean that the book ignores the socioeconomic roots of the revolutionary spirit among Ethiopian students and intellectuals. A whole chapter sets out the rising discontent stemming from economic hardships and the lack of tangible reforms. Even so, the major argument of the study maintains that while socioeconomic problems certainly explain the pressing need for change, they do not account for the attraction that Marxism-Leninism had on Ethiopian students and intellectuals. The explanation for the attraction lies in the cultural crisis caused by the internalization of the Eurocentrist outlook. Accordingly, a full and accurate picture of the radicalization of the educated elite emerges only when socioeconomic problems are viewed less as the direct cause of radicalization than as a symptom of a cultural malaise involving exogenous factors and endogenous predispositions. Marxism-Leninism became enticing to the extent that the doctrine of class struggle and the total socioeconomic transformation it advocates gave tangible and uncompromising expression to the cultural alienation of the educated elite. Since the explanation appeals to a complex process, and so avoids the one-sided method that generally prevails in studies dealing with revolutionism, it does seem a suitable approach to study a phenomenon that so forcefully reveals the active involvement of human agency.

Before engaging the complex process of radicalization, I should provide a note explaining the focus of this study on the Christian dimension of Ethiopian culture. As already indicated, though Muslims represent half of Ethiopia's population, the situation prior to the 1974 Revolution was that the Christian part, mostly located in the northern Amhara and Tigray regions, almost exclusively provided the political elite and the overwhelming majority of students and intellectuals. The number of Muslim university students was actually negligible before the Revolution. According to statistical data combined by the Department of Sociology of the then Haile Selassie I University, Muslims made up just 5.2 percent of students.[7] As one Ethiopian scholar correctly stated, "The most important outcome of the Ethiopian revolution was the rise of the people of the South to public visibility."[8] In neglecting the Islamic component, this study does not suggest that Ethiopian Islamic culture is not worth studying, but that such a review does not enlighten the question of radicalization, given that the radicalization of the early 1970s occurred mainly among students who came from Christian regions.

I hasten to add that Ethiopia's modernization is unthinkable without the full and active participation of the Muslim community. Similarly, the equality of the various ethnic groups composing modern Ethiopia is another sine qua non for modernization. Since the Revolution things have changed in the direction of equality, though much remains to be done, especially in terms of power sharing. One of the challenges is how the two religious communities and the various ethnic groups can evolve national characteristics through the inheritance of the cultural and historical legacies of traditional Ethiopia, also known as Abyssinia. As we shall see, for the Ethiopian student movement the exclusive solution was socialism, in line with the prevailing belief of the time, and this meant the reconstruction of Ethiopian society on a completely new foundation by leaving said legacies in the museum, so to speak. Herein lies the great difference between liberalism and radicalism in the Ethiopian context. While the latter targeted a tabula rasa type of change, with the great risk of breaking the country apart, liberalism necessarily posited continuity. Liberalism can only advise reforms, and reformism does not advocate a total break with the legacy; on the contrary, it argues in favor of maintaining many aspects of the past, including the class structure.

This analysis of the causes of the radical orientation invites a fresh approach. The reference to liberalism illustrates the ideological choices presented at the time to students but does not overlook the problems associated with borrowings from an external source. To the extent that liberalism belongs to different historical and cultural legacies, a beneficial application to the Ethiopian situation requires a serious and creative work of adaptation. No less than revolutionism, the commitment to simply copy Western liberalism is expressive of uprootedness. Hence the need to find new ways of integrating the traditional and the modern: a society that fails to integrate loses its continuity, that is, its anchorage, thereby becoming a peripheral entity. For more information on this question, I refer the reader to my book *Survival and Modernization—Ethiopia's Enigmatic Present,* which discusses the nature of Ethiopia's historical and cultural legacies and offers some suggestions on how the traditional and the modern could be integrated.[9]

1

The Rise of Student Radicalism in Ethiopia

As in Russia, China, Cuba, and elsewhere, students and intellectuals have been the carriers of revolutionary ideology in Ethiopia. By all accounts, by the mid-1960s Haile Selassie I University had become the center of a student movement that was rapidly gathering momentum toward extreme forms of political activism. The African scholar Ali A. Mazrui, who gave a talk to the student body in December 1973, characterized Ethiopian students as "the most radical African students [he] had ever addressed."[1] Any study of the causes of the Ethiopian Revolution must, therefore, begin by establishing the factors that led to the progressive radicalization of Ethiopian students and intellectuals. One basic reason the elaboration and implementation of a reformist agenda was prevented, at the crucial moment when the imperial regime became weak enough to accept the necessity of serious reforms, was undoubtedly the strong opposition of students and intellectuals, who were committed to nothing less than Marxist-Leninist socialism.

Conditions favorable to reformist solutions had indeed emerged when in February 1974, following social and military protests, Haile Selassie dismissed the old cabinet and nominated Endalkatchew Makonnen as the new prime minister. The latter formed a new cabinet and promised changes, including a land reform proposal. The nomination of Endalkatchew confirms that Haile Selassie had finally understood the necessity of reforms. Unfortunate for the possibility of making reforms, the military overthrew the new prime minister under the pretext of appeasing the continuous protests of students against him. The protests were ultimately ideologically driven, as evidenced, for instance, when "on March 11 (1974), thousands of students demonstrated, and burned the effigy of Prime Minister Endalkatchew Makonnen. For the first time, they openly called for the formation of a 'People's Government.' "[2]

Factors of Student Radicalization

Studies analyzing the causes of student activism abound. To limit ourselves to those dealing with student movements in third world countries, activism is generally attributed to social as well as psychological and intellectual factors. Many studies even recognize protest as an established function of students in transitional societies. As Seymour M. Lipset notes, "In the underdeveloped countries, university students do not just prepare themselves for future roles in public life; they play a significant part in the political life of their countries even during their student period."[3] The reasons for the high level of student activism in the developing world are not hard to find: the weakness of the middle class, the absence of representative governments, bans on political parties and freedom of expression, and the use of repressive methods of government concur in making students "the bearers of public opinion."[4] In developed countries, students need not become the voice of the people, given that the practice of democracy allows parties and groups such as labor unions to express social protests and fight for reforms. Student demonstrations, no doubt frequent in developed countries, often reflect dissident positions that political parties are reluctant to support.

According to many scholars, one factor that encourages the politicization of students is the special treatment that universities usually receive from third world governments. While such governments are quick to repress labor unions and political parties, they typically take "a permissive attitude toward student values and activity" by granting a relative autonomy to their institutions of higher education.[5] A number of reasons explain this special treatment. First, so long as student protests remain confined to campuses and do not spill over into other social sectors, dictatorial governments see no serious threat to their power. Students can neither paralyze the economic life of the country nor constitute an insurrectional force able to remove a government. Second, the embedded link between academic freedom and higher education does not allow a purely repressive policy: short of closing universities, governments have no direct way to shield students from critical ideas. Third, governments acquire a bad reputation when they crack down on universities. It is as though they come up against the advancement of knowledge and free research, not to mention the damage inflicted to the national prestige, which is often symbolized by the erection of a sumptuous university amid urban destitution. Even dictatorial regimes resent being perceived as opponents of enlightenment.

No less conducive to political activism is campus life itself. That a large number of students find themselves "at one location, with similar interests, and subject to similar stimuli from the environment gives a powerful impetus to organizational activities of all kinds."[6] Indeed, the concentration of a large number of students in a relatively isolated location makes communication easy, and so fosters organizational schemes. Ideas spread rapidly and without expensive means, as it is easy to distribute leaflets and organize meetings. What is more, the fact of living together in a secluded environment develops a spirit of solidarity that results in the adoption of common attitudes to external stimuli. We cannot emphasize enough the impact of the development of common attitudes. In addition to creating "a more cohesive community from which to recruit members," the spirit of solidarity drives the majority of students to support the initiatives or the views of a minority, even if they do not individually subscribe to them.[7] A further reason the majority tends to follow the lead of minority groups is that campus life means emancipation from parental authority. The remoteness of parents creates a void of authority that exposes many students to peer influence, especially that of senior students. The development of solidaristic attitudes thus greatly benefits organized and active groups: it facilitates recruitment, just as it tends to prompt the alignment of the majority to the views of activist students.

Scholars of student politics readily connect the tendency to radicalization with the very characteristics of youth. Since "hope and idealism tend to be more a feature of youth than of age," radicalization and the very idea of revolution resonate with youth.[8] Unlike older people, who tend to hold moderate or conservative views, the young are generally attracted by magnanimous ideas. They are especially more sensitive to the suffering of the poor and the lack of justice than any other age group. Aristotle codified the contrast between youth and old age. He found that the young have strong passions and are hot-tempered; they are also generous and trustful as well as courageous and open to noble ideals. By contrast, "the character of Elderly Men—men who are past their prime—may be said to be formed for the most part of elements that are the contrary of all these."[9] Likewise, unlike older people, the lessons of experience, to wit, harsh realities dashing generous aspirations, have not yet hardened the young. While old people are wiser, young people have yet to learn how little reality and idealism make good company. The lack of such responsibilities as making a living and raising a family further assists the idealism of youth. Having not yet developed a vested interest in the social system, they can be easily fired up by revolutionary ideas, just as they can afford the risks of political activism.

Many authors have emphasized how the exposure of third world students to Western education greatly exacerbates the natural tendency of the young to assert their independence by defying existing authorities, especially parental authority. While in developed countries the young and their parents share more or less the same culture, in transitional societies the assimilation of modern education induces the young not only to adopt alien values but also to have contempt for traditions to which their parents are still attached.

This cultural dissociation gives generational conflict such an acute and distressing form that it pushes the young toward revolutionary ideologies. For what else could better express their aggravated rebellion than the adoption of ideas that radically question the traditional society of their parents?

That is why Lewis S. Feuer insists that youth idealism is not enough to explain the radicalization of student movements. A thorough explanation requires the addition of another motivation, namely, the conflict of generations. "The distinctive character of student movements arises from the union in them of motives of youthful love, on the one hand, and those springing from the conflict of generations on the other," he says.[10] While enthusiasm, generosity, self-sacrifice—in a word, idealism—are features of a distinct biological stage, generational conflicts add the social component necessary to detonate the idealist impulse.

Granted the importance of sociopsychological, academic, and biological factors, the study of student radicalization must not lose sight of the decisive impact of social discontent. Commitment to a radical change of the social system is not intelligible outside the heavy presence of social problems. Even if we concede that radical groups are bound to appear regardless of the performances of governments, such groups remain isolated without the dissatisfaction of the majority of students with existing conditions of life. For instance, whatever be the part played by cultural crises, youth radicalization in the United States and France during the late 1960s would not have had the scope it had without the war in Vietnam and France's educational crisis. For radical groups to grow and assume the leadership of student movements, the disaffection of the majority of the student body is a necessary precondition.

Equally true is the understanding that, no matter how grave social problems are, radicalism is unthinkable without cultural dissension. When the issue is to explain the predilection of students for radical changes, and not their mere involvement in politics, the argument according to which the gravity of the social problems dictates the option for radical ideology does not look convincing. It presupposes a type of determinism that amounts to saying that the more acute the social problems, the greater the need for revolutionary changes. Unfortunately, important exceptions challenge this kind of assertion. Though social systems burdened with acute social problems proliferate in the world, revolutions are rare occurrences. Take the case of Indian students:

> although the university student population was the most turbulent in the world, the student radicals do not as a rule make the structures of the larger society and of the university objects of a general critique. Indian student radicals declare no fundamental criticism of their society; they have no schemes for the reconstruction of their universities. They do take stands on public issues. . . . The Indian student

agitation is "occasionalist"; it responds to particular stimuli, local, regional, or national, but grievances do not become generalized and are therefore not persistent.[11]

Given that extreme levels of poverty, further rigidified by the caste system, plagued India, a social situation more conducive to arouse indignation could hardly be imagined, especially among people exposed to modern ideas. Nonetheless, the highly muddled condition only provoked turbulent protests that, however intense and repetitive they may have been, fell short of developing a systematic opposition to the social system, still less of embracing a reconstructive intent. In light of the strong conduciveness of the social conditions, what else could explain the lack of attraction of Indian students to radical ideologies but the resistance emanating from the cultural sphere? The point is that Indian students did not develop a sense of alienation from their culture and tradition. Accordingly, they protested for what needed to be fixed or reformed without, however, harboring a project of total change.

To sum up, cultural factors as much as social conditions are necessary to foster radicalism. Statements assigning radicalism exclusively to structural conditions reflect a deterministic view that excludes the input of different cultural dispositions. The overemphasis on structural conditions forgets that social conflicts usually involve competing elites with specific agendas and goals. According to Charles Tilly, more than the antagonism between the ruling elite and the masses, what creates a revolutionary situation is the conflict between aspiring elites with dissident convictions and interests and the established elite. Rejecting the primacy that theories of revolution, such as Marxism and the theory of relative deprivation, accord to social discontent, Tilly's school of thought rightly emphasizes the impact of elite conflicts. He maintains that "conflict among governments and various organized groups contending for power must be placed at the center of attention to explain collective violence and revolutions."[12]

As expressions of political conflicts, ideologies do not simply crop up from structural conditions; they are strategies by which particular interests and beliefs compete for hegemony. It is not that the situation requires radical solutions; rather, radical solutions are necessary to enthrone special elites. The essential virtue of the radical ideology that is supposed to emanate from structural conditions is not simply to resolve social problems; it is to empower elites that have grown culturally sectarian or unorthodox. Because of their eccentric goals and values, such contenders do not fit in the system, however altered or reformed it may be. Political rivalries involving heterodox elites generate the conditions of social revolutions. What defines the case of India is precisely the nonemergence of culturally marginalized elites. The Ethiopian situation, on the other hand, set forth a political conflict between a traditional aristocracy and an educated elite that, on top of showing discontent over the socioeconomic direction of the country, had become culturally alien.

Radicalizing Factors of Imperial Ethiopia

The factors that radicalized students in other countries were quite manifest in prerevolutionary Ethiopia. Thus, the birthplace and center of the Ethiopian student movement was the secluded and relatively autonomous campus of the then Haile Selassie I University. The suppression of freedom of expression and association by Haile Selassie's autocratic rule had turned the student movement into a representative of public opinion. Compared to other sectors of Ethiopian society, the university was a secluded place in which students had gained—after a bitter struggle, it is true —the right to create their own association, to hold meetings, and to have their own publications. Though such rights were precarious and subject to confiscation each time students concretely challenged the regime, they were nevertheless special treatments compared to the complete silencing of the rest of the country. Such rights, however shaky, were no doubt helpful both in facilitating the spread of radical ideas and generating a sense of solidarity among students. Moreover, as Haile Selassie was especially keen to give the image of a benevolent and modernizing monarch to Western governments and observers, he never launched the full extent of his repressive power against students, even when they directly antagonized him.

As elsewhere in third world countries, the learning process in Ethiopia had a deep alienating effect. Though Haile Selassie relied mostly on expatriate teaching staff of clerical extraction to temper the alienation, especially on Jesuit professors who could not be accused of sympathy for critical ideas, the very fact that the curricula and methods of teaching were squarely modeled on American universities exposed students to ideas and values that were on a collision course with the autocratic regime. What is more, instead of discussing and critically evaluating the radical ideas of Marxist-Leninist literature, most of the teaching staff simply ignored them. This academic censorship colored Marxism-Leninism with the attraction of the forbidden fruit.

The undermining effect of modern education was all the more corrosive the more the regime seemed saddled with an inner contradiction: the need to maintain traditional authority and oligarchic interests clashed with the image of a committed modernizer that the emperor projected of himself. The huge gap between the official discourse and the reality pointed to a blocked society in need of a radical reshaping. Though the modernist discourse of the regime gave prominence to the emerging educated elite, the political system exclusively protected the interests of an outdated landed class. To many educated people, the system offered no other way out than outright rebellion.

In their attempt to decipher the causes of the radicalization of Ethiopian students, many scholars have overstressed, understandably, the impact of structural conditions. The economic failures of the regime led, they say, to the progressive disillusionment of students and intellectuals. This disillusionment took a radical turn when in the late 1960s and early 1970s acute economic crises affected all sectors of Ethiopian society, including university graduates, who suddenly found themselves threatened by unemployment. The economic hardships reached their peak with soaring inflation when in 1973 OPEC quadrupled the price of oil. In the eyes of most scholars, especially those using Marxist methodology, the frustration over these economic woes explains, for the most part, the radicalization of Ethiopian students. For instance, one student of the movement writes, "The prospect of unemployment shattered the aspirations of the younger generation of the intelligentsia, leading to a rapid spread of radicalism among the students."[13] Let us review some representative scholars of this dominant trend.

The Evolutionary Approach

To account for the radicalization of the Ethiopian student movement, the Ethiopian historian Bahru Zewde suggests an evolutionary approach. The radicalization reflected, he writes, "growing impatience with a regime which was not prepared to reform itself. As the century wore on, the medicine prescribed also grew in virulence."[14] While the early intellectuals adopted a reformist stand, those of the sixties and early seventies turned revolutionary because the delay of reforms exacerbated the social problems and induced the belief that the regime was completely resistant to the idea of even moderate reforms. With the loss of hope, there grew the conviction that the initiation of necessary changes required nothing less than the total removal of the regime. Some such awareness prepared the ground for the adoption of Marxist-Leninist formulas, all the more so as the long postponement of reforms so aggravated the contradictions of the regime that a purely reformist approach was no longer feasible. With the sense that the time for reforms had passed, the revolutionary option became hard to resist.

The problem with the evolutionary approach is that it does not seem to confront the real issue. To begin with, to speak of progressive radicalization assumes continuity between the reformist and the revolutionary stands. In reality, the use of different theoretical tools to analyze Ethiopian society at the time caused a break in continuity and led to engagement in a divergent direction. The difference between revolution and reform is one of kind, not of degree. And the shift occurred as a result of Ethiopian realities being read through a completely different theoretical model, namely, Marxism-

Leninism. This different reading, and it alone, explains the prescription of radical therapy. The error is to think that the accumulation and aggravation of social contradictions radicalized the students when in reality the adoption of a radical ideology altered the very perception of the problems. The ideology so affected the reading of the problems that they seemed to require nothing less than a radical solution. In short, what radicalized the movement is not exasperation in the face of the problems but prior commitment to a radical ideology.

Bahru himself seems to endorse the primacy of ideological commitment when, speaking of student publications on the national question, he writes: "Ideological authenticity or rectitude takes precedence over historical reality. The major preoccupation of the authors is not so much with what Ethiopia is as with what Marx, Lenin, and Stalin—particularly the last two—said. The cardinal importance of the national question is asserted in emphatic terms. The 'national question', we are told, is not to be dismissed as a secondary contradiction."[15] In other words, facts were misconstrued in such a way as to justify the prior ideological stand of the student movement. Since Marxism-Leninism decreed that the national question was a fundamental contradiction, Ethiopian history had to be made conformable to the requirement of the theory, even at the expense of historical reality. Even Tigrean students declared Tigray a nation without any record of Tigray having ever existed outside Ethiopia. Clearly, the driving power of radicalization was less the lack of reforms than this prior ideological commitment through which Ethiopian reality was analyzed.

The writing style that was characteristic of student publications best shows the longing for ideological consistency. A cursory look at these writings illustrates how widespread was the method of dismissing opponents by means of quotations. A position is rejected as wrong if one shows that it does not agree with one of Marx's, Lenin's, or Mao's statements, even if it looked factually pertinent. Conformity to the doctrine mattered more than factual analysis and rational scrutiny. And as opponents used other quotations to justify their views, the dismissal by means of quotations could go on indefinitely.

The concern for ideological rectitude was so overwhelming that many students did not hesitate to imitate Lenin's style of writing. Bahru cites the case of Tilahun Gizaw, a famous leader of the movement, who "exhausts the repertoire of abusive epithets bequeathed by Lenin and Stalin in his efforts to annihilate ideologically the ESUNA leadership, which had dared to propose a different solution to a common problem."[16] These attitudinal features clearly back the idea that ideological radicalization came first and then had its impact on the reading of Ethiopian realities. Hence the need to explain first the cultural conditions that welcomed the ideology of Marxism-Leninism before weighing the part played by social problems.

The necessity of according primacy to culture sticks out as soon as we pay attention to the social origins of the revolutionaries. As was the case in other countries, in Ethiopia many radicals came from well-to-do families. As a rule, students coming from poor families were more focused on academic studies, which opened for them the path of social mobility, than were students from wealthy families. The number of radicals who belonged to wealthy, even influential families was so noticeable that Makonnen Bishaw, a moderate who was elected to the USUAA presidency in 1968, has said: "at times, it looked like that some of the students were being used by their ambitious families to effect some kind of a coup."[17] The participation of so many sons and daughters of high officials of the regime in the student movement is believed to have tempered the violent response of the government, thereby encouraging the radicals to become even more daring.

Consider the creation of the All-Ethiopia Socialist Movement (Mela Ethiopia Socialist Neqenaqe), or MEISON, in 1968 at a meeting in Hamburg, Germany. In a recent book written in Amharic, an influential member of the organization enumerates twenty-five founding members all of whom had earned high university degrees.[18] Among them we find neither workers nor peasants; and most of them came from well-to-do families, the only way by which they could have had the opportunity of studying abroad. Stated otherwise, the organization was purely a party of intellectuals from its inception and remained so until the Derg disbanded it. Now it would be difficult to attribute the revolutionary stand of these intellectuals to economic frustration since, however badly the Ethiopian government managed the economy, a bright future awaited most of them. Hence the inevitable question: if the case of revolutionaries coming from wealthy families does not involve economic discontent, what else is left but to look into cultural issues?

Ideology as a Derivation

Another Ethiopian scholar who tackles the question of the radicalization of Ethiopian students at some length is Tesfaye Demmellash. His finding is that the nature of Ethiopia's internal conflicts and the international context combined to make Marxism-Leninism appealing to Ethiopian students. He writes: "Marxism appealed to the Ethiopian student intelligentsia not only because it contained a radical critique of both capitalism and feudalism, but also because it offered them, as no other indigenous or foreign intellectual tradition could, a different structural model of national development and an alternative conception of the good society."[19] One reason why liberalism was not attractive to Ethiopian students was the aggregation of capitalism with feudalism in the Ethiopian context. The addition of a harmful international condition to the already aggravated social contradictions rendered the reformist approach irrelevant. Instead of encouraging liberalization by shattering feudal institutions, imperialist capitalism so intimately coalesced with Haile Selassie's feudal regime that it offered no other solution to Ethiopian students than the adoption of the socialist ideology as the only means to get rid of both feudalism and imperialism.

To explain why Ethiopian students were attracted to Marxism-Leninism, Tesfaye adopts a typical démarche. First he posits the awareness of the problems and then suggests that socialism was adopted because it offered appropriate solutions. He never contemplates the possibility that it may have been the other way round, namely, that the prior adoption of Marxism-Leninism brought about the need for radical solutions—not that serious problems did not exist in Ethiopia, but another theoretical approach would have assessed them differently. Yet, that the ideological conviction was prior to the analysis of the problems is an idea that must have crossed Tesfaye's mind when he points out that many Ethiopian students of the 60s picked up their Marxism during their studies in America. They did not discover the theory in the course of their concrete struggle within the Ethiopian realities; rather, they brought it from outside. For, as specified by Tesfaye himself, the fact "that the ESM [Ethiopian student movement] had no organic links to broader social forces in Ethiopia, especially prior to the February Revolution of 1974, that far from forging such links it was only thinking and acting Marxism *on behalf* of the masses, meant that the movement's Marxist world outlook was a product of little more than pure intellectual construction and socialization."[20]

All the defects of the student movement—such as extremism, dogmatism, and unrealism—point to an activism that a prior ideological conversion propelled. Tesfaye speaks of the adoption of an abstract position that "was not grounded in the historically specific contradictions, political traditions, and cultural practices of Ethiopian society."[21] The term "abstract" does indicate the practice of using Marxism-Leninism as an a priori formula with which things must agree. The theory did not conform to facts; facts were conformed to the theory—that is, they underwent a characteristic reinterpretation that adjusted them to the dictates of the doctrine. To the interesting question why the Ethiopian student movement ended up in complete disarray, the best answer is that abstraction and dogmatism made Marxism-Leninism irrelevant to Ethiopian realities.

The Eclectic Approach

Another Ethiopian scholar who deals with the issue of the radicalization of Ethiopian students is Gebru Mersha, who was himself a former activist and leader. To explain why Marxism-Leninism exercised such a strong attraction on Ethiopian students and intellectuals, Gebru proposes an answer involving multiple causes. After reviewing some authors who dealt with student movements, he concludes: "The radicalization of the intellectuals and their identification with the cause of the oppressed, especially in peripheral formations, stem from a set of interrelated factors: a relatively privileged position in society and their exposure to new and revolutionary ideas and their knowledge of historical processes, career blockages, their realization and disenchantment with the system and its corrupt political practices, its foreign domination, etc."[22] The Ethiopian situation had added one particular cause of radicalization, namely, the Eritrean question, which Gebru characterizes as "possibly the major one," in that it "provoked students to raise one of the most sensitive political issues, the question of nationality."[23]

Commendable though this pluralist approach is, it does not give a clear picture of the issues. Its essential defect is that it remains an eclectic approach that simply enumerates and juxtaposes factors of radicalization without integrating them into a whole. The lack of integration considerably decreases the theoretical significance of the approach, all the more so as none of the enumerated causes calls for radicalization by itself. As already pointed out, the delay of necessary reforms is not enough to explain radicalization. However delayed reforms may have been, a liberal solution was still possible. Scholars forget that the popular movement that overthrew the imperial regime initially expressed democratic demands rather than socialist slogans. The idea of socialist revolution came from above, especially from students and intellectuals. Even the Eritrean question had a perfectly liberal solution: the return to federalism and the concrete democratization of the Ethiopian state would have appeased the majority of Eritreans. There was no reason for students to radicalize over the issue of Eritrea unless they had already accepted the question as a colonial issue, which presupposed a Marxist-Leninist reading of Ethiopian realities.

Let no one brandish the argument that liberalism was more difficult to establish than socialism. Speaking realistically, socialism requires more material and intellectual resources and higher organizational ability than liberalism. Herein lies the major mistake of Gebru and also of many others, namely, the assumption that "liberalism as an alternative ideology did not have a strong material base and even as an incipient tendency was already discredited."[24] Was liberalism discredited because it was judged inadequate to existing conditions or was it so judged because students had already become Marxist-Leninist followers? The rejection of liberalism even as Ethiopians had no any experience of a liberal society suggests that the dismissal was a priori, doctrinal. Gebru's reference to the exposure of students to revolutionary ideas further confirms the primacy of ideological conversion. It asserts that Marxism-Leninism had become so fashionable that liberalism was rejected even before it was discussed.

In terms of undermining feudalism and imperial autocracy, liberalism would have, moreover, been no less efficient than Marxism-Leninism. A liberal position can perfectly express social grievances resulting from lack of democratic rights, corruption, career blockages, foreign domination, and so on. As a country faces these problems, to the extent that it belongs to a lower stage of economic development, what it needs is a bourgeois revolution. Accordingly, a shift to socialism cannot be assigned to the effects of social problems: without the mental orientation that interprets social problems through the lens of the Marxist-Leninist doctrine, liberalization would be simply the commonsense thing to do.

Gebru should have all the more prioritized the ideological component since he denounces the "revolutionary romanticism" of the student movement, together with its "crude and superficial digest of Marxist-Leninist ideas."[25] To speak of romanticism is to underline the detachment of ideas from Ethiopian realities. It also points to the main reason why the movement had to cede the leadership of the 1974 Revolution to a military junta: its inadequate ideological foundations, which could not have emanated from Ethiopia's objective conditions, did not allow the student movement to retain the leadership of the social protests. Since a consistent struggle for democratic rights could have addressed the social demands, the shift to socialism thus reveals an irrational inspiration that can only have come from idealization and the dogmatic reading of Marxism-Leninism.

Toward a Comprehensive Explanation

The Ethiopian scholar who, to my knowledge, has given the most comprehensive explanation of the radicalization of Ethiopian students is Addis Hiwet. After describing the attempt to explain the radicalization of the students in "psychological terms—'alienation,' 'moral distress,' 'moral crisis,' 'generational conflict' [as] all 'Catch-22 like terms,'"Addis lays out the social conditions in conjunction with the cultural component.[26] He thus mentions the cultural tension resulting from the fact that "the imported educational system was, broadly, at ideological variance with the ancient regime, the importer."[27] He also alludes to the impact of the global culture of revolution characteristic of the 1960s, which moved Ethiopian students still further from their native cultural ties. Summarizing the huge impact of this global culture of revolution, he writes, "*The Ethiopian radical intelligentsia was very much a political creature of the sixties—both in its formative consolidation as a caste and in its politicization.*"[28]

Addis has understood that social conditions are not enough to explain the birth of radicalism. In addition to social determinants, we must analyze the cultural conditions that created not only a protesting intelligentsia, but also a revolutionary one. The situation must involve, to use Addis's felicitous expression, "a caste" determined to turn the whole system upside down. In a word, the explanation must be comprehensive enough to account for the rise of a heretical elite. Only where cultural incompatibility develops together with social blockages do conflicts between elites cross the threshold of reformism and move toward social revolutions. It is imperative, therefore, to study the cultural dynamics that bring about the emergence of an alienated and heterodox intelligentsia. When members of an influential sector become adamantly opposed to their own legacy, they no longer seek to establish continuity by integrating the old and the new, the traditional and the modern. They want to erase tradition and build a new society. In thus calling for the eradication of the past, they pursue nothing less than a social revolution.

The Manufacture of Radical Student Movements

Understanding the accession of radical groups to leadership even as the majority of students profess moderate views is one challenge that scholars of student movements face. The Ethiopian case is no exception. Donald L. Donham posits fairly well the problem when he asks: "Why, at the outset, did a small educated vanguard in Ethiopia become so enamored of the notion of revolution? And why, in a matter of only months, did virtually *all* Ethiopian political actors at the center take up Marxism?"[29] Donham's questions amount to asking how radicals, evicting moderates, took the leadership of the social protest movement. Indeed, radicalization does not mean that the majority of students became ardent Marxists, but simply that they acquiesced to the leadership of militant Marxist students.

For the majority of students did not become radical; in fact, for many years the complaint was that Ethiopian students were unusually indifferent to politics. Witness the editorial of March 1965 of *Challenge*, the journal of the Ethiopian Students Association in North America, which complains as follows: "Ethiopia's educated youth, unlike those of other countries, has consistently failed to address itself to them [social issues]. Its history is not one of real concern for Ethiopia but a record of extreme individualistic egoism, opportunism and despair. It is a disunited and uninspiring body. . . . It is not known for an awareness of genuine nationalism like the youth of its generation elsewhere."[30] In light of Ethiopian students being so little politicized, especially compared to counterparts in other third world countries, we can appreciate the extent of the isolation of the few activists in the early years of the movement, but also the amount of work and dedication that they had to apply to finally politicize the majority. Needless to say, the repeated failures of the imperial regime provided a much needed helping hand to the work of politicization.

Data taken from various countries confirm that large numbers of students do not show an intense interest in political issues. In the end, however, such students often come to accept the leadership of organized and militant groups. No doubt, campus seclusion, youth idealism, the spirit of solidarity, and peer influence enter into the rise of radical groups to leadership, but they do not fully explain it. Take the case of the May 1968 student rebellion in France: the majority of students progressively embraced what at first was the preoccupation of a radical minority. The main problem, in France as elsewhere, "is to explain why the protest of this minority was enthusiastically adopted by a large majority of the students."[31]

To understand why the majority of French students came to follow radical groups, one must refer to the predicaments of French society, especially to the crises of the educational system. France's elitist model of higher education was increasingly at odds with the growing number of students coming from lower-middle-class and working-class families. In consequence, the rising number of dropouts and unemployed graduates caused a deep anxiety among students, which resonated with militant groups' denunciation of the entire social system. The wide student revolt was therefore the product of the "conjunction between broad issues proposed by the radical minority and the diffuse dissatisfaction felt by the majority of the students with regard to the university system."[32] Without the dissatisfaction of the majority of students, the radicals would likely have pursued their denunciation of the system, but only as a minority. The dissatisfaction of the majority enabled them to reach out by harnessing the crises of the educational sector to their denunciation of the whole system. This convergence of interests explains why the nonradical majority followed the radicals' leadership.

A similar evolution seems to have taken place in Ethiopia in the early seventies. Not only did the educational system become so dysfunctional that the number of university dropouts dramatically increased, but also the national economy's sluggish growth could not absorb even university graduates. Add to this major crisis the imperial regime's complete reluctance to enact reforms, and you will understand how progressively the majority of students came under the influence of the radicals, who wanted to destroy the system. As we shall see, neither the regime nor the university administration did anything to help moderates have some influence in the student movement. On the contrary, the way they handled protests and demands propelled the radicals to uncontested leadership of the movement.

That the majority of students, first indifferent and apolitical, were gradually drawn into militancy by radical groups, thereby giving birth to what can be called a revolutionary generation, allows the characterization of the generation as a manufactured movement. Ethiopian student radicalism was a product of social contradictions, but even more so of the input of radical groups who progressively politicized the majority of students. John Markakis and Nega Ayele describe well how in Ethiopia a few activists succeeded in fashioning a scattered, discontented social group into a revolutionary movement:

Students and teachers were extremely active agitating, pamphleteering, and demonstrating and provoking others to do the same. They infiltrated other organizations, and sought to influence their position injecting political elements into every conflict and sharpening contradictions whenever possible. Gradually they succeeded in focusing diverse grievances on the regime itself, defining it as the country's essential problem, and the formation of a people's government as the only real solution. "The root of such problems as corrupt officials and similar problems, is the system itself," averred one leaflet, "and the solution to them is a fundamental change of the system and the formation of a people's government."[33]

The quotation clearly shows that as much as, if not more than, the objective conditions, the radical discourse that made the removal of social problems dependent on regime change is responsible for the politicization of the majority of students. Ordinary students complain about corruption, unemployment, the rising costs of living, mismanagement, and the like; the strategy of the radicals is to bring these students into thinking that these problems cannot go away unless the regime is overthrown and replaced by a socialist government. The objective situation is not enough to explain the revolutionary course; equally necessary is the exploitation of the situation by radical groups. Without the influence of the Marxist radicals, the socially discontented would not have abandoned the moderate course of reforms.

If the radicalization of student movements is largely accounted for by the capture of leadership by radical groups, how can one explain that a minority is able to defeat not only conservative students but also the moderates, who most naturally represent the majority? The allusion to a convergence of interests is not entirely satisfactory if only because it does not explain the sidelining of moderates. One possible answer is that the impact of the minority derives from its ability to express the hidden, unconscious desire of the majority of students. As Raymond Aron says, "In any historical period and especially in a revolutionary period, a minority may express the spirit of the time, may translate into actions the ideas or the underlying desire of a generation."[34] Even though revolutions are admittedly the work of minorities, the latter actually carry out what the majority secretly desires. This representative value largely explains the impact of minorities.

There is no doubt that the determined and protracted struggle of the minority awakens the majority to what it wants. But we must go beyond the role of awakening; we must speak of a formative role, which is often called indoctrination. More than the majority recognizing its desires and wishes in the activism of the minority, it is the minority that shapes the majority into wanting a radical form of change. The formative role of minorities attests that revolutionary movements are not the exclusive product of social conditions; the existence of revolutionaries who agitate and lead is equally important.

Of particular interest here is the question of how revolutionary groups emerge in the first place. Without doubt, revolutionary ideologies initially attract individuals "who may be motivated by personal psychological needs, life experiences, disequilibrium-induced tensions, or a combination of all these forces."[35] The introduction of changes through either internal evolution or outside influence always provokes a state of disequilibrium that favors the emergence of dissident views. Notably, changes entail a disharmony between the existing value system and the social environment. When there is dissonance between the value system and the social environment, deviant behaviors multiply at the individual level. While most people yearn for a resynchronization of the system, there are those who go over to rejection. Deviant behaviors can range from the spread of alcoholism, debauchery, and delinquent gangs to the appearance of new religious sects and dissident ideologies. Individuals who become alienated from their society look for a substitute in the creation or adoption of new revolutionary ideologies. And if, failing to reform itself, the society goes through persistent and severe crises, deviant groups find a suitable condition to spread their revolutionary ideology to other individuals and groups, thereby creating a revolutionary movement.

A word of caution: the reference to deviant behaviors does not mean that I equate revolutionism with alcoholism, debauchery, and gangsterism. What I want to establish is that revolutionary impulse appears in societies going through a severe disequilibrium, which is also manifested by unusual attraction toward extremist religious sects as well as by increased alcoholism and other asocial conduct. Needless to say, the difference between revolutionaries and the young people who look for escape in alcohol or drugs or through spiritual pursuits was that the former believed, even as they participated in the same malaise, that political action and change could put an end to the need to escape the gruesome reality through delinquent behavior or religious fervor.

The Emergence of a Marxist-Leninist Core Group

Nothing proves better the manufactured nature of radical opposition movements than the Ethiopian student movement. The case of Ethiopia provides a striking example of how successfully a small group of Marxist-Leninist radicals progressively extended its influence over the majority of students. The process started in the early sixties when a core of militant Marxist students made its appearance among the student body of Haile Selassie I University. Alienation from the larger society and the reading of common Marxist-Leninist literature drew these radical students together. Going beyond ideological affinity, they "formed a loosely organized society called the 'Crocodiles' "during the academic year of 1963–64.[36]

The term "crocodile" needs some clarification. According to Randi Rønning Balsvik, the "name indicated its underground element, secrecy, and dangerous and unpredictable nature."[37] The mysterious nature of the group was such that some scholars doubt its existence while others maintain that it had 50 to 75 members. Obviously, secrecy was necessary for reasons of survival in the context of a highly repressive imperial state. But it also provided the group with a certain aura, all the more so as the early adoption of a radical ideology put the group at variance with the rest of the students. The term "crocodile" conveys the enigmatic and disquieting trait stemming from the ideological disparity of the group.

The view of political militancy as a profession or a vocation was the defining feature of the group. Fully adhering to the Leninist concept of "professional revolutionaries," the members of the group saw the university not so much as a place where one learns and acquires the skills necessary to pursue a professional career as a forum suitable for political agitation. It is important to understand that their militancy was derived from an ideological stand rather than from their own economic plight, obvious as it was that most of them joined the university because their families could afford it. To be sure, social problems had an impact on their ideological transformation, but the point is that a commitment of this nature is primarily made on ideological or moral grounds. As is the case with revolutionaries in other countries, the Ethiopian radicals represented "culturally alienated intellectuals—men and women of well-to-do families who had removed themselves from the orthodox stream of their society's traditional culture."[38] How otherwise could one explain their early adherence to the radical ideology of Marxism-Leninism and their systematic militancy? They did not turn to radicalism via an assessment of the unfeasibility of the reformist stand; they went straight to radicalism consequent to doctrinal conversion.

The formation of the Crocodile group in the university is reminiscent of the group that Mao Tse-tung created when he joined the Hunan Provincial First Normal Teachers' Training School. Mao writes: "Gradually I did build up a group of students around myself, and the nucleus was formed of what later was to become a society that was to have a widespread influence on the affairs and destiny of China."[39] Emphasizing their powerful and eccentric devotion, he adds: "It was a serious-minded little group of men and they had no time to discuss trivialities. Everything they did or said must have a purpose. They had no time for love or 'romance' and considered the times too critical and the need for knowledge too urgent to discuss women or personal matters. I was not interested in women."[40] At the age when most young men enjoy dancing and flirting and are busy planning their future careers, Mao and those who followed him exhibited the idiosyncratic behavior of shunning pleasurable and careerist pursuits. They gave themselves over to an ascetic life completely devoted to the revolutionary cause. Revolution was the ultimate goal for which they lived and sacrificed pleasures and career. In complete agreement with Lenin, revolution had become a profession for them. It would be completely wrong to attribute this overriding commitment to social problems from which they or their family had suffered. Had adverse social conditions caused the commitment, it would not have developed such a systematic and thought-absorbing character. These were people who had become so obsessed with revolution that they had decided to die for it. If they had seen revolution as a means of defending material interests, their activism would not have been systematic, but intermittent and circumstantial.

A similar spirit animated the students who formed the Crocodile group in Ethiopia. Besides recruiting followers and criticizing the university administration and the government, especially for the imposition of policies restricting freedom of expression and organization, their main objective was, from the start, the creation of a strong and united student movement entirely committed to socialist ideology. They did not underestimate the difficulty of the task, but they saw in the seriousness of their own commitment the assurance that they possessed enough energy and single-mindedness to overcome all obstacles.

Conflicts between Moderates and Radicals

The triumph of radicalism in the student movement owes much to the steadfastness of the Crocodile group. A most memorable expression of perseverance is the protracted struggle that the radicals waged to create a citywide association in the capital by dissolving the practice of each campus having its own association. Neither the university administration nor the imperial government liked the idea of such a wide association. Alarmed by the prospect of radical students controlling such a large union, moderate students also opposed the idea. A referendum was organized in November 1966 asking students to choose between the existing campus unions and the citywide union. Its results proved that the proposal of a citywide union "was by no means generally supported."[41] All the campuses situated outside the main campus called *Sidist Kilo* voted to retain their campus unions, while the majority of students in the main campus where the radicals were most active supported the idea of one union. Be it noted that the idea of one union also meant the replacement of the various student publications by one single publication, namely, *Struggle*, which as its name indicates, reflected the views of the radicals and already drew many readers among the student population.

Though the citywide union was inaugurated on April 7, 1966, the mounting opposition made the victory of the radical students precarious. Those who initiated the opposition to the citywide association and advocated the restoration of campus unions acquired the name of "restorers." There was also another group called the " 'Clean Sweep Committee,' " which while not opposed to the idea of citywide union was determined to topple the radical leadership so as to cleanse the association of extremist views.[42] As the fight intensified, a growing number of students came to support the restorers. What was at first an issue of efficiency and better organization turned into an open ideological fight between radicals and moderates. The restorers "strongly opposed what they understood to be a monopoly of USUAA by 'communist' interests and held that students with different views were 'systematically and consistently molested and ridiculed.' "[43]

As it became clear that the conflict between the restorers and the radicals was endangering the very existence of the student union, senior students proposed the resolution of the conflict by means of majority vote. The campaign showed a strong tendency to elect people who were free of ideological allegiance. One election poster of the moderates read: "We shall bow neither to the eastern nor to the western dogmas. . . . Ethiopia shall triumph! Ethiopianism prevail!"[44] Consequently, the seats of president and secretary of USUAA went to Hailu Mengesha and Mesfin Habtu, respectively, who had promised to promote trust and unity within the student body. In one of his speeches, Hailu said: "No problems could be solved unless 'our imported ideologies—ideologies which create division and hatred, disharmony and deterioration' were put aside."[45] The restorers' offensive had produced results: it led to the election of moderates. Another well-known moment that resulted in the election victory of moderation over radicalism occurred in the 1968–69 academic year when the candidate of the Marxist radicals, Tilahun Gizaw, lost the presidency to Makonnen Bishaw, whom the moderates supported.

These election reversals of the radicals demonstrate the existence of a split between moderate and radical leaders since the early years of the student movement. They also indicate that the split had widened to the extent that "the radicals were not unopposed on campus."[46] The seriousness of the moderate opposition underlines the obstacles that the radicals had to overcome to finally triumph and assume the complete leadership of the student movement. The radical orientation of the Ethiopian student movement was neither a spontaneous nor an inevitable outcome; it was the product of the hard work and dedication of a few revolutionary students. As a matter of fact, the ascendance of the moderates was never definitive nor sweeping. They did not succeed in retaining for long the leadership of the movement, still less in reducing the growing influence of Marxist-Leninist students.

The Victory of the Radicals

In order to understand how moderates progressively lost control of the student movement, let us consider the momentous demonstration of February 25, 1965, during which students marched in front of the Parliament building and in the streets of Addis Ababa with the slogan "Land to the Tiller." According to an account of that demonstration, nine months earlier student representatives had submitted a moderate recommendation urging "the government to 'provide protection to the peasant by legalizing the contract between owner and tenants', form producers' cooperatives, and develop saving and credit institutions accessible to farmers."[47] The recommendation stressed the need to create a truly representative parliamentary system by developing democratic institutions. Not only were "the recommendations . . . made within the language of liberal-democratic capitalism," but in a move that betrayed a lingering confidence in the imperial institution, they were also presented directly to the emperor, who showed his appreciation for the students' concern.[48]

Nine months later the University College Union issued a new and different resolution reflecting the resurgence of radicals. The institution of a contract between landowners and tenants was flatly rejected on the grounds that it would only perpetuate the existing system of tenancy. It was replaced by a radical option whose "main slogans were 'Land to the Tiller' and 'Away with Serfdom.' "[49] Unmistakably, these slogans announced the return of radical students to a position of leadership. What explains this return? The discussions in February 1965 in the Chamber of Deputies of a projected law regulating the relationships between landowners and tenants give the answer. The talks bore no fruit: "Pressure from landowning interests inside and outside parliament ensured that no vote was taken, despite the fact that the emperor was understood to favor the proposal, and Sweden had threatened to discontinue agricultural development assistance if it did not pass."[50] The blockage worked for the radicals, who had the easy task of convincing students that the imperial government and the feudal class were not willing to make even minor reforms. In light of this open reluctance to make the slightest change to the existing system, no other choice was left but to step up the struggle in the direction of overthrowing the regime.

The main reason why the moderates, who had the confidence of the majority, progressively lost the leadership to Marxist radicals is thus clear enough. The government's refusal to deal with the burning question of tenancy undermined the position of moderates in favor of radicals. Reformism would have prevailed if the government had supported reformist students by listening to some of their suggestions. Moderate leaders could then have argued that they were obtaining results, that reformism was the way to go. In rejecting even minor reforms, the government did nothing less than push most students into supporting the views of the radicals. With no reform forthcoming, a confrontational attitude supplanted both dialogue and constructive criticism.

When, on top of rejecting reforms, governments engage in a policy of systematic repression, the chance for moderates to retain the leadership of student movements becomes close to zero. Of the Ethiopian case, Balsvik astutely writes: "The government might have been able to enlist a loyal opposition; moderate forces were still strong among the students. Instead, it rejected the contribution and exchange of ideas from those who thought it was their particular moral duty to speak out against injustice. Confrontation was inevitable."[51] Even if students had snatched the right to have their own publication and association after a bitter struggle, the Ethiopian government displayed the pattern of closing the university and removing the recognized rights each time that students demonstrated over some social issue. Those rights were reinstated anew until a new demonstration put them again in jeopardy. This repressive cycle enabled the radicals to claim the situation was hopeless and that all forms of moderation were utterly inappropriate and inefficient.

In addition to blocking reforms and creating despair, a repressive state actually works toward the promotion of radical leaders. When, frightened by repression, moderate leaders leave the scene, radical students step in both to air demands specific to the student population and to spread their ideological beliefs. The withdrawal of moderate leaders confirms the extent to which repression cripples moderation. In the face of sacrifices and risks, the radicals have an uncontestable edge, given their initial commitment to the cause of revolution. The more dangerous the situation becomes, the greater is the prospect for radical students to come to the forefront of the struggle. Here we witness how political conditions can propel radical groups to the leadership of a movement that is composed in the majority of moderate students. As Misagh Parsa puts it, "Government repression may weaken or eliminate elite or moderate challengers and consequently polarize the opposition in favor of the hegemony of radical or revolutionary challengers."[52] Repression does not create radicalism, which is always the affair of a minority and appears in conjunction with specific theoretical and ideological influences; but it opens the leadership of the protests to radical groups by effectively eliminating or scaring off moderates.

Concrete instances of Ethiopian government policy undermining the position of moderate leaders abound. Take the imperial government's Proclamation on Peaceful Public Demonstrations issued on February 11, 1967. It stipulated that no demonstration is allowed unless organizers apply for a permit a week in advance giving the time, place, and purpose of the demonstration. Naturally, "the students viewed the proclamation as directed mainly against their political agitation."[53] They discussed the proclamation in a general assembly meeting and, by a majority vote, adopted the resolution to stage a demonstration. The demonstration led to a clash between the demonstrators and the police and resulted in the arrest of many students. Students then refused to attend classes until every arrested student had been released. The government issued the ultimatum that unless students returned to classes the university would be closed. Students rejected the ultimatum and the university was effectively shut down. The incident clearly shows what drove many students to side with Marxist-Leninist radicals. A reactionary law was promulgated that no reformist student could dare defend. The suggestion of the radicals to stage a demonstration emerged as the only choice left, even in the eyes of the moderate majority. The government's use of force and imprisonment to disband the demonstration merely shored up the arguments of the radicals.

Another representative case is the incident over the fashion show during March 1968. Organized by the University Women's Club and some Peace Corps volunteers in the main hall of the university, the show staged Ethiopian women students wearing the latest European fashion. Under the instigation of radicals, students protested against the spectacle, which they assimilated to "'cultural imperialism' promoted by 'aristocratic Ethiopian women and American imperialism.'"[54] Interestingly, the show became the occasion for male students to vent their condescending attitude toward female students. Linking the participation of university women to a lack of awareness about the detrimental effects of neocolonial influence, an article in *Struggle* bluntly stated: "Our sisters' heads have been washed by western soap."[55] Complaints about the low level of political consciousness of female students intensified. For instance, the radicals attributed the loss of the presidency of the student movement to female votes in favor of the moderate Makonnen.

To the disruption of the fashion show, the government reacted with its usual repressive manner. It closed the university, banned student unions and publications, and arrested student leaders and dozens of others. Yet, the fashion show was a cause that mobilized many students because of its highly nationalistic implication. Instead of supporting the students for their nationalist stand, the repressive response of the government allowed the radicals to portray themselves in patriotic terms, that is, as defenders of the national culture.

Equally supportive of the radicals was the inability of the imperial government to stick to repressive measures. It followed a vacillating pattern: a confrontation would occur over some issue, and the government reacted by abolishing already acquired rights and at times by closing the university. The tension persisted until the government presented conditions for the opening of the university. The university would reopen but the conditions were never applied. Finally, when the university administration backed down, the curtailed rights were restored. Both the reopening of the university and the restoration of rights invariably appeared as a victory for the activists, who thus became heroes. The implication of this enhanced authority of the activists was to consecrate confrontation as the only and right way to deal with the government.

One amazing outcome of the study of the Ethiopian student movement is discovery of the extent to which the imperial government was heedless of the consequences of its repressive policy. Though officials knew that radicals were leading the protest, they did not understand that a repressive policy was strengthening the radicals' hegemony, the reason being that repression was falsely believed to be having a discouraging effect. In reality, even moderates were increasingly attracted to radicalism the more the negative responses of the government convinced them of their own inefficiency. Engaging in self-criticism, many able moderate leaders joined the camp of the radicals.

I hasten to add that the repressive and conservative policy of the imperial government was just one factor, no doubt important, in the radicalization of students. There were other factors, mostly originating from an ideological commitment so absolute and categorical that it justified the use of any means to achieve victory. Let us come back to the incident of the fashion show. The hostile campaign that radicals initiated against the spectacle is best represented by the comment of an activist in *Struggle*: "How can a hall in our University, where our national culture is believed to be preserved and developed be used for girls stalking along showing western rags?"[56] Though the radicals had a low opinion of Ethiopian national culture, which in other writings they characterized as feudal, reactionary, and outdated, they used the fashion show to present themselves as guardians of the national culture. They knew the resonance that this cultural nationalism would have on many students and used it to boost their image among students.

Intimidation, name-calling, and even physical threats were, according to many prominent testimonies, among the methods radicals used to assert their hegemony. Faithful to the very style of Leninism, the radicals' preferred tactic was smearing their opponents. Thus those who held moderate views were characterized as CIA or government agents. And when smearing was not enough, the next step was the threat of physical violence. In the e-mail exchange to which I have already alluded, Makonnen Bishaw himself has confirmed to me that he had experienced firsthand this tactic when he was elected president of USUAA. He added that the pressure of intimidation converted some students to radicalism.[57] The method was apparently successful, as fewer and fewer students dared to challenge the radicals openly.

As I have noted, the radicals owed their ascendance over the moderates primarily to their ideological commitment. Again according to Makonnen, many students resented the radicals for their extremism, their choice of violent opposition, their rejection of Ethiopian traditions, and their support for Eritrean secessionist groups.[58] Unfortunately, the moderate groups had neither a clear ideology nor any rudimentary organization. They wanted change, but they did not articulate the nature of desired reforms in such a way as to really offer a viable alternative. It is no exaggeration to say that many students followed the lead of the radical group by default. No doubt, the ideological hegemony of Marxism-Leninism in the sixties and early seventies greatly contributed to the victory of activists over moderates. The theory had become a fashion that spontaneously attracted many of the young and the educated in third world countries. By contrast, the moderates had nothing to offer that could counter the authority of Marxism-Leninism: liberalism and reformism were in theoretical retreat. Aside from the failures of the imperial government, the era favored Marxist-Leninist activists.

The absence of a credible alternative could not but present the moderates as disguised defenders of the status quo. The radicals had no trouble in saying that, though moderates spoke of change, what they offered was no different from the usual tired liberalism, which had so dramatically failed elsewhere in the developing world. The fact that many restorers were American Field Service returnees leant credibility to the accusation that they were propagandists of the American way of life. And since the U.S. government was a staunch supporter of the imperial regime, the enthusiasm of these former American Field Service returnees for American liberalism appeared to be at variance with their stand against the imperial regime. For students fighting the imperial regime, any allegiance to the system that supported Haile Selassie was simply contradictory and unacceptable.

A major strength of the radicals thus came from the nature of their ideology, which advocated neither the pursuit of compromise nor a wait-and-see attitude. On the contrary, as a radical opposition, it constantly put students in a position of confrontation with the hated regime. As such, it appeared as the only genuine and sincere opposition, as the only stand determined to achieve something. In addition to inculcating a combative mood into the student body, Marxism-Leninism armed students with a clear goal: to fight both the imperial regime and its imperialist allies. It also provided the ideological and conceptual framework by which students and the regime appeared absolutely polarized, just as it charted a confident course of socioeconomic development. Not only was Marxism-Leninism in great vogue, but also, as any doctrine propelled by social messianism, it inspired a bold and dedicated activism. On top of supplying a powerful tool of social analysis, its messianic inspiration filled followers with a sense of mission like no other social theory could. This sense of mission largely accounts for the boldness of activist students. Where moderates hesitate, radicals are ready to pay any price, make any sacrifice for their cause, including the ultimate sacrifice, and this degree of commitment has a magnetic power on students.

Unlike the absolutely committed activists, the moderates viewed political action as one activity among others. Not being as single-minded as the radicals, who had become professional revolutionaries, the moderates avoided a continuous fight; nor were they willing to use any means to triumph. Though they understood the need to fight the radicals, they did not wage a systematic and sustained struggle. Their involvement was intermittent, and so lacked the methodical quality of the radicals' efforts. One reason the radicals retook the leadership of the student union after being defeated in the 1968 election was their sheer determination. According to Makonnen, once that election was over, moderates returned to their usual activity.[59] Their electoral victory was thus short-lived because a program of constant activity aimed at dislodging the radicals from all positions of leadership was not followed. The lack of follow-up allowed the radicals to stage their comeback and regain control of the movement.

To sum up, the victory of the radicals over the moderates, which resulted in the conversion of many students to activism, cannot be explained without the enthusiasm inspired by the Marxist-Leninist doctrine itself. To the extent that the enthusiasm fostered dedication, single-mindedness, and organizational ability, it is an essential component of victory alongside sociopolitical conditions. Add to this the fact that the university was in no position to provide any critical tools by which students could temper their enthusiasm for Marxism-Leninism. The complete absence of freedom of expression prevented the professors from engaging in a critical dialogue with the students. Granting academic freedom was, however, in the long-term interest of the government. When ideas are out in the open and debated, moderation and common sense can hope to prevail, as students become exposed to the pros and cons of any controversial theory. But when a theory is banned, as was Marxism-Leninism, in addition to having free publicity and drawing the attraction of the forbidden fruit, it takes the character of being true without any examination of its actual merits. If it is banned, so students say, it must be true.

Cultural Unorthodoxy and Revolutionism

We have already established that leadership by heretical elites is a defining characteristic of social revolutions. An account of social revolutions remains singularly deficient if it does not give an insight into the factors that produce such kind of elites. This study has already alluded to the presence of an unorthodox elite in prerevolutionary Ethiopia through use of the Leninist term "professional revolutionaries"; it also has referred to their uncommon dedication.

What defines such elites is the eccentricity of their values and beliefs. This characteristic isolates them from the rest of the society until lingering social dissatisfactions give them the opportunity to cast the social frustration in terms of their cultural eccentricity. When they succeed in seizing the opportunity, these elites rise to the leadership of social protests. To study revolutions is thus to follow "sparks across national borders, carried by small groups and idiosyncratic individuals who created an incendiary legacy of ideas."[60] The process of social revolution evolves as small groups composed of eccentric personalities bent on secrecy and conspiratorial behavior progressively expand their sway. The case of Ethiopia reproduced this general pattern: we saw the appearance of a radical group named "Crocodile" whose essential characteristics were secrecy, single-mindedness, and complete devotion to the cause of the revolution. We also followed how Ethiopian social conditions and the repressive policy of the government combined to propel the radicals to the leadership of the student movement to the detriment of the moderates.

To underline the importance of the notion of unorthodox elite, it is instructive to discuss an article comparing Ethiopian and Nepalese students. The authors of the study, Peter Koehn and Louis D. Hayes, see striking similarities between Ethiopia and Nepal and their respective student movements. They also detect differences due essentially to Ethiopian students being more radical than Nepalese students. While Ethiopian students were committed to the violent overthrow of the monarchy and the establishment of socialism, "during the same period, students in Nepal consistently supported the monarchy."[61] The study attempts to explain this major difference.

Let us begin by establishing that students in Nepal and Ethiopia indeed faced similar sociopolitical conditions. Traditional autocratic regimes led by conservative monarchs exercising absolute power ruled both countries. The ideological apparatuses justifying the exercise of absolute power in both countries were also comparable in that they advocated the fusion of the political and the sacred: "In Ethiopia and Nepal, monarchical authority is founded on a long history of rule by royal families and myths of divine authority. The Ethiopian Orthodox Church affirms the divine nature of imperial authority. In Nepal, the king is considered a reincarnation of the Hindu god Vishnu."[62] Moreover, both countries were not subject to prolonged colonial rule; nor did they receive massive amounts of foreign investment. As a result, they were overwhelmingly rural, nonliterate, and poor. Similarities are found in the educational systems as well. To train indigenous technical, professional, and administrative cadres, both countries gave great importance to modern education, which they tried to develop by appealing to expatriate academic faculties.

How, then, could so similar social and political conditions lead to such dissimilar student attitudes? Why did Ethiopian students challenge the legitimacy of the monarchy and opt for socialism, while Nepalese students expressed similar discontents but fell short of questioning the monarchy's legitimacy, limiting their demands to the establishment of a constitutional monarchy? To quote Koehn and Hayes: "What accounts for such divergent perceptions of regime legitimacy in similar polities? Existential conditions of poverty, illiteracy, and vast social and economic inequities are found in both Nepal and Ethiopia during the period under investigation. Yet, only Ethiopian students attribute these conditions to the political system."[63]

To explain the disparity in radicalization, the authors review the reactions of the two regimes to student opposition. Thus, unlike the Ethiopian government, which opted for continued repression, the Nepalese government showed an "accommodative pattern of political control."[64] In addition to allowing students to demonstrate and protest, it agreed in principle with some of their demands, such as the establishment of a free press, the reform of the educational system, and the removal of the ban on political parties. Another important difference was the lack of marginalized ethnic or religious groups: "the discontent with ethnic, religious, or regional group progress manifested by some Ethiopian students was not an issue in Nepal."[65] Lastly, owing to the greater isolation of the country, Nepalese students were not as exposed to radical ideologies as Ethiopian students were.

Are the mentioned differences really enough to explain the greater radicalization of Ethiopian students? Surely, the less repressive reaction of the Nepalese government did not favor the radicals. The authors allude to the appearance among Nepalese students of radical groups that tried to assume the leadership of a nationwide strike of students over reform issues. During the strike, "ideological and revolutionary slogans were employed to an unprecedented extent. Violent police reaction to student processions resulted in many arrests and a new level of student radicalization."[66] However, following this escalation, something that never happened in Ethiopia occurred in Nepal: the student movement divided and, most of all, "when revolutionary slogans began to appear, moderate students withdrew support for the strike."[67] We must understand what caused the withdrawal of the moderates' support and why they were able to break up the student movement. That the Nepalese government was less repressive is not sufficient cause, since the withdrawal of the moderates' support occurred at a time of heightened confrontation.

The withdrawal of the Nepalese moderates expressed their commitment to reformism, that is, their enduring confidence in the availability of reformist solutions to the existing social problems, however severe they may be. What we need to understand is why moderation did not prevail among Ethiopian students. For we cannot deduce a Marxist-Leninist type of radicalization from the existence of grave economic, ethnic, and religious problems in Ethiopia, since students in countries with comparable problems did not go through a similar ideological metamorphosis. The mistake is to assume that the majority of the students became radicalized because definite and serious problems existed. The problem must be stated otherwise. Radical groups may exist always and anywhere; the question is under what conditions do such groups assume the leadership of student protests, thereby radicalizing the movement. Radical groups existed in Nepal, but the conditions allowing them to take up the leadership never completely developed. As

Koehn and Hayes noted, the majority of students refused to follow the course advocated by radical students.

What else could explain the attitude of the majority but the refusal to question the traditional legitimacy of the monarchy? Despite the accumulation of social problems, there was a threshold that the majority of Nepalese students refused to cross. Instead of favoring the radicals, the escalation of the conflict with the government set off the alarm of an irreparable polarization that most Nepalese students rejected. The disparity between Ethiopian and Nepalese students remains unexplained so long as we do not know why Nepalese students saw boundaries where Ethiopian students saw none.

In whichever way we consider the problem, the explanation for the establishment of boundaries points to the cultural disposition of Nepalese students. However appalling social conditions may have been, there never developed a large movement of cultural heterodoxy in Nepal. Accordingly, the conflict was confined to social issues; it did not spill over to the realm of values and beliefs. Had it done so, the need for total change would have displaced reformism. All the more reason to pose the problem in cultural terms is Koehn and Hayes's insistence that the main safeguard against the radicalization of Nepalese students was their commitment to the sacred legitimacy of the monarchy. Nepalese students refused the path of radicalization because of their religious belief.

In Ethiopia, too, so long as the religious justification of the monarchy prevailed, people blamed, not the emperor, but his entourage. The religious justification soon declined in Ethiopia, while it persisted in Nepal. Why? No social or political reasons can fully explain the decline since they were more or less similar in both countries. What then remains but the cultural difference? Put otherwise, the decline of the monarchy's religious underpinning in Ethiopia was the product of a change that occurred at the cultural level. So stated, the problem amounts to asking why Hinduism resisted better than Christianity, given that Ethiopia's revolutionary students came predominantly from Orthodox Christian families.

The reason for the weaker resistance of Ethiopian culture is not hard to find: because of a common Christian background with the West, Ethiopian students were more receptive to Western ideas, and by extension to Marxism, than were Nepalese students. Western statements and accomplishments did not appear as detrimental to Ethiopian identity. Not so with the Nepalese: being non-Christians, attachment to Hinduism meant the defense of their identity. While for Ethiopian students the West appeared as a developed form of what they are, as their future, for Nepalese students it meant self-denial. Hence the stronger attachment of Nepalese students to Hinduism, as opposed to the "tradable" religion of Ethiopian students.

For modern-educated Ethiopians, the West had already shown the right path by overthrowing monarchies, establishing republics, and instituting the separation of church and state while remaining ostensibly Christian. This is to say that the introduction of Western education could not have the same impact on Nepalese and Ethiopian students. While in Nepal it provoked a reaction leading to cultural conservatism as a means of defending identity, in Ethiopia it stimulated cultural disaffection because the common Christian background could not but portray the West as the future of backward Ethiopia. There developed a cultural chasm between the modern educated elite and the traditional ruling elite the consequence of which was the gathering of conditions favorable to extreme polarization. The cultural divorce with the traditional elite left the rising elite in a state of mental wandering that made it vulnerable to the discourse of the radicals. With the multiplication of social problems and the intensification of repression, nothing was left that could counter the temptation of a total shakeup.

Add to this temptation the Ethiopian predisposition to messianism inherited from the Christian legacy. As will be amply shown in chapter 6, Hindu culture is less receptive to radical ideology. Because it does not place a great tension between the mundane and the otherworldly, Hinduism does not incite millenarian or utopian thinking. By contrast, the Christian belief more sharply distinguishes the temporal and the otherworldly. It hopes to resolve the tension when the advent of the kingdom of God brings about the final triumph of justice and freedom. The affinity that so many studies underscore between millenarian thinking and revolutionary ideologies of the Marxist type should enter into the explanation of the disparity between Ethiopian and Nepalese students. The Ethiopian cultural predisposition to revolutionary ideology is an important factor in the explanation not only of the emergence of radical groups but also of their greater ability—compared to Nepalese radicals—to attract many followers and assume the leadership of the student movement. Not that the majority of students really became radical, rather radical groups could easily touch a sensitive cord that facilitated their rise to leadership.

The upcoming chapters will study the cultural conditions that led to the appearance of unorthodox groups and the concrete process that facilitated their ideological hegemony over the Ethiopian educated elite. The process was complex, involving various mental outcomes in combination with definite sociopolitical parameters. The next chapter assesses the deep implications of the introduction of Western education in Ethiopia.

2

Eurocentrism and Haile Selassie's Educational Precept

An inquiry into the origin of the revolutionary mind in Ethiopia must begin by exploring the effects of Western education on the country's youth. According to Bahru Zewde, the introduction of modern education in Ethiopia produced not only Ethiopians trained in modern administrative and technical skills but also "intellectuals who woke up to a disturbing awareness of their country's backwardness and became committed to the introduction of reforms."[1] Unfortunately, Ethiopia's continuous political crises and economic stagnation since the Revolution of 1974—that is, since the Ethiopian educated elite took charge of the destiny of the country—flatly contradict the assumption that the system of education has produced enlightened reformers. In lieu of producing expedient reforms, the social promotion of the educated elite has inaugurated polarizing and confrontational methods of political competition. The wide adherence to the Marxist idea of class struggle and to ethnonationalism gives evidence of the attraction toward divisive ideologies. Since the appropriation of Western education defines the new elite, the question whether the nature of the system of education was instrumental to the receptivity to divisive ideologies emerges as a primary object of inquiry.

In adding to the predicaments issuing from a frozen sociopolitical system the cultural pathology of the educated elite, this approach goes beyond the usual explanation of the Ethiopian Revolution. The assumption that appalling social problems made radicalism attractive only partially explains why Ethiopia engaged in a revolutionary instead of reformist course. In reality, the revolutionary course resulted from a combination of social problems with mental disorientation imparted by exposure to Western education. The purpose of this chapter is to unravel the corrosive effects of Western education on the native educated elite.

The Function of Modern Education in Transitional Societies

We have already indicated that some studies dealing with student radicalism give more importance to cultural crises than economic factors. Their main argument is that student movements, be they in developed or developing countries, typically recruit people of elite family backgrounds who are, therefore, not primarily angered by downturns in the economy. The tendency to pin student protests on cultural factors chiefly implicates the development of "a sharp disjunction between the values and expectations embodied in the traditional families in a society and the values and expectations prevailing in the occupational sphere."[2] Inasmuch as this line of thinking speaks of the inevitable conflict between traditional and modern values, it detects the incubation of intense cultural crises in the very making of the intelligentsia of third world countries.

That the early exposure to Western education is the primary source of the clash between traditional cultures and Western values and beliefs in the mind of educated elites in third world countries can hardly be denied. If revolutionism is first of all an expression of general disagreement with the existing society, then even before the advent of a particular economic or political grudge, the divorce is caused by the impact of Western education. The assimilation of Western ideas generates a split between the existing society and the educated elite. The economic failures of existing regimes only add up to a split already consummated, an alienation already accomplished. Western ideas present traditional societies as anachronistic, backward, and so as ordained for a major transformation even before the hatching of sensitivity to economic or political falloffs. In alienating educated elites from their society, these ideas cause the primary fracture, which is therefore cultural.

The revolutionary attitude can easily grow from an alienated mind, which naturally assumes the mission of extirpating barbarism and backwardness from the native soil. Let there be no misunderstanding: the revolutionary orientation of students and intellectuals cannot be exclusively ascribed to the nature of the educational system. Many factors intervene, such as economic failures and blockage of social mobility. But it is also evident that the educational system creates a predisposition that the addition of other factors easily inflames.

The factor that needs to be underlined is the type of relationship that the introduction of Western education establishes between recipient and donor cultures. Besides invading the traditional culture with new ideas and values as well as with the awareness of its lag, Western education's portrayal of the donor culture as superior demeans the recipient culture. A normal, self-centered contact between two different cultures involves a free exchange resulting in the mutual benefit of both cultures. Each culture maintains its own norms and appropriates ideas in a selective manner so as to avoid harm to its integrity and growth. Not so if the one culture is construed as superior: the ability to select gives way to a normative subordination as a result of which the recipient culture comes to despise itself and tries to model itself on the donor culture. By this self-empting posture, the dominated culture takes in not only ideas and techniques but also norms.

Unlike modernization theorists, who often fail to see the whole picture, many scholars of culture change "have called attention to the effects of modern schooling, usually to point out its disintegrating results on tribal communities and tribal culture."[3] The process of modern education does not simply pour new ideas into the recipient culture; it also undermines existing beliefs and values, leading to disorientation, conflict of values, negative views of one's legacy, and a sense of inferiority. Since the dominant culture wants to mold the recipient culture in its own image, the former cannot do so without dissolving the latter's identity, pride, and autonomy. Denouncing the upshot of modern education in Africa, one scholar accurately said: "The African was treated as a *tabula rasa* upon which could be written a completely new civilization."[4]

We miss the issue if, following Seymour M. Lipset, we assume that "the tasks of the universities in the underdeveloped countries of the world are fundamentally not very different from what they are in more highly developed societies."[5] The purpose of universities in developed countries is to transmit the cultural heritage of their society and train people in skills pertaining to science, technology, management, and administration. In underdeveloped countries, universities forfeit the function of transmitting the culture of their society. Since their curriculum is copied from the developed world, they transmit the heritage not of their society but essentially of the Western world. Far from transmitting indigenous cultures, they promote their dismissal on the ground that modernization means the adoption of Western values and institutions.

Lipset maintains that, besides the transmission of the "universal" culture, universities have the simultaneous role of "cultivating and developing the indigenous, actual or potential national culture and enhancing national life."[6] For one thing, he forgets that the so-called "universal culture" is none other than Western culture passing itself off as universal culture. For another, he concedes that "the situation is not made easier politically and pedagogically by the fact that in Africa, and in major areas of Asia, university teaching and scientific writing are still conducted in the languages of the former colonial powers."[7] If native universities use alien languages, then it is not clear how they can go about developing national cultures.

This Eurocentric orientation clearly shows that universities in underdeveloped countries have a different mission than in developed countries. In developing countries, the mission of higher education is to civilize, to modernize indigenous societies in the image of the West, while the mission of universities in developed countries is to pursue the progress of the existing society by the further development of knowledge and technology. Any society needs the two functions of education, to wit, progress and continuity. When change is produced from within a culture or introduced by a similar culture, continuity is hardly an issue, as integration occurs almost naturally. That is why, favoring change over stability, Westerners "seldom consider [education] as a means of achieving cultural continuity or of building social stability and cohesion."[8] The situation is different in third world countries: the invasion of an alien and denigrating culture turns the issue of continuity into a major problem, all the more so as the capacity of education for bringing about positive changes depends on the extent to which the recipient culture conserves its integrity.

The Need to Decolonize Education

Let us make sure that the real dimension of the problem is correctly grasped. When the problem of modern education is discussed in Africa, the consensus is to deplore its unsuitability to the needs of Africans. The culprit is, of course, "the survival of colonial influences," which survival "means that in varying degrees education is badly adapted to national realities and the needs, situation and aspirations of the people."[9] The solution seems no less obvious: modern education would become relevant if Africans applied a systematic policy of Africanization. "There is a great feeling that first, the staff should be Africanized and secondly, the curriculum should be Africanized."[10]

The central question is what exactly does Africanization mean. If it means the introduction of Africa's past and present realities while using Western concepts and views to understand those realities, what we have is not Africanization, but Africa still viewed through a Western lens. In whichever way we contrive the borrowed concepts and views, they will invariably give a negative portrayal of African realities. Measured against the Western model, African characteristics will continue to appear deficient, backward, and in serious need of total remodeling. Though African universities have increasingly included the study of African realities in their curricula, Africanization remains a failed attempt because the Western paradigm still controls the acquisition of knowledge and the teaching process. Africanization succeeds only when African realities are perceived and understood in their own terms, that is, only when the entire curriculum and the teaching staff are first decolonized. The work essentially requires that concepts and theories be emptied of their strongly Eurocentric content.

Take the attempt to Africanize the teaching of history. Great efforts have been and are being made to give the teaching of African history a prominent place in the curriculum. Notably, the impediment due to the lack of written documents has been partially removed by "the acceptance and refinement of the methodology of oral traditions as a means for recapturing the African voices from the past."[11] Nonetheless, significant though these efforts are, they are still a long way from producing a real African historiography. Unless a way of interpreting history independently of Western norms and philosophical assumptions is found, the evolutionary scheme that makes African societies into backward formations remains. The incorporation of oral traditions into African historiography is not enough if concepts conserving Eurocentric meanings are used to interpret these traditions. Describing the remaining challenge, B. A. Ogot writes: "We have struggled hard to reject a conceptual framework which is Western both in its origins as well as its orientations. But we have not yet succeeded in evolving an autonomous body of theoretical thinking. Herein lies the root of our cultural dependence."[12]

Unless the work of decolonization is seriously carried out, the harmful consequences of the imported Western system of education are simply unavoidable. The harm even invalidates the widely held portrayal of modern education as the best means to achieve rapid modernization. When given outside the particular and historical context of third world countries, modern education yields a very superficial understanding of modernity. Because many of the ideas drawn from alien contexts are delivered to students without any sense of their relevance to local conditions, they are hardly useful for analysis and understanding. Once divorced from the concrete conditions that gave them rise, ideas cease to be instruments of analysis; they become norms to which local conditions must be made conformable. Instead of enhancing comprehension, borrowed concepts mystify the recipient culture by imparting a normative stature to whatever comes from the West. In thus failing to be reflections of existing and particular conditions, they activate infatuation rather than the propensity to an insightful form of thinking. The normative subordination stemming from Western scientific and technological advances becomes, in the end, so overwhelming that Africans see no other explanation for their lag than through the endorsement of racial inequalities. Given that "the sense of awe toward the West becomes a foundation for subsequent intellectual dependency," the learning of self-debasement and of Africa's insignificance, more than the acquisition of skills and enlightenment, defines Western education.[13]

The concept of Platonization best describes the nature of modern education in third world countries. As one Ethiopian scholar correctly stated, "Infatuated with . . . [Western] ideas, college students tend to maintain an extreme and idealistic position."[14] Just as for Plato the world of ideas provides the norms of truth and goodness to the visible and lesser world, so too modern education depicts the Western world as a Platonic ideal world to which the non-Western world must conform. The native intellectual represents the "philosopher-king" who, having visited the upper world, returns to shape the visible world in the image of the ideal. An educational system based on Platonic premises hardly helps students develop a practical, pragmatic connection with the local realities they face; they rather become copyists, imitators. Moreover, the sense of visiting a higher, normative world sets off the tendency to radicalism, which is none other than the mission to redeem the native world from the perversities of primitiveness.

Confusing Nationalism with Elitism

A largely shared assumption maintains that the emergence of nationalist elites was one of the unwanted consequences of the introduction of colonial education in Africa. Referring to the assumption, Ali A. Mazrui writes: "During the colonial period in Africa, education served the purpose of creating not only a reservoir of qualified people which the government could use, but also a pool of potential qualified nationalists who came to challenge the colonial presence itself."[15] Scholars who underline this positive impact of Western education are often at odds with their other statements in which they denounce its alienating effect. How could the same education impart at once alienation and nationalism when we know that the latter presupposes some attachment to native legacies? Moreover, postindependence developments strongly contest the belief in the emergence of consistent nationalist elites in Africa. First, though the expectation was that Western education would detribalize African elites, in postindependent Africa tribal conflicts actually multiplied. Secondly, African developments did not confirm the assumption that one important factor of nationalism is "the predominance of modern political values and ideals," such as democracy and economic prosperity.[16] Instead, dictatorship, nepotism, economic mismanagement, and stagnation became the defining features of postcolonial Africa.

The truth is that cultural dependency stands in the way of a real nationalist positioning of African educated elites. Only when colonial rule is perceived as an intolerable offense and humiliation to a culture with which one identifies does the premise of a nationalist reaction emerge. Nationalism is thus defensive; as such, it is anti-Western in the sense that it challenges the superiority of the West, a good example being the case of Japan. It is a political and ideological stand inspired by a resisting and combating culture. But since the end result of Western education has been to instill the idea that the cultural legacy is not worth defending, its first impact is not to instigate the rise of nationalism, but to suppress it. Mazrui brings out the unsuitability of Westernized education to nationalism when he notes: "All educated Africans to a man (and to a woman) are still cultural captives of the West. The range is from Samora Machel (a captive of Marxism as a western ideology) to Léopold Senghor (a captive of French philosophical traditions), from

Charles Njonjo (a profoundly anglicized Kenyan) to Wole Soyinka (the angry westernized rebel with a Yoruba accent)."[17]

The confusion of nationalism with elitism explains the mistaken diagnosis about African educated elites. Where these elites rose against the colonial rule and ultimately managed to wrest political power from colonizers, the explanation is to be found not so much in their nationalist drive as in their situation of competition with metropolitan elites. The competitive situation originated from the very premise of Western education. Since the justification of colonization was that advanced people had the right to rule over retarded people so as to civilize them, native elites who partook of the same enlightenment acquired the right to rule. The right to take the place of the colonizer implies, it should be noted, the acceptance and continuation of the definition of political rule as a civilizing mission. A further reason for educated Africans to believe in their right to supplant colonizers is their better suitability to fulfill the civilizing mission. Being natives, they have the ability to resolve the Western contradiction of a civilizing mission undercut by racism. Native elites are thus the correctors of the colonial system in that they alone can implement the ideas of equality, democracy, and economic prosperity.

This idea of being the true implementer of enlightenment explains the attraction of African intellectuals to theories that criticize the West, such as Marxism and postmodernism. These theories confirm these Africans' perception that they are the true sons of the values that the West discovered but disfigured. The perception unleashes what Mazrui calls *"aggressive dependency,"* the outcome of which is that educated Africans posit themselves as the authentic heirs to the best of Western culture, henceforth endowed with a universal significance.[18] When Western ideas are used against the West, it is less out of nationalism than out of the aggressive dependency making African intellectuals into the rescuers of a betrayed legacy.

That African intellectuals are often ferociously critical of the Western world because of their tendency to define themselves as authentic heirs to the Western legacy is best evidenced by the great impact that Marxist diatribes against capitalism has had on them. By vigorously denouncing the duplicity of Western civilization and calling for its complete turnover, Marxism appears as a transfigured African voice to many African intellectuals. Mazrui writes: "We are against Europe so we go Marxist. We forget that Marxism is simply another European tradition—a tradition of dissent indeed; a tradition of rebellion; a heresy within Europe, but still an intellectual tradition of Europe."[19] If Africans missed the Eurocentric inspiration of Marxism, it is because they had already defined themselves as rectifiers of that inspiration rather than as nationalists, and this definition put them in the good company of the dissenting position of Marxism. Furthermore, the Leninist component of Marxism flattered their political ambition by investing them with the historical task of leading their people toward liberation and prosperity. Just as Lenin had predicted, no other class than the Western educated elite can direct African societies toward modernization, bogged down as all the other classes are by their alliances with imperialist forces.

Would-Be Europeans

What is said here seems to contradict my assessment underlining the failure of African modernization. How comes it that African societies proved unable to get out of underdevelopment even as elites claiming to be the authentic heirs to the best of Western culture were their guides? The contradiction is only apparent, for the simple reason that the kind of elites that African societies have does not match with the ascetic or puritan elites that have launched industrialization in such countries as China, Russia, and Japan. Unlike the Chinese and Russian Marxists or Japanese samurai, a huge gap between theory and practice encumbers the African educated class. Despite lofty discourses about modernity, capitalism, or socialism, African educated elites have so far shunned the determined and systematic pursuit of these lofty discourses about attaining modernity. Their undertakings have been repeatedly spoiled by adverse practices and lack of single-mindedness.

For many scholars, the impairment resulting from the conflict between tradition and modernity explains the lack of determination of educated Africans. For instance, Stanislav Andreski writes, "Their exposure to clashing scales of values has turned them into practical cynics and theoretical ideologues."[20] The fact that educated Africans are persons of two incompatible worlds—the native world from which they inherited traditional values and the modern world to which their education gave them access—entails a clash of values that can only be confusing and paralyzing. To begin with, the clash disturbs the process of acculturation and turns the modernity of the elite into a superficial acquisition. It also provokes a conflict of loyalty between traditional and modern values, thereby making the commitment to modern values hesitant and contradictory. The gap between theory and practice widens as a result of this conflict of loyalty. Unable to realize all the necessary conditions of modernization, the educated elite compensates its deficiency in practical realizations by an excess of theoretical assurance.

My own analysis does not fully agree with the role given to the conflict of loyalty—not that I deny the existence of such a conflict, but because I question its alleged importance. To give great importance to the clash of values presupposes that educated Africans still value their traditions, that they are really torn between two equally important commitments. How can it be so when we know that the major fallout of Western education is uprootedness, that is, the loss of allegiance to tradition? On account of this loss, I contested the characterization of the educated elite as a nationalist class. Let us see whether uprootedness itself accounts for the gap between theory and practice.

We have already indicated that theoretical learning that excludes local realities causes infatuation with ideas. This type of learning inverts the order of things: instead of ideas reflecting reality, it is reality that must conform to ideas taken as norms. The normalization of the West and the subsequent attempt to transpose its norms to alien local realities produce a characteristic disjunction that discourages practice in favor of exhortation. The cleavage between the borrowed theory and the local reality becomes so sharp that it disables the practical will. In other words, the gap between theory and practice is none other than the expression of the alienation of African educated elites from African realities. As though their mind had become too big and too important for the African body, concern for practical realization becomes secondary, almost unworthy. Instead, pure, unmixed enchantment with ideas matters most to the elites, as it is proof of their transition to the higher and normative world.

The loss of commitment to tradition also explains the lack of determination from the moral angle. This loss leads to the feeling that the educated African is not accountable to the native society, that he/she is above its rules and authority. Here is the irony: though African educated elites perceive themselves as rectifiers of the civilizing mission perverted by racism, because they retain the same mission they cannot get beyond the colonial mentality. So long as "the attraction of the foreign model [is] associated with a revulsion against the backwardness of indigenous institutions," African elite cannot shake off the mentality of the colonizer, despite their good will.[21] Indeed, what else does the attraction signify but the perversion of native elites by the colonial mentality, which proved unable to implement those values in the name of which it justified colonization? The gap between theory and practice, mainly expressed by the failure of modernization and the proliferation of dictatorial regimes in Africa, is thus a fallout of the contamination of the educated elite by the colonial mentality.[22]

The Belated Colonization of Ethiopia

What singles out Ethiopia among African countries is that it escaped colonization. Owing to a series of military victories over colonial forces and cunning diplomatic connections, Ethiopia successfully foiled the design of colonial powers. The Italian occupation of the country from 1936 to 1941 was too short to produce any lasting impact, not to mention its failure to crush the resistance of nationalist forces. Undeniable as these facts are, the prevailing consensus portraying Ethiopia as a noncolonized country is, however, quite misleading. Far from me to deny the reality of Ethiopian independence, but colonization meant more than just the loss of political sovereignty. The most enduring and detrimental impact of colonization is actually cultural colonization to which Ethiopia was subjected since the introduction of modern education. The illusion of having been independent all along made Ethiopians so insensitive to the issue of alienation that they did not feel the need to redefine and revive their legacy and identity, as did so many colonized people. Ethiopians preferred to deny their alienation rather than admit that the independence of which they are so proud got lost somewhere along the way to modernization.

No better way exists to validate the thesis of the belated colonization of Ethiopia than to show that all the flaws that beset African educated elites are also those of the Ethiopian educated elite. Despite the preservation of its sovereignty, the bare and distressing fact is that Ethiopia adopted a system of education that had and still has all the characteristics of colonial education. Like other African countries, the Ethiopian society was judged backward, and the purpose of modern education was to civilize, to modernize. The function of education was to produce a new elite that, having internalized Western values and institutions, would bring about modernization by remodeling traditional society on the Western model. Because of this goal, the educational system focused on learning the Western world, that is, on internalizing its values, institutions, and achievements while pushing aside whatever is native and traditional. Modernization was not posed in terms of rivalry with the West, but in terms of Westernization. While the former presupposed the defense of identity, the latter advocated its dissolution. Tekeste Negash unravels the ambiguity of Haile Selassie's educational policy in the following terms: "The official policy during the period of Emperor Haile Sellassie was that Ethiopia, as an ancient and civilized society, should opt for a carefully selected adaptation of European ideas and systems. In practice, however, the Imperial regime did very little to inculcate respect for Ethiopian traditions of social and political organization. It left the curriculum and most of the teaching in secondary schools to expatriates who quite naturally spread the gospel of modernization."[23] Haile Selassie's complete reliance on expatriate faculty both to design the curriculum and to do the teaching indeed jeopardized whatever desire he had to preserve the Ethiopian heritage. The conclusion is obvious: even though Ethiopia was never colonized, its educational system used a curriculum that had "a strikingly colonial character."[24]

Before some Western-educated Ethiopians realized the duplicity of Western education, a senior cleric and a leading scholar of the Ethiopian Church during Haile Selassie's heydays, Aleqa Asres Yenesew, had already warned about the colonizing goal of Western education. In one of his books, he writes: "although Italy's army was driven out, its politics was not."[25] The military defeat of the colonizer did not put an end to the colonial project; it has simply compelled colonizers to proceed cautiously and to use other more subtle means. Chief among such means of preserving their original design was Western schools. That is why colonizers were so eager to open schools and send teachers. What better means were there for realizing their colonial project than the propagation of their books and the creation of a Westernized Ethiopian elite? Aleqa Asres was so firmly convinced that the so-called modern-educated Ethiopians were the instrument of Ethiopia's colonization in default of military means that he asks: what else is their role but "to appropriate and expand what originates from the enemy and pass it on to youngsters?"[26] To change "modernized" Ethiopians into turncoats, Western education had first to "denationalize their mind" by denigrating the traditional education and encouraging individualism and social ambition.[27] Westernized Ethiopians are essentially unhappy with their place in the social hierarchy because they have been talked into believing that exposure to Western education alone should determine status and authority. In thus isolating them from the rest of the community and inducing frustration over their place in the social hierarchy, Western teachers changed them into rebels.

It must not be made to seem that the introduction of modern education was smooth. It actually aroused the strong resistance of many influential members of the nobility and especially of the Ethiopian church. According to the prevailing interpretation, the church opposed modern education, not only because it took away the church's major function as the sole educator of the society, but also because the church was already a rigid, dogmatic institution little open to innovation and change. Great merit is attributed to Haile Selassie for his stubborn and consistent battle in favor of the spread of modern education, even against the combined powerful forces of the conservative nobility and the church.

The reduction of opposition to a simple reaction of conservatism, to the refusal of progress and change on the part of the nobility and the church, is a partial view. One must also see the other side of the question, namely, the nationalist reaction triggered by legitimate concerns over the integrity of Ethiopian identity and centrality. The precautions that Emperor Menelik II took when in 1908 he opened the first school that carries his name show the extent to which the traditional ruling class feared the danger of alienation. Convinced that the best way to combat alienation is to bring in expatriate teachers who had religious beliefs similar to Ethiopian students, he made sure that "instruction was safely left to Coptic teachers," who were brought from Egypt.[28] How else than in terms of sane nationalist reaction can we describe this attempt to reconcile modern education with the national cultural heritage?

With the rise of Haile Selassie, for reasons that will be discussed in the next chapter, the need to protect the national identity progressively decreased. As a result, the new education became not so much modern as

Western, all the more so as Western missionaries established the first schools. As Bahru remarks, "As in many parts of Africa, its (modern education) introduction coincided with the arrival of missionaries, who saw the provision of educational facilities as the most effective way of winning over new converts. They thus set up schools and sent the more promising ones for studies in metropolitan institutions abroad. The Catholics (both Lazarist and Capuchin) and the Protestants (the CMS and the Swedish evangelists) vied with each other in these endeavours."[29] The danger was so palpable that even people who supported the introduction of modern education argued that the national content of the education must be safeguarded by immediate drastic measures. Bahru mentions an Ethiopian lady, Abbabach Waykaman, who very early on "emphasized in particular the need to break the dependency on foreign teachers by training Ethiopians, both male and female."[30] He also cites the case of an American educational adviser to the government, Ernest Work, who in 1931 defended both the use of Amharic as a medium of instruction instead of English or French and "the Ethiopianization of curricula and textbooks."[31]

Uprooting Education

According to many scholars, the defects of Haile Selassie's educational system were numerous. They consisted of (1) the distribution of modern education among the various regions was unequal, with most schools concentrated in urban centers, such as Addis Ababa and Asmara; (2) enrollment ranked the lowest among African nations, especially in primary and secondary education; and (3) government expenditure on education, among "the lowest in Africa," was insufficient. The resulting consequences included overcrowded classrooms, lack of teaching materials, unqualified teachers, and a high number of dropouts.[32] But the gravest defect of all was, in the eyes of many scholars, the uprooting character of the educational system. As Teshome Wagaw states: "The most glaring of its shortcomings arose from the fact that both its objectives and the experiences it offered to children and youth were unrelated to Ethiopian realities, and thus its product was a younger generation unaware of and unappreciative of its own cultural heritage and roots."[33]

The root cause of this detrimental orientation can be traced back to the decisive role that foreign advisers, administrators, and teachers played in the establishment and expansion of Ethiopia's educational system. Partly because very few Ethiopians were qualified in matters dealing with modern education and partly because the prevailing bias exclusively confined whatever is modern to Western experts, Haile Selassie and his government relied totally on expatriate staff to lay the foundation of modern education. As "appointed foreign advisers tended to think that what had proved successful in their countries would also benefit Ethiopian development," curricula and teaching materials in the new Ethiopian schools naturally tended to reflect at all levels those of Western countries.[34] Besides financial, infrastructural, and technical problems, the introduction and development of modern education thus faced the paramount issue of Ethiopianization. To quote Randi Rønning Balsvik,

> Modern education in Ethiopia was imported from Great Britain and the United States, was influenced by various other western countries, and was not attuned to the country's needs. Patterns of education, curricula, and textbooks intended to further the interests of the most highly industrialized countries were transplanted into one of the least developed rural economies in the world. There was little of relevance to the basic and immediate needs of Ethiopian society. To the average child the school was essentially an alien institution about which his own parents were usually ignorant.[35]

Since the learning process focused on inculcating the normativeness of the West, in addition to being irrelevant to Ethiopian conditions, it induced copyism and imitativeness. Nowhere was the system inspired by the goal of creating persons capable of interpreting, enriching, and adapting their heritage to new needs and changing conditions. Instead of defining modernization as a challenge to tradition, the educational system made modernization conditional on the liquidation of tradition in favor of Western culture. Just like the colonial system of education, modern education in Ethiopia targeted the tabula rasa of a fresh start. The lack of continuity between the traditional and the modern "gave birth to a system of education altogether new, if not alien, to the cultural pattern of the nation."[36] As the traditional system of education was literally abandoned, the new system had no root in the past; worse yet, it was openly depreciative of the Ethiopian heritage. This does not mean that the traditional system of education was not defective. Far from it, its defects were as numerous as they were serious. Even so, the detrimental shift is best illustrated by comparing modern education with the traditional system of education.

The Ethiopian Traditional System of Education

Scholars who have reflected on the traditional system of education agree on its Ethiocentric orientation and content. The Ethiopian Orthodox Church assumed the exclusive task of designing and propagating an educational system whose central subjects were the religious beliefs, values, and practices of the Ethiopian church. Besides religious instruction, the teaching had a secular component that dealt with Ethiopia's history and sociopolitical organization. Teaching was so tied up with the church that scholars speak of

"Church schools which bore the main burden of education for sixteen centuries," that is, until they were progressively supplanted by modern schools.[37] What is said here about the traditional system does not include traditional Islamic education for the simple reason that such inclusion would have no enlightening effect on the issue of radicalization, which, as already stated, essentially affected students from the Christian parts of Ethiopia.

A brief review of the curriculum is enough to show the Ethiocentric orientation of traditional education. The system had three distinct and successive stages, which can be said to correspond to elementary, secondary, and higher levels. The first level "taught reading and writing in Ge'ez, and Amharic…and simple arithmetic. The emphasis was upon reading the Scriptures in Ge'ez, the original language of the Church ritual."[38] This elementary education was dispensed to students who became ordinary priests and deacons. Students who wanted to pursue higher levels of study had to go to the great churches and monasteries.

Higher studies began with the "*Zema Bet*" (School of Music) in which students studied the musical composition and the liturgy of the Ethiopian church.[39] The next stage was called "*Kiné Bet*," which means "School of Poetry."[40] It focused on "church music, the composition of poetry . . . theology and history, painting . . . manuscript writing."[41] In addition to these subjects, the *Kiné* level comprised the teaching of philosophy based on a main text, the "*Metsahafe-Falasfa Tabiban* (Book of Wise Philosophers), with passages from Plato, Aristotle, Diogenes, Cicero, etc."[42] The third level, called "*Metsahaf Bet*" (Schools of Texts, or Books), provided an in-depth study of the sacred books of the Old and New Testaments as well as of books related to monastic life.[43] It also included the study of three major books of Ethiopian history and code of laws, namely, "*Tarike-Negest* (monarchic history), *Kibre-Negest* (Glory of the Kings), *Fetha-Negest* (laws of the Kings)."[44] World history was taught at the third level: the ancient world and the histories of the Jews and the Arabs made up the substance of the teaching. The student who successfully went through the three stages earned the title of "*Liq*" or "*debtera.*"

The focus on Christian doctrine and values, the use of indigenous languages, and the extensive reading of books and textbooks that are pregnant with native content bear witness to the fact that the subject of study was Ethiopia, its legacies, characteristics, and history. Not only did the materials deal with Ethiopian history, customs, languages, and values, but the spirit of traditional education was also to produce scholars able to serve the church and, by extension, the country with a sense of dedication to its characteristics and sense of mission. Describing the requirement of the School of Poetry, Sylvia Pankhurst says the teaching "must be rich in content, revealing a deep knowledge of the Bible, of Ethiopian history, and of the stories and legends which have gathered during the centuries around the great personalities and events of religious and national tradition."[45]

Take the Ethiopic text known as the *Kibre Negast*: it establishes kinship between the rulers of Ethiopia and King Solomon of Israel, the favorite nation of God. The epic narrates the visit of an Ethiopian queen, Sheba or Makeda, to King Solomon and the subsequent birth of a son who became the king of Ethiopia under the name of Menelik I. Besides stating the blood ties of Ethiopian rulers with the Solomonic dynasty, the epic relates the transfer of God's favor from Israel to Ethiopia. The reason for the shift of God's favor is, undoubtedly, Christianity. Unlike the Jewish people, acceptance of Christianity promoted Ethiopians to the rank of God's chosen people.

This way of tying Christianity to a given territory, people, and emperorship turns the *Kibre Negast* into a national epic. It lays the foundation for the merger of church and state, and so "defines the secular and religious foundation of Ethiopian nationhood."[46] It also imparts a direction to history such that Ethiopia is where the sun rises and sets. Indeed, the whole purpose of relating Ethiopian rulers to King Solomon originated not so much from the desire to claim a Judaic racial identity as from the need of a messianic history uniquely able to give Ethiopia the confidence it needed to defend its Christian identity in a region increasingly dominated by Islam. Surrounded by Muslim countries, Ethiopia could not hope to survive unless it had the guarantee of a special relationship with God, emanating from the sense of being God's favored nation. The following passage taken from the chronicles of King Amda-Seyon, who was Emperor of Ethiopia from 1314 to 1344, gives a clear sense of the divine guarantee:

> As for us, we have heard and we know from the Holy Scriptures that the kingdom of the Moslems, established for but seven hundred years, shall cease to be at the proper time. But the kingdom of the Christians shall continue till the second coming of the Son of God, according to the words of Holy Scripture; and above all (we know) that the kingdom of Ethiopia shall endure till the coming of Christ, of which David prophesied saying "Ethiopia shall stretch her hand unto God."[47]

The promise of the final triumph of Ethiopia gave the direction and the ultimate goal of world history. Since the Apocalypse means the survival of Ethiopia when everything else is destroyed, the obligation to stand fast becomes Ethiopia's scriptural vocation. Clearly, the impregnation of students with the spirit of *Kibre Negast* enabled them to see the world from the viewpoint of Ethiopia. In a word, the discourse centered Ethiopia by endowing it with a specific mission, which became the repository of its national identity.

Compare for one moment this traditional understanding of history with the Hegelian vision of history, which largely underpins the modern, that is, Western, teaching of history. Resolutely making Europe the center of history, Hegel writes: "the History of the World travels from East to West, for Europe is absolutely the end of History."[48] Since what happened outside Europe was either a mere prelude to Europe or something insignificant, the real development and consummation of history take place in Europe. Being backward, non-European countries are only fit to be towed by the European engine.

Such is not the manner of the *Kibre Negast*'s conception of world history. It purposefully centers Ethiopia by construing world history as a background, an introduction to the Ethiopian epic of survival. The driving force of history is Ethiopia's resistance and fidelity to the authentic Christian faith. History is not defined in terms of new technological or cultural inventions; the preservation of genuine Christianity amid adverse forces, such as Islam, paganism, and heretical Christian doctrines, is the defining concept of history. The epic of Ethiopian survival is none other than the final triumph of good over evil.

The emphasis on serving the church did not entail the exclusive confinement of the traditional system to the formation of priests, deacons, and church teachers. Religious education extended to the secular realm, since "church education also produced civil servants . . . such as judges, governors, scribes, treasurers, and general administrators."[49] This extension to secular society was a natural consequence of the basic and all-embracing function of religion in Ethiopia. Religious instruction conveyed the norms of social behavior, the meaning of the social hierarchy, and the rights and duties attached to the social status of individuals. Traditional education was thus both mundane and spiritual: it taught a religious belief that was inextricably intertwined with a definite social system and a mode of life. According to the renowned Ethiopian novelist and essayist Addis Alemayehu, traditional education had served as "a powerful means to unite the spiritual existence with the secular mode of life."[50]

In addition to its highly integrative and nationalistic function, the other virtue of the traditional system was its freedom from political influence and vicissitudes. This freedom emanated from the complete autonomy of the church from the state in terms of education. Because traditional schools were "run by the Church without the intervention of the state," education was not politicized.[51] On the contrary, church education transcended political rivalries to concentrate on what was permanently Ethiopian, and so was an agent of unity and national cohesion. As one author writes, "Acting as the sole repository of Christian culture and identity, an educated elite of priests and *debteras* preserved a heritage which for fifteen centuries united the Christian community against surrounding alien cultural influences."[52]

Playing the Sorcerer's Apprentice

Modern critics of Ethiopia's traditional system of education have, of course, no trouble exposing its severe shortcomings. Thus, Mulugeta Wodajo points out that the techniques and content of the education were not particularly apt to develop the understanding; nor were they likely to cultivate the intellectual faculties of creativity, criticism, and imagination. These deficiencies sprang from the emphasis on "the role of rote memory" in the traditional educational system.[53] Worse, the teaching used a language that was not current and familiar to students, as "all the texts are in Ge'ez and hence are meaningless for the child."[54] However, the recognition that the high level of poetry made "great use of the imagination and creative mind of the pupil" tempers Mulugeta's negative evaluation.[55] He even adds: "It is a source of sorrow to see the decline of the '*Zema Bet*' without any worthwhile substitute in the Government schools."[56] Some critics have underlined the discriminatory nature of the church's education, since only parents who were Orthodox Christian could send their children to the traditional schools. "Church schools did not serve the whole nation, therefore, and so cannot be considered impartial or democratic," says one such critic.[57]

Critics are unanimous and most vociferous in their denunciation of the total expulsion of scientific courses from the traditional system of education. Being basically religious, the teaching had little inclination to include scientific and technological components. The reluctance changed into outright rejection as the religious doctrine progressively turned into rigid dogma. The dismissal of whatever was not in line with transmitted beliefs was so endemic that Teshome Wagaw speaks of an approach to education that "became increasingly rigid, to the point of ossification."[58] The educational system simply stuck to the old belief according to which "as the heavens and the earth are ruled by God all enquiries into the working of the heavenly bodies and the laws of nature were and are regarded as sinful."[59]

As so rigid and antiscientific a system was particularly unfit for modernization, Ethiopia, like most third world countries, reached the conclusion that the best way to get out of the disabilities of the traditional system and catch up with the economic and social advances of Western countries was through the resolute sidelining of traditional schools and the rapid spread of modern education. The latter is a shortcut to development: an appropriate system of education can capture and rapidly disseminate what Europe has achieved through a long and gradual process of evolution. And as science, technology, and enlightened beliefs and values are the distinctive features of modernity, no better means exists to effect a rapid modernization than through the adoption of the Western system of education.

For Ethiopia, the adoption of the Western system meant an abrupt shift from the religious content of the traditional system to secular subject matter. It also made the inculcation of the innovative spirit characteristic of modernity conditional on the dissolution of traditional conservatism. Accordingly, the formation of an educated elite entirely opposed to the characteristics of the traditional elite became the major goal of the new system. The task of modernization was particularly difficult: the traditional system directly coun-teracted the effort by its very purpose of producing a mind that repudiates whatever tradition has not sanctioned. To show how diametrically the tradi-tional system was opposed to the spirit of modernity, Teshome writes: "The purpose of church education is not to extend man's understanding of the world, but rather to lead men to accepting the existing order of things as it is, to preserve whatever has been handed down through the years, and in turn to pass it on unchanged to the next generation."[60] Given its complete opposition and irrelevance to the modern world, the traditional system of education was beyond salvation. It had to be entirely rejected and replaced by modern schools.

Before making a judgment on the wisdom of the decision to virtually elim-inate church schools, we must reflect on the characteristics of the system that replaced the traditional system. Let there be no misunderstanding: the argu-ment that church schools should have been preserved is not the basis of my assessment of modern education in Ethiopia. As Addis Alemayehu noted, given the realities of the modern world and the new challenges it poses, "it is very difficult to say that an education restricted to the teaching of religion and mode of life can fulfill the needs of the society."[61]

It is one thing to say that the system had to be changed, but quite another to entirely throw away the old in favor of an alien system. The path taken by Ethiopia was not to update and modernize the traditional system; it was to erase past practices so as to implement the new. The question of whether such a policy was wise is all the more legitimate the more the expected ben-efits of the new system proved elusive. Indeed, so radical and rapid a shift was bound to encounter great difficulties. Even those who are very harsh about Ethiopia's traditional education admit that modern education has lamenta-bly failed. In particular, many scholars, as we saw, have deplored its alienat-ing impact.

The causes of the failure are no doubt multiple. Some of them emanate from the inability to provide the appropriate material and human condi-tions. Others are products of misconceptions and policy impediments. However grave the defects of the traditional system of education may have been, since modern education initiated the country's belated colonization, its adoption was nothing less than a bad deal for Ethiopia. How, then, is one to explain the eagerness and the determination of the imperial regime to introduce and expand an educational system with such detrimental conse-quences? Was it lack of awareness? Or was it the outcome of a flawed approach to education? The next chapter will try to answer this disturbing question.

3

Origins and Purpose of Haile Selassie's Educational Policy

The traditional system of education in Ethiopia, however serious its defects may have been, gives us a clear idea of what a national system of education looks like. A review of the system of modern education introduced by the imperial regime confirms that, more than the shortcomings due to deficient material and human conditions, the inculcation of alienation was its most serious deficiency. What needs to be firmly established is that the deficiency was itself a product of the lack of national ideology.

The Lack of National Ideology

Strange as it may seem, though Haile Selassie consistently presented himself as an ardent promoter and patron of modern education and supported this role by regularly visiting schools, handing out certificates and prizes, sending students abroad, and stressing the importance of education to development in many of his speeches, he never clearly fastened his educational policy to the goal of national development. An in-depth study of the entire educational system, known as "the sector review" of 1971, has straightforwardly pointed out the lack of policy articulation. In light of the increasing number of dropouts and unemployed and the glaring inadequacy of the educational system to the needs of the country, the Ministry of Education decided to undertake a review of the entire educational system. The project involved Ethiopian scholars and experts from Haile Selassie I University, the Ministries of Agriculture and Community Development, and the Planning Commission. It also included foreign members from UNESCO, the International Labor Organization, the Ford Foundation, and Harvard University Development Advisory Service. The final report of this serious and extensive assessment deplored "the lack of a clear statement of national ideology."[1]

Nothing could better illustrate the nonnational orientation of the educational system than the manner in which Haile Selassie I University was founded and organized. The responsibility of supplying the necessary administrative and teaching staff to what was at first only a college went to American Jesuits. The Mormons replaced the Jesuits when "in 1961 a University of Utah survey team organized the graduation of the college into Haile Selassie I University."[2] The predominantly American origin of the administrative and academic staff inevitably entailed the modeling of the university on American universities: teaching as well as organizational structures reproduced the American model, and the United States also provided the textbooks.

Though Orthodox Christianity was the traditional and official religion of Ethiopia, it was not given a place at the university, and Ethiopian students were placed under the influence of Catholic and Protestant academic staff. The dominance of expatriate staff with alien religious affiliations indicated from the beginning that the university had forsaken the goal of defending and promoting the national culture, which was interwoven with Ethiopia's religious legacy. The main difference with traditional education occurred here. As we saw, the protection and dissemination of the national culture was the overriding goal of traditional education.

Let us ponder on the Ethiopian paradox. How to endow modern education with a national content and direction is a problem that Ethiopia shares with other African countries. As already indicated, all studies deplore the irrelevance and alienating effects of the African educational system. However, whereas most African countries can impute the lack of national direction to colonization and its aftermath, Ethiopia offers the unique case of failing to inaugurate and develop a national system of education while not being hampered by colonial rule. The preceding chapter explained the Ethiopian miscarriage: the introduction of modern education was itself an instrument of colonization. The insidious and creeping nature of this form of colonization caught most Ethiopians off guard. Consequently, beyond missing the opportunity to harness education to a national policy of development, the Ethiopian system took a turn that was even less protective of the national identity than the system prevailing in the colonized African countries.

Consider the study of history. Given the exceptional status of Ethiopia as an African country that safeguarded its independence by pushing back colonial forces and the great pride the victory inspires in Ethiopians, one might assume that an essential component of history courses at various levels would be devoted to explaining the reasons for Ethiopia's independence. Nothing of the kind took place: because history courses reproduced the scheme of Western history, there was no provision for the Ethiopian exception. Asked to give an idea of how history courses described Ethiopia, a former student said: "We were only told that she had preserved her independence."[3] And as the preservation of independence was not explained, it appeared as an aberration or an accident. This omission ceases to be surprising when one recalls that the history course for eighth-grade students used for many years a bulky textbook titled *The Old World—Past and Present.* On top of designating Africa as "the Dark Continent," the textbook "mentions Ethiopia as Abyssinia in only one paragraph, referring to it as an 'Italian colony.'"[4] Though Ethiopians are proud of their independence, the introduction of a system of education with a marked colonial character took from them much of the benefit of having withstood colonial powers.

My own experience corroborates the utter heedlessness of the officials of the Ministry of Education to the issue of national ideology. Soon after I finished my high school at the French school of Lycée Guebre Mariam, the French government offered me a scholarship to study philosophy in France. But officials of the Ethiopian Ministry of Education opposed the idea and demanded the cancellation of the scholarship. After much wrangling, I was finally allowed to go to France, mainly because I refused to study any other subject and the cultural attaché of the French Embassy strongly backed my position. Not surprisingly, one of the reasons for the opposition was the government's strong suspicion vis-à-vis philosophical studies. I remember one official asking me why I insisted on studying philosophy, whether I had any revolutionary intent. However, the central objection came from the conviction that the country needed not philosophers but medical doctors and engineers. Besides, the reduction of the Philosophy Department of Haile Selassie I University to one faculty member with a Canadian Jesuit teaching mostly logic for many years made apparent the indifference of the imperial regime to ideological matters.

The Gap between Intention and Practice

Haile Selassie and officials of his regime were hardly unaware of the serious shortcomings of the modern educational system. Official speeches repeatedly stressed the need to correct the system, "to Ethiopianize the entire curriculum."[5] Underlining the fundamental role of the university as guardian of Ethiopian culture, Haile Selassie said in his 1961 inaugural address:

> A fundamental objective of the University must be the safeguarding and the developing of the culture of the people which it serves. This University is a product of that culture; it is the grouping together of those capable of understanding and using the accumulated heritage of the Ethiopian people. In this University men and women will, working in association with one another, study the well-springs of our culture, trace its development, and mould its future.[6]

This major speech ascertains the connection between education and modernization: the fundamental goal of education is to modernize Ethiopia, but to modernize it in the spirit of its traditions and culture.

The study of Ethiopian culture becomes essential because, first, Ethiopia's legacy is useful and galvanizing, and second, modern education is put at the service of the society only when it connects with the culture of the Ethiopian people. Education must serve the nation, and it can do so only by promoting national culture. Development cannot occur if the beliefs and traditions of the people are demeaned or ignored. Haile Selassie reiterated the need to base development on the Ethiopian legacy: "Although such education may be technical, . . . it must nonetheless be founded on Ethiopia's cultural heritage if it is to bear fruit and if the student is to be well adapted to his environment and the effective use of his skills facilitated."[7] One of the basic tasks of the university is, therefore, to build bridges between the past and the new so as to achieve historical continuity.

Haile Selassie recommended the study and development of Ethiopia's cultural heritage as the best way to fight iconoclastic ideologies. In an apparent reference to socialist ideology, he said: "These young people face a world beset with the most effectively organized program of deceptive propaganda and of thinly screened operations ever known; they deserve the best that can be taught by their parents, by religious institutions and by the University, to prepare them for a wise choice among contending ideals."[8] The elaborate propaganda designed to mislead young and impressionable students into wrong beliefs and attitudes is effectively countered if they are taught that their heritage provides either the values they admire in other cultures or their equivalents. People desist from converting to alien ideologies if they are shown that what they have matches the best of other cultures.

None of these loudly proclaimed directives was put to work. Though the speeches called for a syncretic approach to modernization, the real practice was to hand over Ethiopian schools and higher education to expatriate staff, thereby chasing the representatives of the traditional culture out of modern institutions. True, attempts were made to inject courses dealing with Ethiopian realities into the curriculum. Thus, at the university level, the study of Ethiopian history progressively acquired a noticeable place; likewise, courses on Ethiopian geography and law were given a much needed boost. Mention should also be made of the creation of the Institute of Ethiopian Studies with its museum and library in which researchers and students could find appreciable documentation on Ethiopia.

Granted these efforts to Ethiopianize, the issue that needs to be discussed is whether the efforts successfully redirected the content of teaching. Indeed, the issue being one of ideological reorientation rather than of quantitative increase of courses devoted to Ethiopia, it is proper to ask, "To what degree did [Ethiopianization] take place and to what extent did agreement exist as to the university's role as a force for change and development in Ethiopia?"[9] It is safe to say that courses dealing with Ethiopian legacy, environment, and socioeconomic problems were simply appended to a curriculum that remained largely Eurocentric both in its inspiration and content. Moreover, the university could hardly become an engine for change and development without a free and critical examination of Ethiopia's problems. Haile Selassie's autocratic rule did not grant such a right even to the university. This suggests that the lack of national direction of the educational system may have been due to the nature of the imperial regime itself.

The Expulsion of Traditional Education

While official discourse called for a system of education that integrated the modern with the traditional, Haile Selassie, scholars are unanimous, never pushed for a serious integrative effort, which alone would have provided modern education with a national orientation. "The greatest shortcoming of the education system in Africa in general and in Ethiopia in particular is that it is poorly related to and interlinked with the traditions of education which predate the coming of the modern school," writes Tekeste Negash, an acute critic of the Ethiopian system.[10]

Nor did the resistance of the Ethiopian church make such integration impossible. The attempt to set church against modernity simply overlooks that "the Churches in Europe managed to lay down the basis for most of secular higher learning."[11] In Europe, modernity grew out of Christianity such that there was historical continuity between the religious and the secular. Being ruled by a Christian elite, Ethiopia could conceivably have gone through a similar evolution. Accordingly, the problem was not so much the resistance of the church as Haile Selassie's reluctance to encourage its reformation. For reasons that we will discuss later, rather than involving the church in the process of modernization, he opted for a policy that blocked such involvement.

In failing to integrate the modern with the traditional, the system produced students with a declining sense of national identity—indeed, with a marked contempt for their own legacy. Without the involvement of the moral and cultural values and the specific features of the national heritage, the educational system could not have a national goal. A draft paper on "educational objectives" by a task force composed of three Ethiopian experts who were involved in "the sector review" of 1971 prophetically stated: "An educational system that merely provided knowledge and skills without the essential blend of such [moral and cultural] values is in danger of producing soulless and rootless robots."[12] The Ethiopian educational system failed to accomplish the basic task of any education, namely, the transmission of the cultural legacy of the country to the next generation. To go further, by propagating the Eurocentric paradigm, the system was but denigrating Ethiopia's legacy. In so doing, what else could it produce but "a rootless social caste"?[13]

Another important author who has shown the link between the denationalization of Ethiopia's educational system and the exclusion of traditional education is Addis Alemayehu. In analyzing the reasons why modern education was not successful in Ethiopia, Addis first establishes the difference between modern and traditional education. As indicated already, because the clergy provided a system of education based on common religious beliefs and values and, moreover, without the intervention of the state, the traditional system of education was a source of unity and common identity. In addition to imparting common beliefs and values, traditional education was unifying because the nonintervention of the state left it unpoliticized. On the contrary, the church transcended political rivalries to focus on what was permanently Ethiopian. As a result, says Addis, "without changing its Ethiopian features and nature and without deflecting from its basic direction and loosening the unity of the people, the traditional education has succeeded in bringing Ethiopia where it is today through a long historical path."[14]

Nowhere is Addis advocating the preservation of traditional education. We saw in the previous chapter that he unequivocally supported the replacement of church schools by modern schools. For him, a system of education confined to the transmission of religious beliefs was singularly not adaptable to the challenges of the modern world. But here is the hitch: if "we ask the question of knowing whether these modern schools can be really called Ethiopian, the answer seems to me difficult," says Addis.[15]

Because on the one hand the Ethiopian state finances the schools and their administration and an Ethiopian staff teaches young Ethiopians who will be serving Ethiopian society, we can call them Ethiopian. On the other hand, since the main subject matter is not Ethiopia and since nothing of what defines Ethiopia is taught, the characterization of modern schools as Ethiopian is misleading. For Addis, "[It is] only when the teaching of modern schools synchronizes with Ethiopia's history, administration, social system, tradition, customs, and other distinguishing features and is taught in the language of the society that modern schools really deserve to be called Ethiopian."[16] Whatever enlightenment modern education is said to have provided, the bare truth is that, in failing to take up the task of transmitting the features that define Ethiopia and safeguard its cohesion, it has deserted its national mission.

The lack of national ideology entailed a state of disarticulation between the goal of social development and modern education. Though the need to connect the two was repeatedly stated, the absence of a national ideology created a situation where modern education became more a means to

individuals' hedonistic pursuits than a service to the nation. Modern education turns into an instrument of development when it is clearly articulated
with a social purpose; otherwise it is reduced to the level of a vehicle for individual consumerism and hedonistic gratification. Owing to the absence of a
national ideology, the disarticulation between personal pursuits and commitment to social purpose became at one point so pervasive among the
Ethiopian educated elite that it was customary to ask "whether education primarily had succeeded in producing 'a privileged group of parasites' as
'impotent' as they were 'selfish.' "[17]

Comparing Japan to Ethiopia

A comparison with Japan is most instructive. The way Japan introduced modern education is singularly different from the Ethiopian experience. The difference does not spring from Japan not importing or importing less from the
Western educational system. Rather, it borrowed from the West extensively,
both through the use of foreign instructors and textbooks and by sending
Japanese youths to Western countries for higher studies. As Kaigo Tokiomi
writes: "The methods for constructing a modernized curriculum were modeled
after European and American schools, and necessary materials and tools for
teaching were introduced from those countries."[18] The great difference, however, is that the Japanese ruling elite very soon realized the danger of alienation. Without a firm foundation in the traditional heritage, an educational
system modeled on the West would foster uprootedness. In effect, since the
introduction of Western education, "the impact of foreign influences upon the
traditional culture of Japan had resulted in a state of social disturbance and ideological confusion such as Japan had never before experienced."[19]

Unless Japanese students quickly countered the borrowed system with a
commitment to their own traditions and values, modern education was going
to give way to an imperceptible but forceful colonization. Hence the government decree known as "the *Kyôgaku Taishi* (Principles of Education) of 1879,"
which introduced the traditional Confucian philosophy and ethics into the
modern educational system. The declaration emphasized the importance of
"the virtues of benevolence, responsibility, loyalty and fidelity based on the
precepts of [Japanese] ancestors" and added that "in the teaching of morality, the Confucian morality will be primary."[20] In other words, the Japanese
said yes to Western education but no to the expulsion of traditional teaching.
The design of a syncretic approach inaugurated the appropriation of Western
science and technology by a mind that remained Japanese, thereby investing
modern education with a national foundation and purpose.

In this way, the introduction of modern education amounted to the process
of reforming and adapting traditional Japanese teaching to the modern
world. Unlike the Ethiopian path, the Japanese understood that the prevention

of the formation of an ideological vacuum among students is the best defense against the subversive influence of the West and other alien ideologies. The more the educational system assumed the task of enhancing and glorifying Japan's cultural heritage, the stronger the counteroffensive against the demeaning impact of Western education became. The display of the good things that tradition has to offer assured the success of the crusade against alienation.

The other important disparity between Japan and Ethiopia is the use of the national language. Japanese leaders have encouraged the limited learning of foreign languages for the purpose of translating books into Japanese and giving access to Western knowledge. This strictly utilitarian function barred foreign languages from usurping the traditional prerogatives of the national language for the wider student population. The preservation of the national language as a medium of instruction, supplemented by translations, made modern knowledge easily accessible to a large number of people. More importantly, it provided a good basis for the defense of the culture itself by avoiding the expulsion of the native language from the realm of modern studies and research. If "the Japanese borrowed more techniques than values from the West," unlike Africans, it is because they "undertook their modernization primarily through the Japanese language, and did not become linguistic converts to an alien idiom."[21] Though Amharic was given the status of a national language in Ethiopia, it was used as a medium of instruction only at the elementary level. This limitation no doubt suggested to young Ethiopians that the national language was congenitally inadequate to the expression of higher levels of knowledge.

If, while imperial proclamations reiterated the necessity of providing education with a national component, actual practice showed a different outcome, the attribution of the lack of national ideology to negligence, ignorance, or mistaken policy strikes me as indefensible. Instead, internal reasons must be sought for the gap between official discourse and practice. Two basic reasons immediately stand out: (1) Haile Selassie and his close associates had basically endorsed the colonial idea according to which non-Western societies were backward, thereby conceiving of modernization as the internalization of Western values and institutions; (2) Haile Selassie was all the more willing to push for Westernization as the marginalization of Ethiopia's traditional values and institutions was the sine qua non for the establishment of his autocratic rule. Let us first examine the conception of modernization.

The Ideological Origin of the Imperial System of Education

To understand the roots and main function of modern education in Ethiopia's imperial system, it is necessary to refer to the very conception that

Haile Selassie and his close followers and advisers had of modernization. Since knowing the causes of Ethiopia's developmental retardation would provide an indication of what must be done to catch up with Europe, their conception of modernization also included an assessment of why Ethiopia lagged behind European countries. That Ethiopia shared with the West a Christian belief and had preserved its independence for so long made the question of its retardation all the more problematic.

The retardation turns into an enigma when we note that Ethiopia had reached a high level of civilization at a time when most inhabitants of Europe lived in caves and survived by hunting and fishing. Aksum and its Amhara extension had produced, by any standard, the basic ingredients of a civilization that could be accurately defined as powerful, advanced, and refined. About the greatness of Aksumite civilization, which came to full blossom at the end of the first century AD, a recent study says: "At the height of their power, the kings of Axum ruled an empire that extended from the Upper Nile Valley in the west to Yemen in the East and was considered together with Rome, Persia, and China one of the four great empires that divided ancient Eurasia and Africa between them."[22]

Since Ethiopia had shown great advances in the past, only the occurrence of obstacles that interrupted the course of progress can explain its lag. Among the early intellectuals who supported Haile Selassie's modernizing tendency, the two most prominent ones, namely, Afework Gebreyesus and Gebrehiwot Baykedagn, assign Ethiopia's decline to the rise of warlordism subsequent to the weakening of the imperial power in favor of regional lords. The decline of the central power started in the mid-seventeenth century and plunged Ethiopia into a state of continuous political instability. Internal conflicts and wars blocked socioeconomic progress and the development of knowledge by promoting warlike values and plunder as a noble way of life. "Whereas other peoples were progressing thanks to their knowledge and know-how, we [Ethiopians] remained so far behind because of our conflicts," writes Gebrehiwot.[23]

For Afework, too, the culprit for Ethiopia's backwardness was the social condition created by the decline of the imperial authority and the rise of warlordism. He describes Ethiopia as a country ruled for centuries by authorities who, on top of mercilessly robbing the people, did nothing but "eat, drink, and sleep, like sheep being fattened for Easter."[24] A more recent thinker, Kebede Mikael, attributes the cessation of progress in Ethiopia not so much to evil social and political developments as to the country's isolation since the rise and spread of Islam. "Ethiopia," he writes, "isolated from the world, to which the route was barred to her, existed for a long time in the impossibility of making contact with the modern world."[25] Cut off from the major centers of civilization by the Islamic encirclement, Ethiopian creativity and progress could not but decay.

In whichever way Ethiopian intellectuals analyzed the country's retardation, the consensus was that Ethiopia, which had a brilliant past, entered into a slumbering existence that caused its massive lag behind Europe. The solution, they said, is to awaken from this lethargic state—and modernization is just this act of waking up. That is why writings and speeches predating the 1935 Italian invasion defined modernity as "light" or "dawn" and analogized the transition from traditional culture to modernity as a passage from darkness to light, from night to day, from sleep to wakefulness.

For instance, a book published in 1924 in which statements of Ethiopians are collected refers to a newspaper, characteristically called "the Dawn of Ethiopia," that defines modernization as the moment when the people of the world are "awakened from their sleep."[26] Modernization defined as light and awakening suggests that Europe, too, had slept for a long time. However, compared to Ethiopia, European countries woke up earlier. The book reproduces the poem of an Ethiopian by the name of Mambaru that says:

> The people of Europe were like us:
> By the increase of knowledge and work,
> They mounted to the sky in order to float there.[27]

The whole secret of the Ethiopian conceptualization of modernity lies in the translation of the Eurocentric "civilized versus primitive" or "superior race versus inferior peoples" into "light versus darkness," "awakening versus sleepiness." In thus putting everybody in the same initial condition of ignorance and darkness, the conception affirms the fundamental sameness of all humans, regardless of their race or nationality. To speak in terms of dawn and awakening also stipulates the equal potential of all humans to be awakened.

Haile Selassie totally adhered to the conception of modernity as light and awakening. For instance, in one of his important statements he talked of Ethiopia as a "Sleeping Beauty . . . that is beginning to awaken from her sleep."[28] He also named the newspaper he founded *Berhanena Selam*, which means "Light and Peace." These expressions clearly reveal that Ethiopian leaders themselves had endorsed the idea of a backward Ethiopia being awakened by the arrival of Westerners, the providers of light. Some such conception of modernization turns Westerners into tutors and Ethiopians into tutees. The upshot of this view of modernization is that Ethiopian schools and colleges must reproduce an imported Western curriculum. The essential purpose of education is to learn from Europe so as to imitate its values, institutions, and achievements.

The Normativeness of the West

If Haile Selassie strongly supported the need to defend the Ethiopian legacy in many of his speeches while doing practically nothing to ensure its protection, one of the reasons must be that he blamed tradition for the lack of progress. What has been achieved in a state of slumber had no intrinsic value; it was rather an obstacle to progress. Hence the resolution not to push for the incorporation of the traditional into the modern: the formula for progress was modernity versus tradition. Haile Selassie having thus fully accepted the Western view of Ethiopia, "everything really appeared as though," in the words of two French scholars, "the emperor were working toward the mental colonization of his own people as a superspy in the service of Westerners!"[29]

One major implication of Ethiopian leaders' acceptance of backwardness is that modernization was not posed in terms of defending a national identity, still less of competing against the West. Again, a comparison with Japan is quite instructive. Unlike the Ethiopian conception, the Japanese understanding of modernization was from the start confrontational. The major objective of modernization was to provide Japan with the power to resist Western countries; better still, it was to raise Japan to a level of parity with the West. Accordingly, the West was not viewed as a model, but as an adversary, and "Japan could hope successfully to compete in the modern world only if the rulers of the state were supported by a trained as well as united people."[30] Since modernization was coined in terms of competition with Western powers, the Japanese conception of modernization discarded the idea of a passive imitation of the West. On the contrary, it advocated the use of all available resources to win the competition, including those traditional elements that gave advantages to Japan.

The Meiji Restoration is a good illustration of the usage of tradition. Squarely revoking the motto "Modernity versus tradition," the restoration of the traditional emperor with his divine attribute created a powerful center of loyalty from which emanated the command to modernize and save Japan from colonial powers. When the West is taken as a model, the idea of competition is put aside in favor of reproducing Western values and norms. Imitation rules out deviations from the model, which dictates the norms of modernization. By contrast, the perception of the West as an opponent encourages deviations to secure the mobilization of those traditional characteristics and peculiarities that bolster the competitive edge of the developing country.

For the imitative paradigm, modernization is the process by which lagging societies catch up with advanced societies. The operation amounts to refashioning the lagging society in the image of the Western model. Unfortunately, the outcome does not meet the expectation: far from catching up, the lagging society is relegated to the periphery, as a satellite of the model. Given that imitation does no more than suppress local initiatives and reduce people to passive imitators of an external mode, no wonder marginalization is its outcome. "If both modernization and development are seen as a struggle to 'catch up with the West,' " writes Mazrui, "the twin processes carry considerable risks of imitation and dependency for the Third World."[31]

Haile Selassie's view of modernization was not impregnated with a competitive spirit. Considering Western countries as benevolent tutors, especially after he regained his throne in 1941 thanks to the assistance of the British, he saw the West both as an ally and a model. Such was not the view of Menelik II, his predecessor, who understood modernization as a competition with the West rather than as Westernization. Menelik is reported to have said: "We need educated people in order to ensure our peace, to reconstruct our country and to enable it to exist as a great nation in the face of the European powers."[32] So defined, modernization combines the borrowing of Western technology with the defense of national identity and the mobilization of the country's traditional assets. Compare Menelik's statement with the speech that Haile Selassie, still regent, made in 1925 while visiting the Tafari Makonnen Lyceum:

> Of Ethiopia's greatness and antiquity, and especially of the long years when, surrounded by pagans, she struggled for her faith and her freedom, we ourselves, her own children, can indeed bear witness. . . . But it is not what she was that can profit Ethiopia, but what she may become. . . . Knowledge must be sought and found whereby Ethiopia too, an African state which has preserved her independence, may be led towards progress and may attain political stability and the well-being of her people.[33]

The Ethiopian past is devalued if only because it is stripped of any regenerative power. When, challenged by the West, other nations turned to their glorious past for inspiration (a good example being Japan), Haile Selassie looked up to the West. Nothing could be more alien to his understanding of modernization than the statement of a Japanese scholar who said: "The best way to look forward is by looking backward."[34] Moreover, modernization is described in terms of progress resulting in political stability and material well-being. The emphasis is not on the confrontation with the West, which is no longer seen as the enemy or the threat. This conception of modernization activates not the spirit of rivalry but the zeal of the copyist who tries to secure the benefits of the model.

The Sociopolitical Roots of the Imperial System of Education

The imputation of Haile Selassie's reluctance to defend tradition to his own alienation, which some scholars trace back to the fact that "unlike many of his compatriots, [he] had an early exposure to Western culture," would be a partial view.[35] While it is true to say that he did nothing to integrate the traditional legacy into modern education, it is also undeniable that he preserved and even enhanced many traditional features. In one of his speeches, he even said: "Ethiopia is a country with her own cultures and mores. These, our cultures and customs, more than being the legacy of our historical past, are characteristics of our Ethiopianness. We do not want our legacies and traditions to be lost. Our wish and desire is that education develop, enrich, and modify them."[36]

Insofar as the statement loudly advocates a syncretic approach to modernization, the lack of a serious effort to save the Ethiopian legacy looks incomprehensible. Yet, the imperial inconsistency can be easily explained if one recalls that Haile Selassie wanted education to develop those Ethiopian features that lend themselves to an absolutist interpretation. In his eyes, tradition saved and enriched is the manner through which his autocracy finds roots in the past, the best example being his frequent reference to the traditional title of the emperor as the elect of God.

All the features that Haile Selassie preserved from the past are those that either justified or effectively supported his absolute power. The imperial institution, the nobility, and the church are among the most important features that Haile Selassie preserved. But, be it noted, he preserved them in such a way that they reinforced the exercise of absolutism. Thus, the nobility and the church were conserved after they had been dispossessed of their traditional autonomy and power base. In the name of modernization, Haile Selassie applied a tight centralization policy that stripped the nobility of its traditional administrative and military prerogatives and the church of its educational role and internal autonomy.

The commitment to a sweeping form of centralization confirms that the imperial ambiguity in the defense of tradition resulted from alienation working in conjunction with the need to take from tradition elements that supported absolutism while leaving out those that went against it. This selective dealing with tradition explains why traditional elements were banned from modern schools but conserved, albeit in altered forms, in other institutions. In preserving a nobility divested of its traditional functions, the imperial system created a parasitic class that was entirely dependent on its protection and largesse. In return, the emperor could totally rely on the loyalty of such a nobility to his autocratic regime.

The enhancement of imperial power through the selective use of tradition provides one explanation for Haile Selassie's easy acceptance of the status of Ethiopia as a peripheral state to the West. Overwhelmed by the West and yet aware of having inherited a proud history, he eased himself into the acceptance of his country's marginality by transferring the past greatness of Ethiopia to his own person. As an individual, he will play a great international role, thereby substituting his personal megalomania for Ethiopia's past glory. Although he acquiesced to rule over a peripheral country, his reign will be great as a result of his becoming a leading figure in the non-Western world.

Understandably, in order to have this leading role, Haile Selassie had first to build political institutions that would allow him to achieve absolute power in his own country.

To reduce Haile Selassie's building of autocracy to the exclusive pursuit of personal ambition would be a one-sided view. Absolutism also emanated from the very understanding of Ethiopia's lag, which, as we saw, was attributed to the decline of imperial power in favor of the regional nobility. The decline had created a state of political anarchy with incessant conflicts and destructive wars that halted Ethiopia's progress. Getting out of this predicament meant nothing less than the establishment of a central power strong enough to marginalize the warlords. Moreover, to the extent that centuries of ignorance and warlike values had spoiled Ethiopian culture, modernization required the enlightened leadership of an absolute monarch who would use all his power to lead the country out of backwardness. Put otherwise, the theory of Ethiopia's retardation combined with Haile Selassie's megalomania to point out autocratic centralization as the key to Ethiopia's path to modernization.

Modernization under absolutism dismissed the establishment of a liberal system as much as it demanded the creation of a bureaucracy entirely committed to the emperor and emancipated from traditional obligations to the church and the nobility. Here, then, is an important goal of the educational system implemented under Haile Selassie's rule: it was inspired less by the purpose of transforming the country than by "the need of having a bureaucracy free from the umbrella of the church and the feudal lords, and thus the creation of an elite which owed an unswerving loyalty directly to him."[37] Could there be a better method of creating a monopolized bureaucracy than the institution of an alien system of education entirely copied from the West? The uprooting impact of this type of education effectively cut off the educated elite from its traditions and confined its allegiance to the emperor alone. Just as Haile Selassie had made the nobility and the church dependent on him by becoming the protector of privileges inserted into a modernizing system, so too he had designed an educational system whose main function was to create a new elite divorced from the people and hence loyal only to him.

Let us agree, then, that the Westernization of education in Ethiopia was not meant to train people who would serve as agents of development; rather, it was devised to produce an uprooted elite entirely shaped to serve autocratic rule. Disconnected from traditional life and values, which it even learned to despise, such an elite would be committed to the task of marginalizing the nobility and the church. It would promote centralization by hailing absolutism as the only way to modernize the country.

A system of education entirely modeled on the Western system was also in line with the imperial regime's acceptance of the peripheral status of

Ethiopia. The lack of a national ideology clearly harnessing modern education to Ethiopia's developmental needs was a manifestation of this status. In becoming a peripheral country, Ethiopia had ceased to have its own objectives and course of action. Its integration into the imperialist world as a dependent partner required the production of a local bureaucracy trained to serve as a connecting link with the capitalist economy. The task of implementing the directives of core countries called for a denationalized bureaucracy, which was best fashioned by an imported system of education.

Let us not overlook the ideological interest of Western countries: in assisting the Ethiopian emperor to create an uprooted bureaucracy and intelligentsia, hopefully with some penchant for liberal values, Western nations, especially the United States, were advancing their goal of containing communism. The global policy of containment of communism in third world countries induced the United States to invest "heavily in the ideological sector (i.e. education) of its 'anticommunist' campaign."[38] Because of its history, its symbolic value as the only noncolonized country, and its leading role in African politics, Ethiopia was a central focus of the campaign. Keeping Ethiopia within the orbit of the liberal camp had an exemplary value for the rest of Africa. In any case, Ethiopia was the only country that could come under American influence as former colonial powers maintained control over other African countries. As a result, "Ethiopia was the main beneficiary of the Peace Corps program when it was launched in 1962."[39]

Haile Selassie had justified absolutism as the only way to extract the country from backwardness. His students professed the same pattern of thought, albeit under the different name of "Marxist-Leninist vanguard elite." They too advocated the elimination of tradition and a theory entirely committed to centralization and development from above. No doubt, what was designed as an instrument of autocracy rebelled, but only to succumb to similar wanderings. This convergence testifies to the similarity of their inspiration, to the fact that they are parallel tracks of the same derailment. The students who revolted were not the remedy for Haile Selassie's bankruptcy; they were rather its exasperated expression. When the whole issue should have been the recentering of Ethiopia, the ideological movement from autocracy to the extreme left simply deepened the loss of national direction by favoring first the Leninization and then the ethnicization of the Ethiopian intelligentsia.

4

Radicalism as a Fallout of Uprootedness and Globality

The last chapter unraveled the ultimate purpose of Haile Selassie's educational policy. It also showed how modern education was used as an instrument for his autocratic project. However, what was devised to produce a docile instrument of autocracy and satellization backfired: having lost its attachment to tradition and being cut off from the people, the Ethiopian educated elite became increasingly receptive to revolutionary appeals. The ideological root of this receptivity was none other than the endorsement of the causes of Ethiopia's retardation propagated both by the imperial regime and by Western teachers and textbooks. This chapter begins the task of demonstrating how concretely the major flaws of modern education in Ethiopia created a mind-set eager for radical ideas. Since uprootedness has been diagnosed as the fundamental cause, let us see how it served as bedrock for radicalization.

Uprootedness and the Temptation of Tabula Rasa

Though many authors have reflected on the alienating impact of Western education, few actually link the alienation with the propensity to espouse radical ideas. In their eyes, repression and the lack of freedom are the primary causes of student radicalization in Ethiopia. Yet, what else could the alienating impact of modern education induce but radicalism? Because what was taught was so disparaging to Ethiopian culture and history, it unleashed the desire to get rid of everything and start anew.

The rise of destroyers consequent to the cutting of the umbilical cord finds a poignant expression in the following poem of an Ethiopian student:

> Gone are those days when we were innocently playful
> Gone too with them is the vigor of life;

> Cold is the heart that once was warm with love,
> And the hot and lively blood,
> Has given way to coldness,
> The coldness that heralds
> The nearing of the end[1]

The poem vividly unravels the effect of Western education: how it took away from Ethiopians their innocence and confidence, including their perception of Ethiopia as the elect of God. All that Ethiopians had venerated was declared backward in the schools they were sent to. The vigor of life was indeed gone. In its place was planted the coldness of those who must destroy what had been venerated for centuries. The ferocity of the disenchanted Westernized natives was to do for Ethiopia what colonizers did elsewhere in Africa. These natives were able to develop a patricidal urge, because their love had been twisted into hatred. Such coldness of heart fomented by disenchantment unleashed a craving for ideas of social change that advocated total destruction, such as Marxist ideas.

What the Westernized elite wanted was not mere change, but change that implicated a total break. The normal process of change reconciles novelty with heritage, and so achieves continuity. The impact of Western education on native peoples is qualitatively different: it calls for a fundamental rupture with the past. As we saw, the colonial characteristics of the Ethiopian educational system stemmed from a theoretical construct that opposed modernity to tradition, and so put the blame for Ethiopia's technological lag on its traditions. Nowhere did the educational system make a provision for an alternative view describing Ethiopian society as an autonomous civilization that pursued goals different from those of Western countries. The qualification "backward" makes sense only through the assumption that Ethiopia had goals that were similar to the West's, especially as regards the technological conquest of nature. Not only is such an assumption factually indefensible, but it is also based on the idea that Western civilization is universal. The claim reflects a theoretical construct that fraudulently interprets an idiosyncratic pursuit as a universal characteristic.

Since the teaching fully endorsed the universality of the West, its modus operandi consisted in opposing two societies, one of which was taken as a norm. The operation did not plead for continuity with the indigenous legacy but for rupture, thereby creating a predisposition to revolutionary ideas. History is no longer the framework of continuity moving toward the future; it is how arrested societies get towed by another's history. The rise of radical intellectuals is, therefore, part of the process of modernization of countries that are latecomers: the contrast of their society with those of the West produces a characteristic disenchantment and dissociation that set them apart as liquidators.

Internalizing Western Normativeness

Had Ethiopian students perceived their legacy not as backwardness but as the manifestation of a sui generis civilization defined by different values and pursuits, the need to defend their legacy would have taken hold of them. Modernization would have been conceptualized as necessary to defend their particularity rather than as a means of catching up with the West. Instead of seeing themselves as liquidators "campaigning for a clean break with the country's history and tradition," they would have produced a competitive spirit that would make use of modern methods to enhance Ethiopian identity in lieu of merely imitating the West.[2] The internalization of Western historiography blocked these developments by generating the view of tradition as an arrested history that simply needed to be liquidated.

The following quotation taken from an editorial in *Challenge*, the journal of the Ethiopian Students Association in North America, gives a good idea of Ethiopian students' drastic rejection of particularism:

> Those who try to write off Africa or Ethiopia from the main stream of historical development by either conjuring up the dead past of an African socialism or citing the uniqueness of Africa are not only evading the outstanding problems of our time, but also do fall right in the laps of the racist theory that tries to exclude Africa from the best achievements of history. We believe that there are law-governed principles that operate in all kinds of human society regardless of race, sex or origin.[3]

Particularism is portrayed as demeaning and racist because it implies that universal laws do not govern African societies. Such an implication propels Western realizations outside the reach of Africans. The more Ethiopians claim their uniqueness, the further they move away from the Western type of achievement, such as science and technology. The system of education taught Ethiopian students everything except the insight into the manner an eccentric history is fraudulently promoted to the rank of universal history. As good students, they showed their great diligence by the uncritical endorsement of a linear historical process, which made them very sensitive to the idea of backwardness.

Herein lies the main difference between African and Ethiopian intellectuals. Ethiopia's Westernized elite never engaged in the task of defining the Ethiopian legacy as the outcome of a different cultural line, as was attempted by some theoretical developments in Africa. I have particularly in mind the theory of negritude, which refused the qualification of backward or primitive, arguing that African cultural trends were dissimilar from those of the West.[4] While the Western trend pursued the conquest of nature, African cultures followed the path of harmony and integration. Denouncing the Eurocentric interpretation of history, Léopold Sédar Senghor writes:

The Europeans claimed that they were the only ones who had thought out a Civilization to the level and the dimension of Universality. From this to maintaining that European civilization was to be identified with the *Civilization of the Universal* is only a step and one which was taken many years ago. It was not difficult for us to show that every "exotic civilization" had also thought on a universal scale and that the only merit of Europe on this point was that through its conquests and its technology, it had diffused its own civilization throughout the world.[5]

The Ethiopian educated elite utterly refused to dissociate itself culturally from the West, which it considered as an embodiment of universal norms.

The need to conform to the Western historical scheme explains why educated Ethiopians were quick to characterize their society by the term "feudal," even though many scholars argued that Ethiopia presents characteristics dissimilar to feudalism as it existed in Europe. For example, Gene Ellis writes that feudalism "can be applied to Ethiopia only with the greatest of generality. . . . There are numerous significant differences between European feudalism and Ethiopian experience."[6] Some of the differences underlined by scholars are actually important: they are (1) the absence of hereditary nobility and of rigid class distinction between lords and peasants; (2) the nonexistence of serfs, that is, of landless peasants, owing to the *rist* system, which recognizes ownership right to the cultivator while giving tax right to the lord; (3) the lack of cultural distinction between lords and peasants; (4) the subjection of the cultivating class to military service as opposed to Europe's class of specialized warriors.

Despite these important differences, the prevailing tendency among Ethiopian intellectuals was to safeguard the Western historical scheme by considering these differences not as particularities, as distinctive features, but as anomalies, as deviations from the pure model of European feudalism. To admit that Ethiopia is not feudal would challenge the universal and progressive paradigm of the Western conception of history. It would mean that there is no such thing as a universal history, with the important consequence that countries do not pass through similar stages. So intolerable had become such an assumption that Ethiopian intellectuals preferred to stretch the concept of feudalism to the point of disfigurement than to admit the singularity of European history, and with it, the inappropriateness of the term "feudal" to define the Ethiopian experience. What they liked about the term was not so much its conceptual accuracy as its usefulness to characterize the imperial regime as a backward, obsolete social system.

The use of the concept of feudalism clearly shows that the bashing of Ethiopian history and culture is an outcome of the internalization of the colonial discourse, which is best manifested in modern schools' portrayal of the West as a normative reference. The normative universalization of the history and values of Western societies forced Ethiopian intellectuals to construe their culture and history negatively, that is, as products of historical blockage. Given the mental bent generated by Western education, it is not surprising that Ethiopian students and intellectuals became prey to what an Ethiopian scholar called "national self-hatred and nihilism."[7] It is even less surprising that given the loss of the national sentiment they looked for a substitute in the commitment to Marxism.

As the national sentiment weakened under the constant assault of Eurocentric notions on the Ethiopian legacy, a natural reaction aimed at refurbishing the sentiment took place. A distinction radically opposing the oppressor and the oppressed gradually replaced the traditional attachment to Ethiopia. The distinction diverted the attachment to the oppressed, and the nihilist disposition was sublimated into a revolutionary ethos. Marxism-Leninism replaced the love of Ethiopia by its touted compassion for working people. When the love of tradition is denounced as love for the oppressor, that love naturally turns toward the victims of the system and start idealizing them. The following quotation taken from S*truggle*, the journal of the USUAA, dramatically epitomizes the movement from national nihilism to Marxism: "In our Ethiopian context, the true revolutionary is one who has shattered all sentimental and ideological ties with feudal Ethiopia. . . . Our rallying points are not a common history, a feudal boundary, the legendary Solomonic fairy tale, religious institutions, regional ethnic, linguistic affiliations, but the cause of the oppressed classes, who are the ultimate makers of history. That is why we are internationalist, because the masses have no nation, no home."[8]

This passage is unbelievable in its exaltation of uprootedness and self-denial and its offer of revolutionism as a substitute for Ethiopianness. Instead of common history and culture, both rejected on account of being feudal, the commitment to an internationalist view championing the unity of the oppressed is suggested as a much more worthy goal. The resolution to eradicate sentimentality and any attachment to Ethiopian characteristics clearly indicates that the rejection of tradition is not based on the examination of its negative and positive aspects. It is the product of a boundless, indiscriminate ideological hatred that targets nothing less than a complete shakeup.

This ultimate deconstruction sees Ethiopia as yet to be born, redesigned as it should be around the struggle and the cause of the masses. For such a deconstructive project, nothing of Ethiopia is sacred or untouchable, not even national unity. Thus, *Challenge* takes pride in the position of the ESUNA because it "reiterated its unconditional support for the right of the Eritrean people to self-determination including independence."[9] Once a common legacy is rejected, no reason remains to condemn secessionist movements. An equally valid way of getting rid of oppression, however, would have been the struggle for democratization. But since Ethiopia must be redesigned, the recognition of the right to secede to resolve what is but a democratic issue is a forced component of the revolutionary project.

Globality and Hegemonic Ideology

One major manifestation of uprootedness is globality, which denotes a thinking pattern outwardly oriented. When a mind is bombarded with the idea that norms come from outside, naturally it develops a marked tendency to extroversion. Global notions and events impress such a mind, and its impressionability is proportional to the scope of its peripherization, of its exclusion from the center. Most of all, acquiescence to the external origination of norms creates a mind-set sensitive to globalist ideologies of modernization, such as Marxism and liberalism.

Speaking of the outward-lookingness of the Ethiopian educated elite as a result of the inculcation of the normativeness of the West, Addis Hiwet writes: "The intelligentsia was dynamically marked by globality. The educational system of which it was a product was its mark of globality, and quite literally. In this the Ethiopian intelligentsia was, as it were, a local variation on a truly global theme, from Afghanistan to Zanzibar."[10] The impact of an extroverted disposition went so deep that external events directly conditioned Ethiopian students. They did not simply watch these events as curious but detached spectators; the events produced profound resonances in their psyches. Consequently, the polarizing atmosphere of the Cold War and the subsequent struggle for ideological hegemony between Marxism-Leninism and liberalism had a powerful bearing on Ethiopian students. Naturally, this same extroverted orientation imparted by Western education made them particularly receptive to the ideological message of socialism as an expression of global resistance uniting peripheral countries, Western left-wing movements, and socialist countries against imperialist forces and their local allies. This heightened receptivity is what many observers have in mind when they assert that Ethiopian students became Marxists because Marxism was in fashion at that time.

Pursuing his analysis, Addis shows how globality determined the attitude of students, their combative mood as well as their radicalism. Ethiopia could not be that country where nothing was happening when revolution was on the march worldwide. Ethiopian students could not feel part of a global culture of resistance without echoing its major demand, namely, the denunciation of reaction and imperialism. Being members of a global culture, Ethiopian students "could only aspire for the most advanced ideology associated with the embattled movements on a global scale. The ostracization of politics domestically and an exceptionally politicizing international conjuncture expedited the process of radicalization."[11] Rightly, Addis combines the explanation of radicalization by globality with domestic problems. While the epoch of the Cold War and the competition between capitalism and socialism played a part, radicalization became effective in conjunction with social problems inherent in the imperial regime.

However undeniable the conjunction may be, for the issue of the Marxist versus the reformist orientation of students, the globality factor should have precedence over social conditions. More than social dissatisfactions, the ideological hegemony of Marxism-Leninism conditioned Ethiopian students to think that reformism was ineffective. Globality preserves its autonomous causal impact only if it is not overwhelmed by local structural conditions.

The fact that internal conflicts in Ethiopia were still in their infancy proves that students did not radicalize because of local conditions. Ethiopian students, Addis himself admits, were "isolated domestically from fundamental social classes," so their political program, such as "Land to the Tiller" and socialism, was raised "in the *absence* of a working class movement or peasant jacquery."[12] In fact, they fought the regime alone for many years in a country that seemed resigned or indifferent. If students' revolutionism was manifesting in the name of conflicts that were not yet formed, the explanation lies in their globalist orientation. The ongoing struggle between reaction and revolution on the global scale painted the Ethiopian situation as an anomaly. From the perception of anomaly there emerged the calling of the Ethiopian students as rectifiers. Imbued with a revolutionary ethos by their globalist orientation, Ethiopian students could no longer tolerate living in a situation of nonrevolution, and so embarked on the hazardous task of provoking revolutionary conditions.

The sense of belonging to a global generation rising against the old world is reflected in the following quotations taken from an article published in *Struggle* under the title "The New Generation":

> In all the corners of the world, the young generation is restless and is often referred to as the chaotic generation. This generation of diverse attitudes, colors, creeds, and races has been witnessed to have no single common demand. Nevertheless, it manifests its demands through more and more outward, frank and sincere ways such as violence, annihilation of existing systems and phobia towards the old generation.[13]

> We belong to the universal new generation in that we fight against the past and the precedent.[14]

This interesting self-portrait refers to a generational conflict whose particularity is universalism and revolutionism. Like any generational conflict, the movement reproduced the rebellion of the young against traditional authority but with the added emphasis on the rebellion being global and a carrier of a radical goal of social change. Take the late sixties: while French students protested against the system of education and American students against the war in Vietnam, third world students, be they in Latin America, Asia, or Africa, denounced in unison American imperialism, apartheid, neocolonialism, and internal reaction. Actually, the May 1968 student rebellion in France had a direct galvanizing impact on Ethiopian students who talked about" 'justified violence' and about turning the university into a 'Sorbonne.' "[15] This worldwide generational protest reveals how resistance against radicalism, hence against Marxism, was difficult for the young. Since the epoch defined youth by the standard of radical rebellion, it created an image, a norm with a strong pressure to conform.

The Causal Scope of Globality

Theories exist that contest the reality of globality as a force of its own. Thus, according to Mark N. Hagopian, if revolution seems to spread to other countries, as was the case in Europe when the French Revolution exploded, the phenomenon is accountable to similar structural causes producing similar effects. Such an explanation of revolutionary fever in eighteenth-century Europe "deemphasizes contagion and imitation in favor of common structural weaknesses to explain the near collapse of so many 'absolute' monarchies."[16] According to structuralist scholars, the trouble with the approach emphasizing contagion is the underlying assumption that the ideological factor is the essential cause of revolutions. What else does contagion signify but ideas traveling from one country to another regardless of structural conditions? The approach simply forgets that "revolutions are more responses to indigenous patterns of social conflict than manifestations of a transnational wave."[17] In fact, where structural similarities do not support the movement, the imitation remains superficial and has no lasting effect.

The ephemerality of imitation in situations where structural conditions are insufficient does not refute the power of contagion. On the contrary, it shows that the sheer power of inspiration drives people to repeat the same prowess even where conditions are not ripe. Revolution is a normative, galvanizing event; it cannot but influence other countries down the same path. The problem for the structuralist objection is that, even though social problems have intensified today, no movement claims to be revolutionary for the simple reason that utopian theories of social change have been discredited, at least temporarily. The loss of the ability to fire up the imagination of people, and not the absence of intense social conflicts, explains the lack of current revolutionary movements.

Even studies of the radicalization of Ethiopian students that refer to the radical milieu often back down from assigning a causal impact to the epoch itself—as if radicalization would have occurred in any period so long as Ethiopia's social problems reached the same degree of severity. The reasoning attributing radicalization to the severity of social problems leaves us wanting each time we ask why the severe social problems of today's Ethiopia do not cause the same kind of radicalization. To account for radicalization, the intensity of social problems is not enough; one must situate these problems in the radical mood of the epoch, essentially defined by the Cold War and the ideological hegemony of Marxism-Leninism.

All the more reason for implicating the revolutionary epoch is that the attraction of Marxism-Leninism seemed to grow in the late sixties and early seventies "when Marxist regimes came to power in so many Third World countries, including South Vietnam, Cambodia, and Laos in Southeast Asia; Ethiopia, Angola, Mozambique, and Guinea-Bissau in Africa; Afghanistan in South Asia; and Grenada and Nicaragua in the Caribbean."[18] In particular, the American defeat in Vietnam seemed to announce the beginning of a general retreat of capitalism around the world. As a result, liberalism was put on the defensive, which further increased the pressure on students and intellectuals to adopt the Marxist-Leninist ideology. In the eyes of many Ethiopian students and intellectuals, the apparent retraction of liberalism meant that it had ceased to be a credible alternative to socialism.

This generalized conviction gave radical students a significant ideological upper hand over moderate students. Even as capitalism became identified with defeat, underdevelopment, and allegiance to the West, socialism increasingly signified victory, economic takeoff, and nationalism. This context of ideological hegemony is crucial to understand why so many Ethiopian students and intellectuals became attracted to Marxism-Leninism. It provoked a shift of reference such that "by 1970, the United States . . . [had] become in the minds of the vanguard of the student movement the arch-villain, the bastion of capitalism and imperialism. The quest for a model of development had shifted to the East—the Soviet Union, China, and Vietnam—and, in the Western world, to Cuba."[19]

Globality and the Progressive Course of Universal History

That epochs can be defined in relation to dominant ideologies is a notion inherent in the very idea of history viewed as both progressive and universal. The notion means that various epochs correspond to the prominence of specific nations that set the pace of progress. The universality of history turns these nations into torchbearers of progress for lagging countries. The belief that advanced nations trace out the road of progress to less developed ones implies that the ideologies characteristic of these nations represent the spirit of the time, that they are the dominant, leading ideas. Defining "the spirit of an epoch," Karl Mannheim says: "The mentality which is commonly attributed to an epoch has its proper seat in one (homogeneous or heterogeneous) social group which acquires special significance at a particular time, and is thus able to put its own intellectual stamp on all the other groups without either destroying or absorbing them."[20]

Mannheim's definition exactly applies to the dominant status of Marxism-Leninism during the sixties and seventies. The theory's intellectual stamp accounts for the shift of the model of development from the West to the East for many third world students and intellectuals. The Leninist definition of imperialism as a decadent, moribund capitalism provided the theoretical basis of the paradigmatic shift. The view that capitalism had lost its historical mission entailed that the torch had passed to the Soviet Union. Lenin sealed the change of global leadership thus: "Imperialism is the eve of the proletarian social revolution. This has been confirmed since 1917 on a world-wide scale."[21]

The evolution of the Chinese student movement after the Russian Revolution gives a good idea of the impact of hegemonic ideological movements. Before the Russian Revolution, the bourgeois type of revolution was the model of change for Chinese students. Even though China faced very serious problems and challenges, the students thought that the appropriate solution resided in the embracing of bourgeois democracy. Reflecting their commitment to liberalism, they adopted the two basic themes of constitutionalism and republicanism. The latter "were so much in the universal spirit of the times that it would have been surprising had they not been in the forefront of student thought."[22] The paradox of countries coexisting while being at different stages in the evolutionary line defined their intellectual horizon; in turn, modernization was portrayed as a catching-up process through the assimilation and implementation of Western liberal ideas and institutions.

With the rise of the Soviet Union and its various successes, the path of liberalism was progressively abandoned by Chinese students in favor of socialism. Less than the intensification of China's social problems, the emergence of a new and successful player that openly challenged the West explains the ideological shift. This new challenger stunned the capitalist world and "whetted the ambitions of the emerging nations by demonstrating that revolutionary state power could, within the space of two generations, transform a backward agrarian county into the second-ranked industrial and military power in the world."[23] Thus was born the myth of socialist revolution, which fired the imaginations of so many third world intellectuals.

Culture of Revolution

Ethiopian students, too, would have hailed liberalism if they had not lived in a period of world history dominated by the Marxist-Leninist ideology. The need to take the impact of global ideologies seriously has convinced one fine student of the Ethiopian Revolution, Forrest D. Colburn, to coin the phrase "intellectual culture of the revolution."[24] The phrase designates the shared commitment to a set of beliefs and practices mostly associated with socialism, such as authoritarian government, a state-led strategy of development, agricultural cooperatives, the formation of neighborhood defense committees, and so on. For Colburn, this culture of revolution has provided "much more than the imperatives of social structure, that has provided the logic of contemporary revolutions."[25] In trying to understand the origin of the common commitment to socialist ideas among third world educated elites, Colburn alludes to similar structural conditions resulting from the ravages of colonialism, imperialism, dictatorship, and economic failure. But more importantly, he invokes the common culture that presented socialism as the right remedy to these social devastations.

Tracing the origin of this common culture, Colburn writes: "A shared educational experience in Europe and the United States by a generation of talented and justifiably disaffected individuals made it possible for a relatively common intellectual culture to arise throughout the poorer countries of the world, from Latin America, to the Middle East, to Africa, and to Asia. Ironically, that intellectual culture was spawned by Europe and the United States, which continued to mediate and swell the flow of ideas and information."[26] The exposure to the same culture diffused from Western intellectual circles—European and American universities being the primary source—and that alone explains how people coming from various parts of the world shared similar radical beliefs. Picture intellectuals already afflicted by the backwardness of their country being exposed to the advanced ideas of socialism, class struggle, democracy, and the like, in European and American universities, and you will understand the eruption of an irresistible temptation to use these same ideas to catch up with the West.

We need to understand the normative dimension of the culture of revolution. The culture was influential to the extent that it was academic, that is, part of the intellectual formation of third world intellectuals. It was also influential because it was Western, and so fed on the intellectual dependency already imparted by the methods and goals of Western education. As a result, many Ethiopian students, including science and engineering students, became radicalized. Colburn cites an Ethiopian professor, himself a student at that time, who remembered that "in those days, not to be a Marxist was considered heretical. Students who were only interested in having a good time were dismissed as 'Jolly Jacks.' "[27] Such was the hegemony of Marxism-Leninism that not to be revolutionary was associated with having a "bourgeois" mentality, which was synonymous with greed, selfishness, petty existence, and national betrayal. What fascinated most Ethiopian students was not the heroes of industry and finance of the capitalist revolution, but the prowess of Che Guevara or Fidel Castro.

We know that Ethiopian students and intellectuals did not succeed in leading the revolution that overthrew the imperial regime in 1974. The military committee known as the Derg took the leadership and initiated drastic measures aimed at implementing a socialist policy. Here too, the radicalization of the Derg is not intelligible without the context defined by the ideological dominance of Marxism-Leninism. Not only was the Derg strongly influenced by radicalized students and intellectuals, but it also adopted socialism as the best way to legitimize its power. The question of the sincerity of its commitment put aside, there is no denying that it used socialism to justify its newfound power, all the more so as the socialist measures strengthened its totalitarian grip on the country.

In the same way as divine mandate justified political power in the past, Marxism-Leninism legitimatized power in the sixties and seventies. What justifies this analysis is the simple observation that no real causal link existed between Ethiopia's problems and the socialist revolution. Though the problems could have been met with simple liberal or democratic solutions, such approaches did not appear viable because the dominant ideology of the time discredited them. The Derg had no need to convince anybody; the country's intelligentsia was simply hearing what it wanted to hear.

All the more reason to underscore external origination is that the ideas propagated by the global ideology of socialism were so advanced that they had no relevance to the actual conditions prevailing in lagging countries, much less did they stem from these conditions. The disparity confirms the purely intellectual origin of revolutions in third world countries. These revolutions did not emerge from the conditions of local realities; they took place because of the exposure of third world educated elites to the revolutionary culture of Western universities. It is no wonder, then, that instead of modernizing these countries, the imported ideas plunged them into conditions of civil war, political instability, and economic calamity, thereby practically demonstrating the ideas' complete inadequacy to local realities. That "those countries that have recently gone through the calamities of a revolution seem 'backward'" only confirms the imported and, consequently, the purely intellectual origin of third world revolutions.[28]

Assessing the Notion of "Culture of Revolution"

Colburn's notion of a "culture of revolution" is theoretically important if only because its arguments in favor of an intellectual origin of revolution go against theories of revolution that give primacy to structural causes, such as class struggle, economic deprivation, or elite conflict. So diverse and disparate were the structural conditions of third world countries that they are unable to explain the emergence of a culture of revolution with similar beliefs and methods. Instead, the impact of a revolutionary culture that was in vogue easily explains the shared ideas under disparate conditions. Common ideas emerged independently of local conditions for the simple reason that the same generation was everywhere exposed to the same intellectual discourse. As one author comments, in Colburn's analysis the "principal intellectual target is in fact the kind of structural explanation, represented by Skocpol, which would render ideological influences irrelevant. His analysis concludes that a culture of revolution among intellectuals was a decisive independent factor in the *initial occurrence* of 'revolutionary' movements and governments."[29]

Moreover, the concept of culture of revolution clarifies the phenomenon of "prior commitment" in that it shows that doctrinal conversion precedes the impact of social problems. Such a precedence validates a causal explanation involving culture, since the primacy of doctrinal commitment activates a process of cultural conditioning. Not only does the conditioning establish that social problems are not enough to explain the radicalization of students, but it also suggests that social problems themselves are analyzed through the prior commitment to Marxism. Put otherwise, the epoch matters because the ideological hegemony of Marxism in the sixties and seventies induced the propensity of the intelligentsia of third world countries to adopt the doctrine prior to assessing the objective needs of their societies.

Granted Colburn's theoretical contribution, the question remains whether the concept of a revolutionary culture being in vogue is enough to explain the radicalization of Ethiopian students. One important issue seems to be missing, namely, the reason most Ethiopian students followed the fashion when other third world student movements retained a moderate direction. Though Marxist groups existed in these countries, non-Marxist groups claiming to represent the majority of students were countering them. The uneven penetration of Marxist-Leninist ideology, the fact that it was more influential in some countries than others, is not explained by the exclusive use of the concept of culture in vogue. One must appeal to the uneven receptivity of native cultures to the Marxist-Leninist ideology. For example, countries with predominantly Christian cultures seemed more attracted to Marxism than countries with Hindu or Islamic cultures.

Though Colburn's thesis relies on the special influence that Western universities have had on third world intellectuals, it does not explain the origin of this powerful influence. Still less does Colburn talk about the dislocating impact of Western education on educated elites of peripheral societies. Without the prior internalization of the normativeness of the West, the impact of radical Western discourse remains inexplicable. Colburn's explanation also leaves out one important aspect: while third world intellectuals felt the hold of Western academia, they also had a wide mistrust toward Western concepts. For no less than Marxist ideas, Western universities were busy extolling the virtues and advantages of liberalism. Why did radical ideas tossed out in the lecture rooms of Western universities have so much impact on third world intellectuals, as opposed to liberal ideas, which Western scholars also defended fiercely?

An approach is needed, therefore, that accounts for the special attraction of some cultures to Marxist-Leninist ideology as well as for the third world intelligentsia's attraction/repulsion attitude toward the West. Once it is admitted that structural conditions do not play the major role, only the addition of particular cultural motives to the receptivity created by academic formation can elucidate the uneven impact of the socialist ideology on third world intellectuals.

5

Imitativeness and Elitism

In evaluating the link that Forrest D. Colburn establishes between the radicalism of third world educated elites and the impact of the radical discourse prevailing in Western universities in the sixties and seventies, we suggested that considerations pertaining to the pernicious effects of the Western educational system on native students must complete the explanation. More than academic formation itself, what impelled students and intellectuals from peripheral countries to espouse radical ideas of social change was the cultural disorientation imparted by modern education. The formation of a culture of revolution presupposes mental disarticulation; more exactly, the culture of revolution is nothing but a clumsy, misguided detour aiming at reinstating cultural integrity and reversing backwardness. The culture of revolution reflects the power of the West as much as it endeavors to break it. It is at once dependence and rebellion. Only by seeing this dual character of third world revolutionism can we understand its intricacies. The aim of this chapter is precisely to reflect on how dependency construes the elimination of backwardness.

The Drawbacks of Imitativeness

An important trend of modernization theory insists that the key to modernity is the formation of a culture of self-reliance. In line with its basic motto "Modernity versus tradition," the trend argues that modernization occurs when traditional values, beliefs, and ways of doing things give way to innovative views and methods. Grant that traditionality is characterized by a hierarchical, ascriptive, and custom-bound social life, and the problem of the transition to modernity credibly boils down to initiating processes that lead to the decline of authoritarian norms and methods. That is why a modernization thinker like David McClelland attributes the rise of modern nations to the emergence of families in which the child-rearing system inculcated self-reliance rather than submission to existing norms. To quote McClelland, achieving boys "usually came from families in which the mothers stressed early self-reliance and mastery. The boys whose mothers did not encourage their early self-reliance, or did not set such high standards of excellence, tended to develop lower need for achievement."[1]

While underlining the necessity of creativity, modernization theorists paradoxically advocate the West as a model and so reduce culture change to the assimilation of Western values and institutions through an imported educational system. In so doing, they encourage the learning not of self-reliance but of dependency and imitation. Like the authoritarian family, the mental dependency on the West blocks self-reliance and innovation in peripheral societies. Obviously, modernization theory's advocacy of Western education as a means to modernize native elites does not tally with its explanation of the rise of modernity.

Speaking of the detrimental impact of the mental dependency of black people, Edward W. Blyden writes: "Without the physical or mental aptitude for the enterprises which they [blacks] are taught to admire and revere, they attempt to copy and imitate them, and share the fate of all copyists and imitators. Bound to move on a lower level, they acquire and retain a practical inferiority, transcribing, very often, the faults rather than the virtues of their models."[2] Innovation goes with self-reliance, which is synonymous for self-respect. Imitation is not your business if you have confidence in your ability. Only the loss of self-respect can persuade you to believe that the best you can do is to try to copy the West. Unmistakably, the building of self-confidence is a necessary condition for producing achieving individuals.

Western education's downgrading of the legacy of Africans in favor of the normativeness of the West thus goes against the need to build up confidence. Such a method can produce neither self-reliance nor innovative capacity. It cannot even produce good copyists, since the loss of self-respect compels Africans to identify themselves with the faults of the model rather than its virtues. For depreciated people, greatness cannot be a goal. The normativeness of the West so deeply depreciates Africans that they end up denying themselves the excellent qualities necessary to reproduce Western achievements. More than from the established socioeconomic gap, Africans suffer from the internalization of Western discourse, which is all the more pernicious since it occurs in the early years of schooling.

Given that the inculcation of dependency suppresses one's ability and lowers oneself, and so results in faulty performances, only the restoration of self-respect can reawaken confidence and the ability to do as well as the original model. In other words, only when the ability is granted to match with the West is there liberation from the goal of copying Western achievements. In such a case, the model turns into an inspiration, better still a challenge to originality, that is, to achieve something different but of equal if not superior value. Indeed, there is a great difference between inspiration and imitation: the latter forces one into passivity and self-depreciation, whereas the former is a stimulation to rival, even surpass, the model.

To show that an important answer to the mystery of the African failure to modernize is found in the drawbacks of a mentality held back by dependency and imitation, Blyden emphasizes the role of autonomy as follows: once the Negro has accepted the stereotypes about his inferiority, whatever his abilities,

> he fancies that he must grind at the mill which is provided for him, putting in the material furnished to his hands, bringing no contribution from his own field; and of course nothing comes out but what is put in. Thus he can never bring any real assistance to the European. He can never attain to that essence of progress which Mr. Herbert Spencer describes as *difference*; and therefore, he never acquires the self-respect or self-reliance of an independent contributor.[3]

While inspiration leads to difference, imitation achieves faulty results by its very aim of reproducing the model. The only way to do as well as the model is not imitation, but deviation. Progress is realized through differentiation, which mobilizes creativity. That which is not unique and original is necessarily hampered by deficiencies on account of being a copy, a reduced realization.

From Imitation to Misplaced Radicalism

Blyden's analysis perfectly applies to the Ethiopian situation: the dismissal of Ethiopian features under the impact of the normativeness of the West realized the blockage of creativity. Its first outcome was uncertainty of direction: although Ethiopian students "can no longer accept the role of the Solomonic tradition and the concept of being 'chosen people' as the basis of the state, any more than they can accept that the Ethiopian Christian Church is fit to be the cement of their society, they are uncertain how to effect a change."[4] The unbearable nature of the uncertainty soon activated imitativeness. The abrupt devaluation of traditional beliefs having blocked all attempt to renovate them, what else was left but the disposition to "seek an alternative philosophy" from outside?[5] Unfortunately, the dismissal of whatever was native encouraged borrowings without any attention to Ethiopian specifics, and hence without any tendency to critically assess imported values and institutions.

Now place this subservient mentality in the epoch of the ideological dominance of Marxism-Leninism, and you secure the characteristic impressionability that explains the infatuation of Ethiopian students with that theory. A dependent mind-set provides, by definition, little safeguard against hegemonic ideologies. Nor can it stand up to the uncritical, dogmatic absorption of such ideologies. Since the mental direction of dependency is not so much to apply borrowed concepts to a concrete and particular reality as to make that reality conformable to the imperatives of the dominant ideology, it unleashes "revolutionary romanticism" as well as a tendency to be satisfied with "a crude and superficial digest of Marxist-Leninist ideas."[6] Because the theory is given a normative rather than an analytical function, it does not set limits and conditions, and so encourages idealism. Also, there is no need to have a sophisticated understanding of the theory when it is up to reality to conform to the theory rather than vice versa. Imitativeness does not analyze; instead, its attempts to subsume reality under alien normative concepts produce the tendency to infatuation for the simple reason that concepts are handled as formulas of incantation rather than as tools of knowledge.

The attempt to make the Ethiopian social system conformable to advanced ideas gleaned from exposure to Western education created a harmful disparity between the thinking of the educated elite and social realities. In addition to inculcating imitativeness, this disparity created impatience. The natural reaction of impatience is to think in terms of catching up with the West. So instead of letting Ethiopian realities mature and change on their own, that is, according to their internal dynamics, the catch-up mode of thinking prompted an interventionist and accelerationist approach, which looked for shortcuts and condensed techniques of socioeconomic growth. Development is no longer a process involving an evolutionary sequence of maturation and self-alteration; it is rather a manufactured outcome in which planning and resolute elimination of hurdles combine to produce a speedy result.

Is it surprising that the Ethiopian impatience was seduced by Marxism-Leninism, which was then credited for the pace of industrialization in the Soviet Union and China that was faster than in any capitalist country? In short, the internalization of the normativeness of the West having provoked impatience, the ideology that promised the most rapid technique of development became irresistible. Far from being excess, radicalism became a virtue, the expression of an unreserved commitment to the fastest course of modernization.

Maoist Heresy

To bring out the harmful nature of imitativeness, let us reflect on the deviations of Maoism. Mao Tse-tung understood very early on that creativity, and not imitation of the Soviet system, was the key to a successful revolution in China. Moreover, he clearly saw that what would sustain creativity was the attempt to synthesize Chinese peculiarities and Marxism. According to Mao:

> If the Chinese Communists, who form a part of the great Chinese nation and are linked with it by flesh and blood, talk about Marxism apart from China's characteristics, that will be only Marxism in the abstract, Marxism in the void. Hence how to turn Marxism into something specifically Chinese, to imbue every manifestation

of it with Chinese characteristics, *i.e.* to apply it in accordance with China's characteristics, becomes a problem which the whole Party must understand and solve immediately.[7]

Mao is not simply defending the truism that Marxism should be adapted to specific conditions. Nor is he merely restating the idea that the integration of Chinese realities is necessary to successfully mobilize the people. He is also showing that a necessary prerequisite to avoiding imitativeness and its harmful effects is the defense of Chinese culture.

From Mao's standpoint "a definite defensive posture emerges regarding Chinese culture, which has been denigrated not only by the imperialists but also by those Chinese, Marxist as well as non-Marxist, who see national salvation only in unqualified Westernization."[8] This defense of Chinese culture against Westernization as well as against Marxism, a product of the West, opened the path for a creative course through the critical and integrative appropriation of Marxism. This process of integrating Marxism into the national culture through the protection of Chinese specifics countered the decentering and disparaging impact of Western concepts. Stated otherwise, Western concepts, including Marxist ones, were viewed less as norms than as useful additions to a valued legacy.

The outcome of this work of integration was that the Chinese ceased to be simply passive imitators of the West. They were engaged in a creative task of interpretation that allowed them to read Western concepts from the Chinese perspective and interest. In this way, they remained culturally centered, thereby escaping the status of periphery of the West. They maintained their autonomy while adopting those Western ideas that they considered to be useful. Paradoxically, then, the only way to become a true and successful Marxist is not to repeat Marx; it is to deviate from Marx, to become a heretic. The Soviets expressed their dissatisfaction with China's creative adaptation of Marxism by pointing out that "there are more references in his [Mao's] writing to Chinese literature and philosophy than to the Marxist classics."[9] In so saying, they were but forgetting that their own version of Marxism, namely Leninism, was also a creative, heretical adaptation to Russian specifics.

Another proof of Mao's deviation is the central place given to the peasantry, which was even promoted to the rank of motor of revolution in lieu of the proletariat. The promotion of the peasantry reflected a mind-set still in tune with traditional Chinese culture. Likewise, the methods of China's revolutionary government revived many Confucian values. One important explanation for these revivalist practices emerges: Mao was a revolutionary intellectual with essentially a traditional background. He knew no Western language—he read all Western philosophers through translations—and did not visit any foreign country before his trip to the Soviet Union in 1949. Because of this cultural seclusion, he was able to give China a view of socialism that was national and practical. The fact that he remained culturally centered allowed him to use Marxism instead of being mesmerized by it.

Failure to Indigenize Borrowings

The Maoist deviation confirms that creativity lies in achieving difference through the renewal of one's national legacy. Such was not the initial urge of Ethiopian students and intellectuals: their imitative tendency precluded any attempt to integrate Marxism with Ethiopian traditional culture. Still less was there any serious endeavor at a retrospective reading of Ethiopia's legacy by means of which, elements of socialist thinking being discovered, socialism could be nationally integrated and defined as restoration. As Beseat Kifle Selassie remarks, "The Ethiopian student movements disregarded cultural factors as important as religion."[10] Instead, the consensus was that the defense of the culture amounted to protecting reactionary beliefs and institutions. Ethiopian students did not see that their call for a tabula rasa deprived them of creativity by committing them to copyism. And, as author B. Kotchy rightly reminds us, "If culture was to play its full part in creating awareness and acting as a source of inventiveness and creativity, it was important for it to be identified, rehabilitated and restored to its true setting."[11]

An even greater reason to revive the Ethiopian legacy was that it could have been used to criticize the imperial regime by exposing to what dangerous extent the ruling elite was drifting away from the traditional norms of independence, self-reliance, social mobility, and regionalism. The amazing survival of Ethiopia, the fact that it subsisted for centuries in a hostile environment, was enough to set the native norms of a viable society that could have discredited the imperial regime. The issue of culture could thus have been raised in such a way as to charge the existing elite with treason and lack of nationalism. Some such cultural revival would have laid the groundwork for the formulation of an Ethiopian Marxism.

The failure to indigenize Marxism largely explains why the Ethiopian Revolution, when it finally broke out, was never able to develop a lasting enthusiasm and energy comparable to that of the Chinese Revolution. Though the Revolution started with great enthusiasm, it soon lost momentum. The intervention of the Derg does not fully explain the loss of enthusiasm and vigor; we must add the disenchantment arising from the impression of taking part in a staged revolution. The political and economic measures were all predictable, déjà vu phenomena. People had the sense of going through a history already played out, of being passive actors of a piece written without their contribution. In thus turning into a huge mimicry of past Soviet and Chinese accomplishments, the Ethiopian Revolution could not nourish the passion that it first stirred up. The feeling of wandering in a secondhand history and of being towed by external forces gave Ethiopians nothing to be passionate about.

Modern Education and Elitism

Another harmful outcome of the educational system was elitism, which was the forced companion of imitativeness. The debasing of the cultural heritage created an unbridgeable generational gap: what was traditional and old being associated with backwardness, whatever appeared as Western and young acquired absolute value, often independently of real merits. Perceived as living fossils, the old lost the authority necessary to transmit the cultural heritage, while the young gained the right not to listen to the old. Consequently, schoolchildren turned into "more sophisticated and infallible 'semi-gods.' Most of those who left school before 1974 believed themselves to be the unspoken leaders of Ethiopian society."[12]

An important source of the narcissism of the educated elite was the great value given to modern education by the very scheme of modernization theory. As Donald L. Donham puts it: "The grand scheme of modernization—the march of advanced nations, followed by backward ones, along a continuum defined by different groups' success in applying science and knowledge—had come to define reality for many of the new Ethiopian educated elite. And as such ideas diffused to the cities and towns of the country, *yetamarē*, educated persons—those who would lead Ethiopia out of backwardness—enjoyed unquestioned prestige."[13] The belief that Ethiopia lagged behind and that modern education was the absolute remedy to get out of backwardness could not but propel the educated elite to political leadership in the very eyes of ordinary people. So awe-inspiring was the prestige of modern education that ordinary people were easily convinced that Ethiopians who happened to possess this education were legitimate leaders, nay, that nothing but good results could come from their leadership. The irony is that the imperial regime's relentless hailing of modern schooling as the one and only key to modernization created the social prestige of the educated elite.

Be it noted that the recognition of leadership was grounded more on cultural enlightenment than on know-how of scientific and technological skills. Both ordinary people and educated individuals endowed modern education with entitlement to social leadership essentially because they believed that culturally Westernized people provided the right remedy to the backwardness perceived as Ethiopia's major social impediment. The technological advance of Westerners was construed as a consequence of their enlightened culture so that the first task was to go after enlightenment. Had modernization been viewed essentially as technological parity rather than enlightenment, as was the case, for instance, in Japan, the educational system would have given primacy to the production of engineers and technicians rather than liberators. But as already indicated, modernization in Ethiopia was posed, from the start, in terms of awakening from a long slumber, and this conception affected educational policy by giving precedence to the import of ideas and institutions over the acquisition of technological mastery. The primacy accorded to Westernization explains why the founders of Haile Selassie I University were American religious scholars, and not technology and science teachers.

The idea of backwardness is at the root both of the politicization of the educated elite and the assignment of a colonizing mission to modern school-ing. As a place of acculturation, the school traded old and backward beliefs with Western ideas. A dramatic illustration of the perception of educated people as enlighteners and liberators is found in the Derg's decision of 1975 to send students and teachers to spread enlightenment in the countryside. The program was called "the Development through Cooperation, Enlightenment, and Work Campaign," and the students were baptized "*ye lewt hawariat*," that is, "apostles of change." The choice of the Amharic word "*zemecha*" (campaign) to define the program added a military connotation to the spread of enlightenment and civilization, thereby likening the whole program to a colonial enterprise. "The students, dressed in khaki uniforms and caps with *zemecha* insignia, would be sent, like an army, to reconquer the countryside," writes Donham.[14]

The deep implication of modern education as a civilizing mission was the delegitimization of the traditional ruling elite in favor of the educated elite, the sole carrier of enlightenment. Students "believed that the major prerequisite for political power should be educational qualification."[15] The way modernization was conceived impacted on the social function of mod-ern educated people by painting political power as their legitimate enti-tlement. In other words, the political calling of the educated elite directly emanated from a system of education that defined modernization in terms of acculturation. Since only the enlightened group was entitled to bring about the modernization of Ethiopia, little wonder Ethiopian students and intellectuals inevitably developed an image of themselves as sole agents of change, and hence as rightful political leaders. By associating moderniza-tion with Westernization, modern education unleashed a fundamental conflict between the traditional elite and the new educated elite whose implication displaced the entitlement to power from the former to the latter.

The exclusive mission of modernizer explains the elitist drift of Ethiopian students and intellectuals. Referring to student publications, Marina and David Ottaway write: "The tone of the writings was quite elitist . . . in that students saw themselves as the only group that could save Ethiopia because of their superior education. Brought up as part of an elitist society, students showed in their publications that they had fully accepted the elitist point of view."[16]

The following quotations taken from *Struggle* and *Challenge* give a good idea of the elitist bent of Ethiopian students and intellectuals: "The future of the old country that still refuses to convince itself that its past glory is merely history now lies in his (the student's) hands. He is at the head of a march and his choice is either to consolidate the constituents of this march from scattered, unequal individuals into a whole united body, or to exploit this situation and become as prosperous and fat as many Ethiopians have already become."[17] Subtitled "The Spirit of Solidarity," one editorial in *Challenge* reads: "Ethiopia's youth, finally aware of its historic mission, called for an end to oppression, injustice and corruption, and demanded the restitution of the inherent rights and liberties of our people. Having liberated itself from the suffocating tradition of fear and mistrust, it set for itself the task of articulating the needs of our country."[18] In the same issue: "The task of awakening our country from her age-old slumber and liberating our people from the iron grip of remorseless tyranny falls on our shoulders. This mission and duty cannot be denied by any Ethiopian, for sooner or later, the tide of history will inevitably herald the victory of our oppressed masses."[19]

These statements did not simply denounce the evil outcomes of imperial policy; they also defined the members of the educated elite as rightful political challengers to the traditional elite on account of their superior knowledge and dedication. The addition of moral rectitude to the intellectual superiority further strengthened the entitlement of the intelligentsia to political leadership. The combination of knowledge with the sense of righteousness created an extreme form of elitism, which claimed to represent the downtrodden masses and speak in their name. In short, it associated elitism with social messianism.

Guilt and Messianic Mentality

The association of elitism with messianism meant that not only knowledge but also social calling set the educated apart as a special group. The belief that those who know, those who have liberated themselves from ignorance and reaction, have the duty to liberate the masses triggered what Tesfaye Demmellash called the "over-eagerness to be a protagonist in revolutionary struggle on *behalf* of the masses rather than *with* them."[20] Zeal thus mobilized the ethical stand demanding students to rise above selfishness so as not to use education as a means of personal gain and enjoyment, for the privilege of being exposed to modern ideas entrusted them with a liberating mission. Thus grew from the mere acquaintance with Western ideas in a social setting allegedly burdened with ignorance and backwardness the sense of a special prerogative of the educated elite, which prerogative gave birth to a messianic complex: of being the rescuer, the liberator of the victims of reaction and imperialism.

Elitism and messianism were all the more encouraged the more Westernization stirred up the guilt of betrayal. Both the great gap that education created between students and their society and the sense of siding with an alien culture against their own legacy activated a secret feeling of betrayal. The only way by which the feeling could be appeased was through the fostering of a messianic mentality: departing from tradition ceases to be betrayal if students come back not only richer and more learned, but also as redeemers, deliverers of their people. Samuel P. Huntington has captured the seduction of guilty feeling with radicalism thus:

> The student thus becomes ashamed of and alienated from his own society; he becomes filled with the desire to reconstruct it completely to bring it into "the front rank of nations." Divorced from his family and from traditional norms and behavior patterns, the student identifies all the more completely with the abstract standards and principles of modernity. These become the absolute standards by which he judges his own society. No goal is sufficient short of the total reconstruction of society.[21]

Radicalism becomes tempting as a remedy against the nagging sense of betrayal because advocacy of moderate or liberal views does no more than accentuate the guilt of betrayal by turning educated Ethiopians into allies and spokespersons of the West. Only by rejecting Western values do they show their independence and commitment to the nation. That is why Marxism fitted so nicely into the mind-set of Ethiopian students: though Western, Marxism criticizes capitalist values and methods and fights for the collapse of capitalism. The Marxist conversion of the criticism of capitalism into the highest expression of modernism could only captivate students disturbed by the gap between their society and the Western world. It gives great relief to know that even those who claimed to be highly advanced were, after all, as defective as traditional societies despite their superior wealth and know-how. In the eyes of student morality, the coexistence of accumulated wealth with great social disparity portrays the Western world as a cynical and depraved civilization.

The sentiment of shame also helps explain the radicalism of many students who belonged to wealthy or influential families. As already noted, studies have shown that the higher the class backgrounds of students, the more intense their radicalism becomes. Neither reasons of economics nor the simple fact of youthful idealism and generosity can account for the overblown radicalization. Scholars have suggested the involvement of an acute form of generational conflict. Only this type of conflict can explain why, for example, in a feudal society educated individuals coming from feudal families often side with the cause of the masses. The fact that they espouse values directly antagonistic to those of their parents strongly suggests the presence of sharp conflict with the values of their own class driven by the failure of their family and class to modernize the country.

The Russian case provides a good illustration of the radicalizing impact of shame. The record shows that many of the radicals who opposed the czarist regime came from aristocratic families. Speaking of the Russian student movement, Lewis S. Feuer notes: "When in the 1860s and 1870s several thousand student youth, inspired by feelings of guilt and responsibility for the backward people, embarked on their 'back-to-the-people' movement, it was an unparalleled collective act of selfless idealism."[22] Though students coming from the upper classes inspired and drove the movement, its distinguishing mark was the refusal to identify with the values of Russian aristocracy. Embracing the cause of the downtrodden masses, many young aristocrats professed socialism; others adopted the anarchist stance. Clearly, before being a doctrinal commitment, the identification with the victims of the system was an act of open rebellion caused by guilty feeling over the disappointing performance of their own class.

The exposure to Western education had revealed Russia's backwardness, but even more so the anachronism of the privileges of its aristocratic class. Add to this the humiliation over Russia's lag behind Europe because of the failure of the ruling aristocracy to pull the country out of backwardness. The accumulated rancor generated a particularly acute form of conflict between the old aristocracy and the young. To quote Feuer:

> The universal theme of generational revolt, which cuts across all societies, produced in Russia a "conflict of generations" of unparalleled intensity because of special social circumstances. The Russian students lived their external lives in a social reality which was absolutist, politically tyrannical, and culturally backward; internally, on the other hand, they lived in a milieu imbued with Western values. Their philosophical and idealistic aims transcended the social system, and were out of keeping with it; the philosophical culture and the social system were at odds with each other, in contradiction.[23]

The increasing bias of young Russian aristocrats toward populism was thus an expression of the need to disavow their aristocratic ties. The guilt and responsibility they felt as members of the aristocratic class triggered the need. The best way to differentiate themselves from their parents was to stand in favor of those whom the czarist system exploited and humiliated. Populism was for them a form of atonement for the failings of their class.

As in Russia, in Ethiopia an established imperial autocracy and nobility failed to make the necessary reforms, preferring to stick to privileges that the exposure to Western values could only present as outdated, if not as ridiculous.

While the absorption of the Western discourse humiliated ordinary educated Ethiopians, it heightened guilt among sons and daughters of aristocratic families because the failure of their families directly affected them. In sharing the blame for the failure of their class, they were naturally driven to express their rebellion by identifying themselves with those that their class mistreated. No economic explanation exists for the great number of sons and daughters of Ethiopia's important families who became radicalized, including those belonging to the upper echelon of the military elite. Still less is the espousal of values diametrically opposed to aristocratic values attributable to their understanding of the necessity of reforms. They did not simply denounce wrongs; in becoming Marxist, they deprived their own class of the legitimacy to rule on account of its unenlightenment, moral decay, and national demission. Only the emotional component of generational conflict can explain why Marxism became more attractive than liberalism to educated youngsters with aristocratic background.

The Love Affair between Elitism and Leninism

Once elitism was born, Marxism-Leninism became irresistible for a number of reasons. We have already indicated that elitism and the subsequent attribution of a messianic, redemptive role to the Western-educated youth carry the supposition that other classes are not fit to lead Ethiopia's modernization process. Together with the traditional elite, the middle class and the petite bourgeoisie are eliminated from the leadership position because they are all judged unable to conceive and apply the right solution to Ethiopia's severe problems. Since all classes are declared unfit, there remain the working masses and their representatives, the radicalized educated elite. Can one fail to see the Leninist origin of this polarizing reading of Ethiopian society? In thus justifying the political ambition of the educated elite, Marxism-Leninism could not but emerge as the only viable philosophy. In a society deprived of progressive forces, only the followers of the ideology that puts modernization in the hands of those who are truly qualified while denouncing other groups as usurpers are entitled to become leaders.

Another attraction was the Marxist-Leninist claim to provide a scientific theory of development. The claim generated a natural acceptance among educated Ethiopians, who felt deep resonance with the term "scientific" subsequent to the awe-inspiring impact of Western scientific and technological achievements on them. Moreover, the alleged scientific approach of Marxism-Leninism meant the possibility of a rapid catch-up with the West, in the manner of the Soviet Union. Equally important was the moral component of Marxism-Leninism, that is, the denunciation of exploitation and injustice and the defense of the poor. It gave Marxism-Leninism the status of an exceptional theory in which science finally goes hand in hand with ethics. For "not only does Marxism have appeal to the downtrodden because of its rejection of past domination and inequality of opportunities, but also because it is perceived as a means of reorganizing the society 'scientifically' to achieve the economic and social objectives of socialism."[24] The alleged union of science and ethics exerted a powerful attraction on Ethiopian intellectuals. In fusing elitism with social messianism, the moral dimension of Marxism transfigured the status of functionary or bureaucrat of the Ethiopian educated elite into that of rescuer.

None of these attractions was as powerful as the Leninist theory of the vanguard party. Lenin makes the realization of socialism essentially dependent on the formation of a party composed of "a select, highly disciplined, and 'theoretical' cadre of professional revolutionaries."[25] No social theory has elevated the educated elite of developing countries as high as Leninism has. To develop a parallel already pointed out, Lenin's theory of a vanguard party realizes Plato's dream of "the philosopher king" by uniting knowledge and politics. Just as for Plato the ideal society comes into existence only when those who have contemplated the world of ideas rule and "political power and philosophy thus come into the same hands," so too for Lenin the political and ideological leadership of revolutionary intellectuals alone can drag workers out of their trade-union consciousness and put them on the revolutionary course of socialism.[26] Strongly rejecting the rise of an independent ideology among workers, Lenin wrote: "We must actively take up the political education of the working class, and the development of its political consciousness."[27] For Leninism, then, revolutionary intellectuals are not mere representatives of the working masses; they are also their tutors in that they educate workers by raising their revolutionary consciousness, and so decide what their long-term interests should be.

A quick comparison with such political thinkers as Thomas Hobbes, John Locke, and Baron de Montesquieu unquestionably justifies the characterization of Leninism as a "pronounced elitism."[28] As theoreticians of the bourgeoisie, the three political philosophers formulated views and forged concepts that allowed the rising bourgeois class to gain ideological hegemony through the identification of its interests with the general interest. None of these thinkers, however, undertook the task of either tutoring the bourgeois class or defining its interests. Such a task would have required a theory advocating the seizure of state power by intellectuals. Unlike these philosophers, Lenin maintained that intellectuals are no longer separate scholars who, transcending partisan politics, try to perceive society objectively. On the contrary, revolutionary intellectuals must be directly involved in the political struggle: in addition to speaking in the name of the classes they claim to represent, they organize themselves for the purpose of seizing power so as to implement the interests of the classes they defend.

Intellectuals are not simply those who conceptualize and propose; they are also political executors and tutors of classes.

The originality of Leninism stands out even better when it is contrasted with the position of Karl Marx himself, who never got anywhere near to assigning a key role to intellectuals. For Marx, "the bourgeoisie and the proletariat were the most powerful actors in modern politics; each was a revolutionary class in its time. Intellectuals, on the other hand, were assigned no independent role by Marx."[29] Lenin, however, transferred the historical role that Marx assigned to the bourgeoisie and the working class to intellectuals. Organized into a party, the latter plan and bring about economic development and guide the working class to socialism. Without the close leadership of revolutionary intellectuals, Lenin insisted, neither workers still less peasants can achieve ideological emancipation, let alone march toward socialism.

What made Leninism so attractive to intellectuals of third world countries is thus obvious: it crowned them as the sole legitimate leaders of underdeveloped societies. To hold a Leninist position was for third world intellectuals to assert their historical mission, and hence their entitlement to power. Add to this legitimation the enticement of voluntarism. According to Lenin, the Bolshevik success demonstrated the great deeds that intellectuals could achieve when they operated organizationally. No need to wait for the realization of necessary material conditions; voluntarism can generate socialism even in underdeveloped societies, provided the subjective conditions of political will, organization, and leadership are gathered. The importance given to subjective factors over structural conditions does show "the contrast between Marxist economic determinism and Leninist voluntarism," just as it explains the strengthening impact of Leninism on the elitist tendency that the educated sector of peripheral societies inherited from its Westernization.[30] The valorization of subjective factors in a situation of economic destitution greatly enhances the ambition of the educated elite both in terms of capabilities and leadership.

Politics as Tutorship

This new role of intellectuals stems from the normativeness of the West yielding a negative perception of traditional societies. Once the conclusion is reached that whatever is old and traditional is an obstacle to modernization, the process of modernization is necessarily defined in terms of replacing the old ruling elite with a new, young, and Western-educated cadre. The problem is so presented because the issue of modernization adds to the usual governing function of the state the role of tutor, which Westernized elites alone can carry out.

Consider the case of the Chinese revolutionary and political leader, Sun Yat-sen. He developed "the notion of tutelage; the necessity of a 'vanguard,' a modernizing elite" very early and before Lenin popularized it, thereby demonstrating that elitism is indeed a direct product of Western education.[31] For him and his followers, "China . . . needed the sustained tutelage of a dedicated student-intellectual elite. By right, the people were sovereign, but they could assume that role and perform their legitimate function only after they had been educated and instructed in both technology and political values."[32] They reached this conclusion while they were committed to Western-style parliamentarism as the best system of government. This gives proof that the real inspirer of elitism is Western education, since Chinese students came to the idea before they espoused Marxism. The impact of Western education on intellectuals from peripheral societies is, therefore, a precondition to the reception of Lenin's notion of a vanguard party.

What Lenin has deeply understood is the incompatibility of the defense of tutelage with bourgeois values. If one is serious about instituting a government of tutorship as a necessary condition to a rapid and successful modernization, the project is obviously at odds with liberalism. Neither the open market system, nor the electoral method of political change, is propitious to the systematic implementation of a tutorial program. Instead, an authoritarian and durable government, which intellectuals rather than politicians or businesspeople run and control, is the way to go. The great consistency of Marxism-Leninism, in the eyes of alienated intellectuals, is that it "sanctions the consolidation of party and state power at the political center to achieve its self-proclaimed ends."[33] Moreover, rapid development is likely to be attained if the center controls, plans, and guides everything. "The Marxist-Leninist emphasis upon vanguard parties, democratic centralism, nationalization and collectivization, planned economies, and popular mobilization" is accordingly the best possible form of tutorship.[34]

Marxism-Leninism thus solved the dilemma of intellectuals who, still attached to liberalism, posited the need for tutelage of the people. Only government by select revolutionary intellectuals is able to fulfill the tutoring task while creating optimal conditions for the transition to the full sovereignty of the people. Such a government plans the economy, educates and mobilizes the people, and gives concrete leadership to the process leading to socialism in which the sovereignty of the working peoples becomes total. The only way tutorship can be effectively applied is through the commitment to a socialist type of development. A free market society cannot harbor the objective of tutoring the masses without challenging its class structure. In a word, tutorship means socialism.

Like the Russian and Chinese students, Ethiopian students reached the conclusion that the traditional elite, being hopelessly inadequate both intellectually and morally, needed to be removed. They also thought that centuries of feudal rule allied with an obscurantist clergy had made the working people unusually ignorant. Given this situation of deep backwardness, their exposure to Western education furnished them with the vocation of tutor of the people. Things would have probably remained at a potential level were it not for the global influence of Marxism-Leninism, which precisely promised a rapid development without the bourgeoisie and under the ideological and political leadership of revolutionary intellectuals. Nothing could flatter more the vocation of tutor assumed by Ethiopian students and intellectuals than the encounter with the principles of Marxism-Leninism. And with its apparently successful outcomes in Russia and elsewhere, the idea of tutorship became definitively tied to the seizure of political power, by which alone the modernizing program could be systematically applied. In other words, the theory of modernity versus tradition, insofar as it brings about elitism and messianism, is the basic root of the attraction to Marxism-Leninism.

The Lack of Homegrown Intellectuals

So far we have reached the following conclusion: having absorbed the values and historical scheme of Eurocentrism, the Ethiopian educated elite fostered a form of elitism that had all the characteristics of a colonial mentality. Being a product of a system of education with strong Eurocentric components and direction, what else could elitism develop but a form of thinking conceiving of modernization in colonial terms? The student movement in Ethiopia as well as abroad and the various political organizations that later emanated from the movement, such as the Ethiopian People's Revolutionary Party (EPRP), the MEISON, and others, despite their ideological differences, all had one thing in common, namely, "an absolutely *dirigiste* conception of [their] relations with 'the people.' "[35]

Neither modernization nor revolution was viewed as a social practice in which people asserted and pursued their interests by remaining active. Social change had to come from the revolutionary elite, which also possessed the exclusive right to enlighten and organize the people. Thus conceived, modernization is a not a lived process, a change arising from the actual life of people—in which case it would be a solution to real problems—it is the imposition of an external model of society considered to be advanced. Such a conception never gives the initiative to the people; on the contrary, it presupposes their passivity as a condition of perfect acculturation. Elites are the real actors so that the masses that they glorify turn into an amorphous material ready to be fashioned at will. As a result, modernization becomes a process uncontrolled by the people and whose purpose escapes them. It is the project of the Westernized elite that takes on itself the job of modernizing a backward society, that is, of constructing modernity on the basis of the colonial model. Modernization is not about letting the people act, decide, choose, and plan; it is about the self-appointed trustee of the West, namely, the educated elite, acting, choosing, and planning on behalf of the unenlightened people.

To come back to a previous analogy, we are dealing here with the demiurgical vocation of native elites. The calling shows the extent to which modernization is conceived in Platonic terms. Plato assigns the mission of fashioning the sensible world in light of eternal ideas to a subordinate deity, the Demiurge. Similarly, modernization theory ascribes the fashioning of traditional societies in accordance with the Western model of society to Westernized native elites. There is thus an ideal world whose conception and access depend on the disparagement of the native society, termed barbaric and backward. Like Plato's sensible world, it blocks access to the superior society. The educated natives are those that Western missionaries and educators freed from the inferior world and took to the upper world to contemplate advanced ideas. Their mission is to go back to their society and rescue their people from traditional ways. For this end, they need to conquer state power and thus become "philosopher-kings," absolute rulers. The basis of their authority is their knowledge drawn from their contemplation of the upper society. Their method of government, which they call modernization, always goes from above to below; its goal is to impose the norms of the upper world on their people and society, both taken as passive and amorphous.

The great tragedy of Ethiopia is, therefore, that it did not produce domestic, homegrown intellectuals, who might have conceived of modernization as an upgrading of the traditional culture. Such intellectuals could have easily risen from the traditional culture if the system of education had established some form of continuity between traditional and Western educational systems. As we saw, the choice was to expel the traditional culture and its representatives from modern schooling with the consequence that a system of education committed to uprooting young Ethiopians totally prevailed. That such intellectuals turned away from the renewal of the traditional culture through purification and reinterpretation is hardly surprising considering their firm resolution to dismiss it.

In his study of the exceptional role that intellectuals play in third world countries, Edward Shils has perfectly described the kind of intellectuals that a country like Ethiopia did not have, that is, those

> men of the traditional culture who were sufficiently sensitive to the impact of modern culture to feel the need to reaffirm their own. Their task was the cleansing of the cultural—and this meant largely religious—inheritance of their society from what they claimed were historically accidental accretions which had brought it into disrepute among modern men and allowed their country to sink in the world's esteem and in its own and, particularly, to appear enfeebled and unworthy in

comparison with Western achievements. They claimed that what was essential in their religious traditions could—by restoration and cleansing or by syncretism—be reformulated in an idiom more appropriate to the modern situation. . . . They claimed that much of what it [Western culture] had to offer—particularly science, technology, and forms of organization—were necessary for the improvement of their countries and the re-establishment of their greatness among the nations. They insisted, however, that their countrymen must not lose their own souls to the West. They must instead rediscover their own essential being by the acceptance of a new and purer version of their own cultural tradition.[36]

Because Ethiopia did not have renovating intellectuals, its modernization was ill-conceived. When it was necessary to go through a cultural renewal to succeed modernization, Ethiopia opted for the barren path of Westernization. In so doing, it coined the implementation of modern schooling and modernization in colonial terms, thereby overlooking the primary task of purifying the culture of all its negative elements so as to integrate modern components through a creative act of reinterpretation.

A pertinent example of cultural renewal is Japan: the Meiji Restoration was a redefinition that made reforms possible, especially by instituting an autonomous prime minister heading a cabinet that got rid of feudalism, while maintaining samurai values and the charismatic role of the emperor. These traditional values were mobilized to achieve rapid industrialization. Likewise, India's Mahatma Gandhi is the perfect incarnation of renewal of tradition through reinterpretation and useful borrowings.

A case in point is Gandhi's rejection of the caste system. He wrote: "Caste has nothing to do with religion. It is a custom whose origin I do not know and do not need to know for the satisfaction of my spiritual hunger. But I do know that it is harmful both to spiritual and national growth."[37] Put otherwise, the so-called sacred texts that justify caste are not authentic; they are products of degeneration. Moreover, if something is harmful, reason tells us that it cannot be attributed to God. These findings call for the purification of Hinduism, not for its rejection. Compare Gandhi's attitude with the position of a revolutionary Indian intellectual, E. V. Ramasami Periyar: "Caste is proof of the fact that our people are not really a civilized people. . . . The cause of untouchability is not political slavery. It is the Hindu religion, pure and simple. Social reformers have perforce to kill the demon of untouchability if necessary by killing the Hindu religion."[38] While Gandhi avoids endorsing the colonial association of non-Western beliefs with being uncivilized, the revolutionary intellectual, who no longer believes in Hinduism as a result of Westernization, does not hesitate to see his own people and culture through the lens of colonial discourse. Gandhi uses modern ideas to renovate tradition; the revolutionary intellectual uses modern ideas to denigrate it.

In raising the issue of religion, this last point provides a suitable transition to the question whether one of the conditions for the rise of radicalism may be found in the manner traditional faiths react to Western education. At any rate, the issue of religion asks us to examine whether components specific to cultures either encourage or thwart the sensitivity to revolutionary ideologies. Whereas Mao advocates the integration of Marxist discourse into traditional Chinese culture, Gandhi prefers the path of purification of Hinduism. What if such a disparity of reaction is due to elements specific to the two cultures? This question is the crucial theme of the next chapter.

6

Ethiopian Messianism

The last chapter has established the radicalizing ingredients of uprootedness fostered by Western education. Yet, not all student movements of third world countries have succumbed to radicalism. In most countries, the majority of students and intellectuals were able to preserve a moderate political stand. For many observers, Ethiopian students and intellectuals were easily and extensively radicalized because of the exceptional gravity of Ethiopia's social and political problems. Here again, in many countries with grave social problems radicalism did not triumph. The reaction against uprootedness even gave birth to revivalist or nationalist ideologies in some countries. This chapter seeks to establish that cultural factors specific to Ethiopia consolidated the drive toward radicalism.

Cultural Disposition to Utopia

To answer the question why Marxism-Leninism supplanted the tradition of a nationalist stand among Ethiopian students and intellectuals, we must venture into cultural issues. The adoption of Marxist-Leninist ideology is facilitated when cultures fractured by Western education fail to show any restorative endeavor. Where a rehabilitative need develops, the attempt to counter cultural alienation and Westernization may find expression in the formulation of a nationalist ideology. As a rule, led by people of petit bourgeois background, often from the military sector, nationalist movements "set out to restore national dignity and promote development."[1] They do so by taking various measures that, they claim, protect the economy from foreign domination, combat corruption and injustice, and accelerate modernization.

One feature of nationalist movements is the association of economic modernization with the protection of the national culture, which nationalists want to renovate, mostly by attempting to "exalt the cultural values of the past (real or imagined)."[2] This commitment to the traditional culture prevents such movements from adhering to Marxism-Leninism, even if they adopt much of its rhetoric. Arab radical regimes, such as those of Nasser of

Egypt and Gadhafi of Libya are good examples of nationalist movements. They claim to be radically opposed to imperialism and internal reactionary forces; they even flirt with some forms of socialism. But they never attack Islam; nor do they attempt to liberate the masses from its influence. The best they can do when they do not openly defend the notion of an Islamic state or Islamic socialism is to establish a secular state that does not engage in any kind of conflict with Islam.

Quite different has been the evolution of Ethiopian students and intellectuals. Anti-imperialism and opposition to internal forces of reaction did not follow the path of a nationalist stand advocating the defense of traditional culture. On the contrary, the dominant trend was to abandon the traditional form of nationalism in favor of Marxism-Leninism. Hence the need to examine whether there are cultural traits that disposed more students to radicalism in Ethiopia than in countries with similar conditions. While other cultures at least strove to counter the uprooting effect of Western education through the revival of a nationalist discourse, most Ethiopian students and intellectuals felt no such need, believing that the right solution came from the adoption of an alien ideology.

One way of explaining the perplexing absence of any attempt to defend the culture is to see whether the alien ideology strikes deep chords in the fractured national culture, even perhaps to the point of emerging as a substitute. No need to revive the past culture if indeed the new ideology satisfies some of its deep longings. No sooner is the problem posited thus than the Christian character of Ethiopian culture and the great affinity that scholars have observed between Christian beliefs and Marxist utopianism spring to mind.

One author who has closely studied the leaning toward social utopia is S. N. Eisenstadt. He notes that the various causes of revolutions that scholars suggest—rising expectations, class struggle, interelite conflicts—do not necessarily lead to radical revolutions of the type that occurred in France, Russia, or China. These social upheavals caused transformations whose intensity and depth went beyond the changes accomplished by such revolutions as the American or English, which only achieved a change of political regime through the alteration of government policy and the political elite. That is why the latter two are defined by the term "political revolution," while revolutions resulting in deeper social transformations, like the French, Russian, and Chinese, "are sometimes referred to as 'great' or 'social' revolutions."[3] In addition to accomplishing the overthrow of a political regime, a social revolution goes deeper and effects transformations that affect the class structure and the cultural sphere. It entails "not only mass mobilization and regime change, but also more or less rapid and fundamental social, economic, and/or cultural change during or soon after the struggle for state power."[4]

Social revolutions are perforce rare occurrences, since the deterioration of social and political conditions are often not enough to even cause political revolutions. In most countries, the emergence of reformist movements prevents the crystallization of social discontent, and hence the eruption of violent protest. Seeing the small number of countries that have undergone social revolution, one must admit that this type of revolution is a special case, a rare form of social change. Hence Eisenstadt's question: "In what circumstances, under what conditions, do such causes give rise to what have been called revolutions and revolutionary transformations?"[5]

The usual answer to this kind of question is that social revolutions occur in imperial or imperial-feudal social systems that delay necessary reforms, the perfect examples being here Russia's czarist regime and imperial China. The structural characteristics of empires, namely, centralization, the social predominance of an agrarian oligarchy, and the use of repressive methods of government, require transformations that go beyond political change. In particular, the removal of the agrarian oligarchy necessitates a revolution such that both the class structure and the social ideology are profoundly modified.

Now, are the structural characteristics of imperial states enough to explain the exceptional occurrence of social revolutions? Let us note that such polities as Japan and the Ottoman Empire, though centralized and dominated by traditional elites, were able to modernize without having recourse to social revolutions. In fact, these examples show that political change is the best way to remove the obstacles originating from imperial states. It is not clear why a society would go through an extreme form of change when moderate solutions are available. Moreover, the shift from political to social revolution has often little to do with the resistance of imperial states, given that the political phase of a revolution begins with the overthrow of the centralized state. This is so true that a social revolution is viewed as the product of radicalization of social movements originally initiated to achieve moderate political change.

According to Eisenstadt, only the addition of specific ideological factors to the structural obstacles can explain the drift toward social revolution. In other words, some cultures must be more susceptible to radical ideologies than others such that social revolutions, which are distinguished by their commitment to a form of total change, have as one of their prerequisites cultural heritages prone to radicalization. Indeed, the line of demarcation between political and social revolutions can be clearly established in relation to their ideological component. Unlike political revolutions, which target emancipation from political tyranny and unfair economic systems, social revolutions involve a utopian inspiration of the type advocating universal freedom and social equality. To quote Eisenstadt, social revolution is "an ultimate expression of autonomous will and of deep emotions, encompassing formidable organizational capacities as well as a highly elaborated ideology of social protest, especially of a utopian or emancipatory image based on symbols of equality, progress, and freedom and on the central assumption that revolutions will create a new and better social order."[6]

One important implication of this approach is that revolutionary ideologies advocating egalitarianism and universal liberation, like Marxism, are less likely to attract cultural trends not vulnerable to utopian temptations. To say that universalist and utopian ideologies do not galvanize cultures with more mundane inspirations does not exclude the possibility of conversion to utopianism of individuals belonging to those cultures. Groups adhering to revolutionary ideologies appear in all countries; the difference is that in some countries they remain small minorities while in others they succeed in firing up a good number of people. The predisposition of cultures to utopianism explains the extension of the beliefs of radical factions to a larger number of people.

Religious Polarization and Social Revolution

There is no doubt that the kind of tension that cultures place between the mundane order and the transcendental or ideal order differentiates them. Some cultures (e.g., Christian, Islamic) see a great tension between the transcendental and the mundane. They attribute to the spiritual order characteristics that sharply contrast with the earthly order. By contrast, Hindu, Buddhist, and African tribal religious cultures are much less eager to accentuate the polarization between the spiritual and the secular. For such cultures, the implication is obvious: "Because of the lack of perception of tension between the cosmic and the mundane order and because of emphasis on the givenness of these orders, there rarely developed within such societies utopian orientations and conceptions of alternative social orders."[7]

Cultures that place a great tension between the spiritual and the worldly are exposed to the pressure of making the secular conformable to the ideal, and so have a particular sensitivity to utopian doctrines of social change. The inner exhortation to bridge the gap drives them to identify "this-worldly activity as the most important means of overcoming the tension between the transcendental-cosmic and the mundane order."[8] To shun the challenge of shaping the world in accordance with the transcendental order is a dereliction of duty that affects salvation.

Thus, recent studies show that one component of the Iranian Revolution originates from a reinterpretation of Shiism in the direction of political activism. This reinterpretation revives a millenarian belief according to which "the twelfth descendant of the Imam, known as the Mahdi, disappeared in 893 to return at the end of time to 'fill the world with justice.' "[9] True, religious beliefs often encourage acceptance of the existing situation until the realization of the ideal condition in the hereafter. When, however, millenarianism promises the return of the authentic leader who would institute the ideal order here on earth, "it can generate a historicist conviction in the final triumph of the right, thereby promoting militancy."[10] Hence the conviction that the political militancy rooted in this reinterpretation of Shiism, as opposed to the quietism that has prevailed in other parts of the Islamic world, provided the ideological root of the Iranian Revolution.

Where no tension between the spiritual and the worldly is perceived, the social order is taken as a given with no exhortation to make it conformable to the ideal realm. As a result, "the focus of salvation is on otherworldly activities rather than a combination of otherworldly and this-worldly activity."[11] Such cultural trends are understandably less likely to warm up to utopian ideas of social change.

Before going further, let us deal with the objection that disputes the pairing of Marxist doctrine with religious aspirations, given not only the secular but also the openly materialist and atheist stand of Marxism. The objection overlooks the fact that what separates a revolutionary doctrine from a religious belief is not so much the absence of utopian beliefs as its commitment to "immediate renovation in the here-and-now."[12] Unlike a religious view, the revolutionary doctrine does not postpone the realization of its ideals to a future heavenly life. Vigorously criticizing the postponement, it poses the secularization of the ideal order as proof of one's sincere commitment to it.

When Marx characterizes religion as "the *opium* of the people," he is stigmatizing the transfer of salvation to an illusory life, but not the quest for salvation.[13] Religion is wrong less because it dreams than because it only dreams; that is, it does nothing to make the dream real here and now. Though the inspiration is laudable, its postponement to a different, imaginary world turns it into an intoxicating promise that justifies the status quo and distracts people from altering the real world through revolutionary practice. To say that Marxism rejects religion because of the former's materialist and atheist philosophy is a truism that hides its originality and the reason for its wide popularity and powerful influence. As already hinted, Marxism differs fundamentally from other forms of materialism because it is not confined to denying religion and its beliefs. Its denial carries the commitment to recover religion's promises of happiness, brotherhood, and equality and realize them here on earth. For Marx, religion yearns, as an expression of real distress, for its dissolution into a revolutionary doctrine.

An extensive literature exists that underlines the numerous affinities between Marxism and Christianity. Marxist theory seems to be grafted onto a Christian worldview: it exalts many important aspects of Christian tradition even as it rejects the belief in the beyond so that it "is in essence a secularized Christian millennialism."[14] Thus, a clear correspondence exists between the biblical story of the fall from Eden and the Marxist account of the emergence of classes through the dissolution of primitive communism. In both cases, the loss of an original state of contentment triggers the conditions of the historical process. Likewise, the Marxist meaning of history is humanity's redemption from evil conditions through the restoration of a prehistoric blissful state, namely, the classless society. This restoration of a lost paradise through a historical process recalls "the linear concept of history so typically associated with Christianity, progressing from a onetime starting point to a onetime end."[15]

Cases of Different Cultural Responses

Once it is established that Marxist atheism does not object to being associated with a religious motivation, we can examine concretely how religion favors or blocks the utopian inspiration so essential to radical revolutionary doctrines. Let us take the case of Japan. We have already indicated that Japan made extensive changes despite the hampering legacy of its imperial-feudal social system. The explanation for Japan's avoidance of the revolutionary path is, of course, the ruling elite's initiative of timely and appropriate reforms. But it may also be that the reformist path became expedient because the revolutionary option was ruled out. The lack of tension between the mundane and the transcendental orders minimized the revolutionary option by blocking utopian inspiration. This very blockage forced Japan to engage in extensive structural changes that fell short of being revolutionary. Deprived of the easy way out of utopianism, Japan had to respond to the Western threat, not by imagining a new social order but by transforming the existing order into an efficient system. Accordingly, "the Japanese case reveals that Imperial-feudal structures unconnected to the perception of tension between the transcendental and the mundane order may experience far-reaching structural transformations but not full-scale revolutions."[16]

Belief in the divinity of the Japanese emperor explains the lack of tension between the transcendental and the mundane. Having assumed a godlike status as the direct descendant of the Sun Goddess, the emperor became the central figure and the source of norms and obligations. A social order based on the sacralization of a mundane figure is taken as a given, with the consequence that it blocks utopian aspirations. Because Japan provided a mundane justification for the social order through the symbolism of the emperor, the cultural sphere did not develop a longing for the ideal. Instead, as illustrated by the leaders of the Meiji Restoration, "the Emperor became the traditional symbol under whose aegis numerous piecemeal changes in daily life and institutions were legitimized."[17] It is important to keep in mind that modernization was not conceived of as the adaptation of the mundane order to the ideal order, but as the mundane order's procurement of greater strength and prosperity. The change "was not legitimized, as in Europe, in terms of a search for transcendental salvation through this-worldly activities but rather in terms of its contribution to the well-being, strength, and expansion of the collectivity," says Eisenstadt.[18]

Another important cultural trend refractory to utopianism is Hinduism. To begin with, Hinduism did not become an expansionist, universal religion; on the contrary, "the religious center or centers became very closely associated with the broad, ethnic Hindu identity."[19] What is more, though Hindu religion polarized the mundane and the transcendental, "there was no concept of overcoming the tension through mundane activity (political, economic, or scientific) oriented toward reshaping or transforming the social and political order, i.e. through this-worldly activity."[20] The caste system and the belief in reincarnation so firmly immobilized the tension that a rigid demarcation separated the transcendental and the mundane. The immutable separation of the two spheres meant the inhibition of utopian longings in favor of obedience to a set of rules of a rigid social order, since "submissiveness in this life was to be rewarded by a rise in the social scale in the next."[21] Social aspirations based on the hope of ascending to the upper class in the next life as a result of fulfilling caste obligations in this life could not but weaken utopian thinking. The emphasis on social mobility through the fulfillment of caste obligations hampered the tendency to reconstruct society on the basis of an ideal vision. Unless the society is viewed as unjust, as in need of rectification in light of a higher order, the aspiration to improve the social order, to institute equality and justice, cannot appear. Contrast the Hindu vision with the Christian inclination constantly to oppose the ideal and the real to the point of portraying the real as illegitimate, unfair, and evil.

The Indian case forcefully underlines the importance of the cultural issue: even though structural conditions were propitious for radicalization, given that India was plagued with chronic and widespread poverty, further aggravated by the caste system, a wide movement toward social revolution never materialized. The Indian Communist Party did not succeed in mobilizing a large and united social protest; neither were radical students able to unite the student movement, which tended toward fragmentation, mainly because of the strong opposition of moderate and radical Hindu students. Thus, the All-India Students Federation, which was a communist-dominated organization, was only "one of many factions within the student movement in India."[22] The thesis that Marxism failed to spread in India not for lack of relevant social conditions but because Hinduism is alien to eschatological beliefs is thus a defensible assertion. The cultural resistance explains why communist groups did not gain the ideological hegemony necessary to generate a wide movement toward social revolution. Even where such groups seemed to have followers, their ideology was used to express protests rather than to signify conversion.

The role of culture stands out even more when comparing the different destinies of China and India. To the question why China and India adopted different paths to modernization while facing comparable socioeconomic problems, answers that point to cultural differences seem most pertinent.

First of all, China's Confucian culture was used to justify an imperial system because, unlike Hinduism, it transcended ethnic, national, and class differences. Moreover, not only did Confucianism place a "tension between the mundane and the transcendental," but it also had "a strong this-worldly focus of overcoming" that tension.[23] The origin of this orientation is to be found in the mythical past of the Great Harmony "when all was common . . . and selfishnesss . . . had not yet torn mankind apart."[24] This blissful age having been lost and replaced by a competitive secular order reaping inequality and injustice, Chinese history was sprinkled with "the periodic dreams of religious rebels to restore the Great Harmony."[25]

The nineteenth century saw a great revival of Confucianism together with emergence of the idea of "the Great Harmony as an ideal *future* stage of development."[26] This longing to restore the Great Harmony certainly contributed to the great attraction of Marxism-Leninism to Chinese students and intellectuals. Speaking of the great impact that the works of K'ang Yu-wei, the nineteenth-century neo-Confucian utopian thinker, especially his *Universal Harmony*, had on him, Mao Tse-tung said: "I read and reread these until I knew them by heart. I worshipped K'ang Yu-wei and Liang Ch'i-ch'ao."[27] The Confucian cultural bent also explains why the attempt to model the existing order on an ideal vision did not disconcert Chinese peasants and workers. In a word, the preexisting harmony between the Chinese cultural makeup and the basic tenets of Marxism-Leninism allowed Chinese radical groups to gain ideological hegemony and expand their influence on the society more easily than Indian radicals were able to do.

Messianic State

In light of cultural trends either favoring or hampering radicalization, we can examine the case of Ethiopia. As an old country with a Christian culture, Ethiopia naturally placed a tension between the mundane and the transcendental. However, the important question is whether the culture had developed views interpreting this-worldly activity as a means of bridging the gap between the mundane and the transcendental. The answer to the question is a straight no; as the Ethiopian historian Merid Wolde Aregay profoundly noted, Ethiopia developed a millenarianism of the "Davidic–messianic type rather than of the truly Christian kind of social protest which developed in Western Europe."[28] Put in other terms, the overriding concern was not so much social issues as the survival of Christian Ethiopia in a hostile environment dominated by heathens and powerful Muslim countries. The all-around and protracted encirclement by hostile forces would have made Ethiopian resistance untenable were it not backed by the development of a form of millenarianism that promised the final triumph of Christian Ethiopia.

In chapter 2, we saw how the legend of the *Kibre Negast* promised the survival of Ethiopia until the Second Coming of Christ. The legend promoted Ethiopia to the rank of God's favorite nation while its king became the elect of God. The bonus for being God's favored country is, of course, the assurance that Ethiopia's enemies will finally be destroyed. Because survival as a Christian country was the most important challenge that Ethiopian society faced, the issue of modeling the social system on the transcendental order became quite secondary. Instead, the need to survive tied closely the church and the state, just as it created a social organization that tended to keep Ethiopians on constant war footing and mobilization.

The inspiring force of state messianism—in lieu of social messianism— clearly emerges when we assess the traditional role of the Ethiopian state. As everywhere else, the universal message of Christianity had justified the formation of a large and expanding kingdom. However, the Ethiopian context put great emphasis on the unity between the political and the religious. The definition of the emperor as the elect of God signified that the main task of the state was to defend the Christian community. In addition to providing law and order, state power became the direct secular weapon of the church. This defining religious mission endowed the state with a messianic vocation. The power of the state meant the strength of the church and the assurance of the final triumph of Christian Ethiopia. So much was this the case that Patrick Gilkes says, not without a bit of exaggeration, "Theocracy is perhaps the best word to use in describing the imperial system. Religion was a major pre-occupation of the Emperors and a main function for the throne was the support for the Church."[29] A proof of the unity binding church and state is that emperors felt obligated to make extensive grants of inalienable lands to the Ethiopian church.

The fusion of the political and the religious had two important implications. First, so essential was the defense of Ethiopian Christianity that the state had no secular goal of its own. Second, from the traditional justification of the state as the guardian of the church arose a cultural bent that could hardly tolerate the idea of a mere secular state. In the eyes of Ethiopians, the legitimacy of the state was congenitally united with the assumption of a messianic role. Before we unravel the secret ligaments binding this type of millenarianism with Marxism-Leninism, let us underline the implications of the indigenization of Christian beliefs through the messianic component of the *Kibre Negast.*

A brief comparison with other African countries reveals a situation specific to Ethiopia, the implication being that the native particularity explains why, from among black African countries, only in Ethiopia did a radical socialist revolution occur. Many scholars subscribe to the judgment according to which the Ethiopian Revolution "was reminiscent not of the recent upsurges in the Third World but of the classic revolutions of Europe—France in 1789 and the February 1917 revolution in Russia."[30] There is no denying that the prior radicalization of Ethiopian students and intellectuals made possible the eruption of a social upheaval of this magnitude. That is why attempts to explain the radical change by the existence of an imperial and "feudal" social system seem highly restrictive in their reduction of the radicalization of the educated elite to the drawbacks of the social structures, thereby failing to raise the question of the radicalizing potential of cultural factors.

Only when, among the reasons for radicalization, the messianic and Christian background of the Ethiopian state is given proper consideration can we explain the radical twist of Ethiopia's social change. The spread of Marxist utopianism in a context dominated by tribal religions and political organizations would certainly be quite restricted. One way of understanding the Ethiopian drift into a radical socialism, as opposed to African socialism— the brand chosen by many African countries—is to note that African cultures did not have "strong universalistic elements that transcend the tribal, ethnic, or national community, as well as strong utopian elements and orientations."[31] The inspirer of the Afrocentric movement, Cheikh Anta Diop, backs this assessment when he suggests that the lack of class divisions and exploitation stifled social utopia in black Africa. Because of the absence of class antagonism, African thinking focused on social integration and unity rather than on the search for the ideal social order. As a result, writes Diop, "there has never been, in Africa, a revolution against the regime."[32]

Many Africans have converted to Christianity and Islam since colonization, but it remains to be seen whether these conversions give birth to indigenized Christian cultures with messianic components, as in the case of Ethiopia, where Christianity was reinterpreted long ago and had assumed native traits in addition to being blended with a specific social order. Nor is it easy to know to what extent Africans who have converted to Christianity have developed utopian or messianic beliefs over and above the pursuit of personal salvation. The irony here is that many African countries refused radical socialism in the name of Africa's communal traditions: in claiming to revive the African tradition of communal life, many African leaders neutralized the revolutionary impact of modern socialism by defending the socialist continuity with tradition. In so doing, they excised the utopian element of socialism, that is, the resolution to re-create society in accordance with an ideal order. The affirmation of continuity freed these leaders from the obligation of building institutions according to the Marxist-Leninist vision.

Traditional Messianism and Marxism-Leninism

In contrast to African developments, what fascinated Ethiopian students and intellectuals was the utopianism that goes with socialism. They ridiculed all attempts to Ethiopianize socialism, just as they rejected African socialism; for them, it was Marxism-Leninism or nothing else. Speaking of the obsession of Ethiopian students with doctrinal purity, Tesfaye Demmellash writes:

> The stress on doctrinal purity and unity within ESUNA in fact entailed the appli-
> cation of methods of scriptural exegesis to Marxist texts, based on the belief that
> there is only one correct interpretation of the writings of Marx, Lenin, Mao, and
> their followers, and that that interpretation is spontaneously given by the texts
> themselves. And the defense of true Marxism so understood, that is, as Holy Writ,
> from "reformist" and "revisionist" heretics became a central ideological concern of
> the ESUNA faithful.[33]

This need to have the right, the true ideology is not intelligible outside the messianic component of Ethiopian culture. Western education, the epoch of the Cold War, the economic and military successes of the Soviet Union and China, the academic hegemony of Marxism, all conspired to point toward socialism as the remedy for Ethiopia's numerous problems. And no version of socialism other than the authentic Marxism-Leninism could satisfy Ethiopia's embedded inclination toward state messianism. Doctrinal purity was essential to set up the framework establishing Ethiopia as the most faithful follower of the doctrine.

While the revolutionary generation firmly believed that it was burying the Solomonic myth once and for all, the way it conceived of its role was analogous to the drama of the *Kibre Negast*. Indeed, just as the Ethiopian queen, Sheba, went to Jerusalem to seek Solomon's wisdom, thereby initiating the events that brought about the election of Ethiopia as God's favored nation, so too the modern educated elite, having gleaned the renowned wisdom of Marx and Lenin, was initiating the process of Ethiopia's becoming the favorite nation of socialism. The extreme radicalization and doctrinal dogmatism of the Ethiopian student movement find a complete explanation only by allusion to the revival of the Davidic-messianic mentality through the taking up of a new national mission. No theory elevates the role of the state as high as Marxism-Leninism. The elevated scenario of the socialist state coming to the rescue of the community fitted nicely into the cultural bent of the *Kibre Negast*.

The unity between church and state, as enshrined in the *Kibre Negast*, had given the state an importance that the socialist state echoed superbly. Not only did the state become the central system of a socialist society, but it also fully realized the ideal definition of the Ethiopian state as the protector of the community by becoming the prime provider of social justice and assuming a direct economic role. Unlike capitalism, which limits the power of the state through the defense of the free market, socialism makes the state an economic agent and a provider of justice and prosperity for the people. The economic, political, and cultural roles of the socialist state thus represented the consummation of the messianic attribute of the Ethiopian state.

Consider the contrast between Ethiopia's magnified status in the *Kibre Negast* and its continued backwardness. Such a disparity frustrated Ethiopian messianism and raised the need to find the right remedy. Equally consistent with messianic frustration was the shift of legitimacy from the old royal family and nobility to the new educated elite. The failure of the existing political elite clashed with the legitimizing ideology of the *Kibre Negast:* the misery and backwardness of Ethiopia hardly matched its alleged status as God's favored nation. The dereliction of the traditional elite vis-à-vis its own legitimizing ideology fully disqualified it, thereby clearing the way for the rise of a new challenger. The messianic discontent also explains why the educated elite squarely defined itself as the new chosen elite, with the consequence that the old elite became completely invalidated. Where legitimacy issues form a sense of being invested with a mission, failure entails nothing short of a complete delegitimization.

An important implication follows: the affinity of Marxism-Leninism with Ethiopia's cultural bent was first established at the level of state messianism. Rather than Marxism's dimension of social reconstruction according to egalitarian principles, it was the Leninist component of rapid and forceful modernization that primarily attracted Ethiopian students. Moreover, the social utopia of equality and justice was perceived less as an outcome of autonomous social struggles than as an expression and allowance of state messianism. Marxist-Leninist discourse became irresistible to the extent that it upgraded the traditional role of the Ethiopian state: going beyond the function of protecting the church, the state now combined developmental function with social altruism. What could be more appealing than this transcription of traditional messianism into a modernizing and benevolent role? And this Leninist vision of the state perfectly agreed with the elitism of the Ethiopian student movement. As we saw, instead of contributing to the generation of a grassroots movement focused on achieving democratic rights, students advocated a form of social development coming from above.

The mystified conception of the Ethiopian state is clearly at the root of the attraction of Marxism-Leninism. So enhanced and ethicized was the role of the socialist state that its accompanying ideology literally seduced the culture. And the more Haile Selassie failed in his mission to modernize Ethiopia, the stronger the revival of messianic longing became among the rising educated elite. No wonder this revival landed many Ethiopian students and intellectuals on the Leninist conception of the socialist state. Given the rudimentary level of political awareness and organization in the country, the commitment to socialism cannot be seriously attributed to the pressure of the oppressed classes. Dig as deep as you want, the infatuation with socialism contains nothing more than the idea of a benevolent state freeing the oppressed from above. This revolutionary project is, in turn, but a refurbished notion of Ethiopian state messianism.

The cultural bent explains why so many of the initiators and followers of the student movement were northern students of the Amhara and Tigray regions. Though Oromo students rightly felt the harsher hand of exploitation and oppression, many of them either adopted moderate positions or succumbed to ethnonationalism. Because of their different cultural milieu, they were less susceptible to surrender to the sirens of the messianic state than were northern students, many of whom were deeply impregnated with the mythical discourse of the *Kibre Negast*. In effect, the coming revolution was coined in missionary terms: it will liberate the Oromos and other southern peoples from the grip of ruthless landlords and an imperial government gone astray. In thus conceiving the ethnic issue in terms of redressing state policy, the student movement naively believed that the altruistic state of socialism was the right remedy to achieve equality among Ethiopians.

Ethiopian Values and Marxist Dialectics

The affinity between socialist ideology and Ethiopian Christianity goes further and touches on other important values. We noted how the capitalist view of the state was at odds with the traditional culture; the disagreement was actually wider: it included the realm of economic activity, all the more extensively as nothing had been done to make traditional values consonant with capitalist values. The traditional culture had contempt for merchants and moneymaking, which it associated with Islam. Moneymaking was identified with greed, selfishness, and lack of higher ideals for life. Moreover, as any people influenced by Christian beliefs, Ethiopians had a deep compassion for the poor and a great admiration for the abnegation of the monk, but even more so for the bravery and service of the warrior.

Nothing, then, could be more in tune with Ethiopian traditional culture than the socialist condemnation of capitalism. Given the culture's contempt for activities associated with moneymaking, which approach to development—liberal or socialist—was likely to attract Ethiopian students and intellectuals was hardly a contest. Not only did socialist ideology revive compassion for the poor and further ennoble the distaste for moneymaking, but the condemnation of social hierarchy based on moneymaking also revamped the traditional social ascendancy of the warrior, who now fights for the emancipation of the poor. In addition, the messianic role of the socialist state enormously heightened the great value that tradition attached to service to the state, martial service constituting the apex of human fulfillment.

Another remarkable axiological affinity between socialist ideology and Ethiopian traditional culture was the conception of social life as strife and rivalry. Few cultures have so thoroughly identified social life with conflict and competition as has Ethiopian traditional thinking. The realization of harmony and cooperation was not the driving goal of social life; still less was society assimilated to a fixed order based on hereditary rights. In line with the traditional belief in *idil*, the ambition of rising to higher positions spurred each individual, even if he/she was born into a lower family. The notion *idil*, which can be loosely translated as "fortune" or "fate," signified the traditional version of social mobility, and the surest means to social ascent was the possession of warlike values.[34] Since each individual was in constant pursuit of his/her fortune, society was viewed as a battlefield where some individuals rose at the expense of many others. And as the rise of one individual required the fall of another, rivalry was considered the normal order of social life.

Scholars have noted that Ethiopians had no problem understanding and agreeing with the Marxist notion of the unity and struggle of opposites. My own experience as a university professor teaching various courses on Marxist-Leninist philosophy for many years at Addis Ababa University perfectly corroborates the observation. Of all Marxist-Leninist concepts, the law of the unity and struggle of opposites was the easiest to understand for Ethiopian students. The reason is not hard to find: the law reflected their understanding of social life as a continuous strife where one individual had to emerge at the expense of other individuals. The other was perceived more as an opponent than as a possible ally or partner. The Marxist-Leninist notion of struggle leading to reversal fitted well with the Ethiopian vision of social mobility. Because the interests and powers of individuals were perceived as exclusive, and thus involved a constant struggle, the fortunes of individuals were held together by their very incompatibility, much like the operation that the law of the unity and struggle of opposites describes.

The only possible form of alliance that this perception authorized was the relationship that I defined in my book *Survival and Modernization—Ethiopia's Enigmatic Present* as clientelism. As a vertical hierarchy, clientelism is how "the domination-subordination relation [instituted] the reciprocal interest of people."[35] In other words, alliance is a utilitarian concept whose principle is that patrons and clients come together and stay in a relationship on condition that it furthers their individual interests. The Ethiopian system of land taxation known as *gult* is a perfect illustration of clientelism: for the support and services that followers provided to kings and regional lords, they were given tax rights on lands owned by peasants. Such rights did not become hereditary: they were revocable as a way of maintaining the followers in a state of dependence.

Beyond the social realm, the law of the unity and struggle of opposites had a hidden affinity with Ethiopian metaphysics, especially with its conception of reality and change. A quick reflection on the Ethiopian notion of time will help set out the matter clearly. As in many cultures, the observation of the given reality has induced Ethiopians to think of time in cyclical terms. The cycles of nature, such as day changing into night, young into old, life into death and vice versa, illustrated for them the fundamental law of being, which is that change happens by reversals and that ultimately nothing new is created. What appears as new is actually nothing more than how opposites alternate. But, then, as Heraclitus profoundly understood, the inner essence of being is struggle: things that cannot happen simultaneously generate a constant struggle that forces them to alternate. One thing rises at the expense of its opposite, but this very victory contains its decline.

To convey the Ethiopian conception of being and time, it is instructive to reproduce a partial and loose translation of a poem, titled "Everything Is Déjà vu," by Kebede Mikael, a renowned novelist, historian, and poet.

> Those who were enemies become friends
> . . . .
> When the rich becomes poor the poor becomes rich
> When one is polluted the other is clean
> . . . .
> That which feels hot gradually becomes cold
> The little is tall and the tall little
> The evil is good and the good evil
> . . . .
> The past as well as the future and the present
> Constitute a cycle; nothing is new in this world[36]

The striking similarity between these statements and some of Heraclitus's aphorisms confirms that we have here a prelude to dialectical thinking. For Heraclitus, too, "it is one and the same thing to be living and dead, awake or asleep, young or old. The former aspect in each case becomes the latter, and the latter becomes the former, by sudden unexpected reversal."[37]

Even if the cycles of nature have impacted on many traditional cultures, the particularity of Ethiopian culture was that the law of alteration, in addition to being perceived as the essence of the material reality, was extended to the social and spiritual realms. It perfectly agreed with the Ethiopian notion of social mobility: the hierarchy binding patrons and clients was never fixed or irreversible. Since the rise of the few was done at the expense of others, the law of alteration pervaded power with a characteristic precariousness. This explains why Ethiopians have always been reluctant to create, at whatever level of the social hierarchy, institutions freezing those who happened to be in power. Incidentally, we note here that Haile Selassie's imposition of a hereditary monarchy was a radical deviation from traditional norms.

We should then suspect that the rapid and extensive infatuation of so many Ethiopians with Marxism-Leninism had to do with the revival of the culture of alteration after the unusually protracted and uneventful rule of Haile Selassie and his closed clique. The philosophy of Marxism-Leninism with its emphasis on the unity and struggle of opposites, became like a wake-up call to a slumbering society that deeply abhorred the perpetuation of a given elite. The ability to revive a deep belief imbued the new philosophy with the attributes of truthfulness and relevance.

The law of alteration was also the very concept that Ethiopians used to define and comprehend the power of God. For them, the precariousness of things was the ultimate expression of God's rule, the manner proper to God to make his absolute power known. The law of alteration underlined the frailty of things, and hence their nothingness. The fact that things are brought into existence only to be destroyed proves their utter nothingness. In particular, it shows that the rise to power is an act of divine promotion that is subject to reversal. It lasts so long as God wants it to last.

The Ethiopian view defending the active involvement of God in a cyclical process creates a tension, given that the proper nature of a cycle is to operate autonomously. What occurs cyclically does not seem to require God's perpetual intervention. Aware of the automatism of reversals, Heraclitus warned: "This universe, which is the same for all, has not been made by any god or man, but it always has been, is, and will be—an ever-living fire, kindling itself by regular measures and going out by regular measures."[38] Moreover, onto the cyclical notion accounting for changes in nature and the rise and fall of individuals in society, the Ethiopians have grafted an eschatological view of time inherited from Christian millenarianism. The process of time cannot be both cyclical and eschatological: a cycle is a rotating movement, whereas the eschatological view implies a process with a direction, a linear movement toward a final goal.

For Ethiopians, the contradiction is only apparent: the eschatological view reveals how the cycle is suddenly put to an end. As such, it expresses the absolute power of God, who decides to end the show that he himself initiated. The eschatological moment is therefore the highest reaffirmation of the power of God: it abruptly stops the cycle, which was going nowhere anyway. The end of the cycle inaugurates a new existence where self-affirmation ceases to implicate conflicts and reversals and where finally humans enjoy the eternal love of God. The belief that things are caught in a macabre movement of rotation highlights the unique role of the *Kibre Negast* with its promise of an exceptional destiny to Ethiopia. The myth protects Ethiopia from the law of alteration in that it guarantees the final victory of Christian Ethiopia over all its enemies. No contradiction is to be noted here since the cycle is the will of God, who naturally reserves a special treatment to his favored nation.

The upshot of all this is that, in addition to giving a secular meaning to the religious ontology of Ethiopians, Marxist dialectics allowed the educated elite to understand its role in apocalyptic terms. Such a conception gave the illusion of restoring the dislocation caused by its newly acquired Eurocentric

formation. In assuming the vocation of redeemer, the educated elite conceived of itself as the long-awaited response to Ethiopia's messianic longing.
As a matter of fact, the decline of traditional society and the corrosion of its
values under the impact of modernization had taken on an apocalyptic
meaning in the eyes of many Ethiopians. To refer to my own experience, I
remember vividly the abundant talk about the nearness of the Apocalypse in
my early youth. Especially, Orthodox monks used to go from house to house
to announce the imminence of the end. Of course, I did not understand the
social meaning of the message at the time, any more than I understood that
what the monks perceived as the end of the world was none other than the
disappearance of the traditional world under the impact of European influences. The reading of modernization as an apocalypse prevented the monks
from seeing that Western-educated Ethiopians rather than outsiders would
be the coming destroyers.

Still less did the monks know that traditional Ethiopian culture itself
would provide the framework enabling the educated elite to assume an
apocalyptic role. Revelation meant revolution, that is, the coming of the last
judgment that ended the cycle and inaugurated a new existence. It crowned
the educated elite with the messianic role of destroying the evil social system
so as to bring forth a new era of prosperity, peace, and justice. It announced
destruction, but for the sake of assuring the final triumph of the good,
thereby secularizing Ethiopia's apocalyptically driven culture. Can one fail to
see the affinity between the self-portrait of the educated elite and the
Leninist conception of revolutionary intellectuals, who receive the calling of
rescuer from their initiation to Marxist doctrine?

To sum up, it is because Marxism-Leninism secularized Ethiopian traditional beliefs in many ways that it gained such a great and rapid ascendancy
among modern Ethiopians. The secularization deeply satisfied their
Eurocentric acquisitions, while the revival of some aspects of traditional culture gave them the illusion that the transition to Marxism-Leninism was but
a salutary correction of past wanderings. The adoption of Marxism-Leninism
would have been harder had it required the effort of going totally against
habitual thinking.

The noted affinity between Ethiopian culture and Marxism-Leninism
hardly gets us off the hook every time we raise the question why an atheist
doctrine so easily seduced a fundamentally religious culture. The observation of affinity, no doubt very useful to pinpoint areas of mutual attraction,
does not fully bridge the huge gap separating religion from atheism. The
purpose of the next chapter is to tackle this issue directly.

7

Religion and Social Utopianism

The conventional explanation suggests that religious cultures may develop attraction to the Marxist-Leninist type of atheism when they become refractory to reforms. Unable to harmonize their modern convictions with beliefs that they increasingly consider archaic, modernized adherents of traditional religions often fall prey to revolutionary atheism. Even if the validity of the explanation cannot be denied, it is imperative to note that the issue is not as simple as saying that people become atheist as a result of losing faith in the promises of religion. This kind of atheism, which we can call academic, is quite different from the militancy of revolutionary atheism if only because the latter retains the emotional and utopian components of religion. Let us begin by clarifying the distinguishing features of militant atheism.

Revolutionary Atheism

Granted that S. N. Eisenstadt's approach gives us a remarkable insight into the reasons why some cultures welcome radical ideologies more than others, it does not help us understand why cultures are attracted by ideologies that expressly go against or reject their otherworldliness. What is more obvious than the contrary goals of religion and social revolution? While religion values the transcendental world to the detriment of the mundane world, "secularization, the separation of religion from politics and the rise of a secular realm with a dignity of its own, is certainly a crucial factor in the phenomenon of revolution."[1] Such was notably the case during the time of the dominance of Marxism-Leninism: on top of revaluating the secular world, revolutionary socialism openly and aggressively advocated atheist beliefs. Without denying affinities between Marxism-Leninism and those religions that place a great tension between the divine and the mundane, one must recognize the paradox of an atheist and materialist philosophy successfully seducing religious cultures.

Our question is the same that Nicholas Berdyaev raised in his attempt to make sense of the paradox of Russia's transformation into a Soviet society.

His question is: "How was it possible for Holy Russia to be turned into an arsenal of militant atheism? How is it that a people who are religious by their very structure and live exclusively by faith have proved to be such a fruitful field for anti-religious propaganda?"[2] Not only was the widespread and robust commitment of Russians to Orthodox Christianity proverbial but also, unlike other European countries, secularization and the expansion of scientific knowledge had not yet put heavy pressure on traditional beliefs. Nor was the proliferation of dissident religions disturbing Russia. Then why, of all countries where atheism had already made some headway, did communism germinate in Russia, which was the least likely to tolerate atheism?

To the question of why Holy Russia became atheist, the most common answer blames the absolute dominance of religion, which was moreover unreformed. The pervasive nature of Russian religion could not but lead to atheism when the need for change arose. The dominance of religion being felt as the deep cause of Russian backwardness, modernized Russians naturally resented the belief and went over to atheism. This kind of answer simply overlooks the important fact that the Russian rejection incorporated many religious elements. The atheism that took hold of Russia was that of Marxism-Leninism, that is, of an apocalyptic philosophy that injected a utopian goal into human history and advocated its fulfillment through an organized and single-minded social militancy. Going beyond the academic or theoretical atheism, which rejects religion essentially on rational grounds, Marxist-Leninist atheism appropriates many of the promises of religion, such as justice, equality, happiness, and claims to give them an earthly reality through the elimination of evil forces.

Hence Berdyaev's idea that Marxism attracted Russians because it satisfied their religious longings: it caused "*a transposition of religious motives and religious psychology into a non-religious or anti-religious sphere, into the region of social problems, so that the spiritual energy of religion flows into social channels, which thereby take on a religious character,* and become a breeding-ground for a peculiar form of social idolatry."[3] Besides underlining that revolutionary atheism is not confined to rejecting religious belief, Berdyaev's explanation shows that this sort of atheism actually taps religious energy and channels toward the goal of social reconstruction. But why did Russians need such a transposition? Why did they direct their religious fervor into something that was not religious? Moreover, is it serious to say that "communism is itself a religion," given that religion offers something fundamental that communism cannot offer, such as the promise of immortality, which is the rationale for the persistence of religiosity itself?[4]

A satisfactory answer to these questions is likely to emerge if we consider the context of educated Russians losing or having serious doubts about their traditional faith. In such a case, the loss of their previous deeply anchored religious faith creates a spiritual vacuum that cries for a substitute. The basic premise here is that adherence to revolutionary ideologies is unlikely if traditional religions have still some impact on people. Facts show that "people who would otherwise join or sympathize with the revolutionary movement are prevented from doing so because of attachment to the religion of their fathers."[5] When the attachment withers away, atheism follows in the form of mere rejection or a rejection that retains the nostalgia of religious hopes. The former may lead to academic atheism; the latter to communist atheism, which is then a negation of the negation, that is, religion negated but also retained.

The communist type of atheism is thus a substitute, a surrogate for religion. The religious mind is still active, still operational, but is directed toward a this-worldly object or goal. This happens when the deception or loss of faith falls short of drying up the religious need. And the stronger the hold of the traditional religion, the harder it becomes to remove it. Given the lack of religious and social reforms in prerevolutionary Russia and the freshness of the wound caused by the loss of a far-ranging and pervasive faith, nothing less than a type of irreligion that preserves some religious longings could appease modernized Russians. The need to take into consideration the grip of the traditional faith shows that secularization is not enough to explain the attraction to ideologies committed to social utopianism. If anything, secularism cannot account for the passion and the fanaticism inspired by revolutionary ideologies. On the other hand, to the extent that a substitute does not give up the religious utopia, it helps explain such characteristics.

The Lack of Reform

What could have caused Russians to be so disappointed with their traditional faith as to look for a substitute, for another messianism? In part, it was the deep frustration resulting from the absorption of Western values and science by a culture that did not go through a prior reformation phase. In particular, the exposure to Enlightenment ideas must have had such an upsetting impact on young educated Russians that a lot of them longed for a substitute through the adoption of socialism. This socialism provided outlets for many aspects of their Christian beliefs, such as the compassion for the poor, the eschatological denouement of human history, the final triumph of good over evil. To back up his explanation, Berdyaev rightly appeals to the authority of the great analyst of the Russian soul, namely, Fyodor Mikhaylovich Dostoyevsky. The understanding that souls tormented by the loss of religious faith tend to consider socialism as a substitute belief convinced Dostoevsky that "Russian Socialism was not a political but a religious question, the question of God, of immortality and the radical reconstruction of all human life."[6]

The Russian case is a perfect example of the uprooting impact of modern ideas on traditional beliefs that had not first gone through a reformist phase. Theoreticians of revolution have observed that social revolutions did not occur in Protestant countries. Even where revolutions happened, as in England, the United States, and the Netherlands, they were strictly political; that is, they did not harbor the project of a utopian reconstruction of social life. By contrast, the only European country that crossed the threshold from political to social revolution is France, a predominantly Catholic country. The question arises as to why Protestant countries proved so resistant to social revolutions. The crucial difference between Protestant countries and countries like France and Russia was the emancipation of their political ideologies from medieval canons, which supported absolute monarchies. The removal of medieval norms encouraged political reforms, for example of the kind leading to modified monarchies, which in turn agreed to "*institutionalize political opposition* through an effective system of parties."[7] In thus legitimizing opposition, societies that adopted Protestantism and parliamentarism prevented the polarization that is so characteristic of social revolutions. The absence of extreme ruptures made socially radical ideologies less attractive.

The restriction of the attractiveness of radical ideologies to the lack of institutionalized opposition does not fully explain the rise of the revolutionary spirit. For the whole question is why the struggle against absolutism shifted from the conquest of political freedom to the utopian reconstruction of society, as happened in France and Russia. We need to bring out the specific contribution of religion, notably by showing the impact of religious reformation. The fact that Protestantism provided a modernized version of Christian belief means that the faith was better tuned to the requirements of scientific thinking and the values of the Enlightenment so that intellectuals had fewer reasons to be in conflict with religious beliefs. The moderation of British social philosophy is a good illustration: "Thanks to the double success of the Reformation and the [English] Revolution, in the sixteenth and seventeenth centuries, the British intelligentsia never found itself in permanent conflict with the Church and the ruling class."[8] The situation in France was quite different. Apart from the faith not being reformed in accordance with the aspirations of the French Enlightenment, the Catholic Church proved to be the main supporter of royal absolutism. This explains why the philosophes focused many of their attacks on the clergy, accusing it of supporting obscurantism and absolutism.

Tocqueville's Insight into the Genesis of the Revolutionary Mind

Among the thinkers of revolution, Alexis de Tocqueville provides the most perspicuous insight into the connection between religion and revolution. He notes that one of the main characteristics of the French Revolution was its virulent attacks on religion: "Among the passions born of the Revolution the first lit and the last extinguished was this passion against religion."[9] He also remarks that the Enlightenment, justly considered as "one of the principal causes of the Revolution, . . . was deeply irreligious."[10] Enlightenment philosophers, he continues, had a "rage against the Church. They attacked its clergy, its hierarchy, its institutions, its dogmas. They wanted to tear Christianity up by the roots."[11]

With their project to reconstruct society on the basis of reason, Enlightenment philosophers inevitably saw religion as the ultimate foundation of social orders established on irrational and obsolete beliefs, and hence as the main obstacle to modernization. For them, revolution transcended the mere removal of an obsolete traditional political elite and its reactionary government; it meant the triumph of enlightenment over ignorance, of reason over tradition, of freedom over authority. Their idea of revolution was social as much as cultural.

A word of caution: irreligion does not cause revolution. Tocqueville knew too well that socioeconomic problems are necessary for the eruption of mass protests. What the loss of faith specifically contributes, however, is the mental condition necessary for the rise of the revolutionary spirit, which is responsible for the drift of political revolution into social revolution. The conditions of social revolution gather when the birth of a revolutionary spirit with its commitment to utopian reconstruction finds the opportunity to assume the leadership of social protests, often caused by economic crises. When this happens, as was the case in Russia with the Bolsheviks or France with the Jacobins, social protests tend to veer toward social revolution.

Tocqueville finds a compelling confirmation of the radicalizing role of irreligion in his comparison of the French and American Revolutions. The main difference between the two social transformations did not originate from the lesser influence of Enlightenment philosophy on the American Revolution; on the contrary, the American Revolution was more faithful on many issues to Enlightenment ideas than the French Revolution. According to Tocqueville, the attitude toward religion provides the main demarcation between the two revolutions: "In political matters, there was not a country in the world where the boldest doctrines of the philosophes of the eighteenth century were more applied than in America; only the antireligious doctrines of the French were never able to make headway there, even with the advantage of unlimited freedom of the press."[12] No factor other than the American rejection of atheism can explain why the same kind of principles led to the moderate and reasonable course of the American Revolution on the one hand and to the extremism of the French Revolution on the other. To wit, what explains the limitation of the American Revolution to political revolution and the overstepping of the French uprising into social revolution is their respective attitude toward religion.

To unravel the manner in which irreligion may activate radicalism, Tocqueville judiciously observes that "when religion deserted souls, it did not leave them, as often happens, empty and debilitated; rather they were briefly filled by feelings and ideas which momentarily took the place of religion, and which at first did not let them be depressed."[13] Since the loss of religion creates a longing for a substitute, the religious impulse does not really disappear. Instead, an intolerable emptiness results, an absence of meaning that propels unbelievers to look for a new utopia, an earthly substitute for the loss of the meaning of life. That religion goes away by leaving behind the spiritual needs means that the desire to make the Absolute available on earth through revolutionary activities spurs the nonbeliever. As a result, the French Revolution itself "became a new kind of religion, an incomplete religion, it is true, without God, without ritual, and without a life after death, but one which nevertheless, like Islam, flooded the earth with its soldiers, apostles, and martyrs."[14] Naturally, when revolution turns into a quest for meaning, it mimics many aspects of religion. It keeps the need and the fervor of the religious mind and channels them toward the construction of a paradisiacal society. Because it aims for the same transcendent goals as religion, it inspires a similar heroism, generosity, and devotion, but directs these character traits toward an earthly project.

Herein lies the great danger of irreligion: when it longs for an earthy substitute, it contemplates a regeneration of the human species such that what Christianity strictly reserves for the hereafter is considered suitable for an earthly existence. In thus denying the ontological gap separating the kingdom of God from the society of humans, and wrongly believing that what is valid for the transcendental life is also applicable in earthly existence, revolutionaries succumb to the most dangerous temptation: the assumption that humankind can conceive and bring into life the perfect society. Once the belief in the endless perfectibility of humans grips the mind, no limits exist to human imagination and audacity of action. Thus, "in the French Revolution, religious laws having been abolished at the same time as civil laws were overturned, the human mind entirely lost its orientation; it no longer knew how to hold on, nor where to stop, and revolutionaries of an unknown species appeared, who took boldness to the point of folly, whom no innovation could surprise, nor scruple hold back, and who never hesitated before the execution of a plan."[15] The American Revolution remained moderate because its commitment to the separation of the divine and the human set limits to the extent of social transformation and advised the institution of mechanisms of control against all kinds of extremist beliefs and actions. Those excessively violent and destructive Revolutions—the French, Russian, Chinese, Khmer Rouge—are compelling testimonies of folly each time humans attempt to fill the absence of God with extravagant social projects.

Substituting Religion

What Tocqueville said about France is largely applicable to the case of Ethiopia. Among Ethiopia's Westernized students and intelligentsia, many progressively developed a deep animosity against the Ethiopian church, including against its beliefs and values. They vilified the church both for being a staunch supporter of the imperial autocracy and for spreading obscurantism among its numerous followers. For them, the enormous authority of the church posited irreligion as a necessary condition of social change in Ethiopia. The anger was all the more intense as, of all the traditional institutions of Ethiopia, the church was the least affected by modernization. Outside some administrative and financial reforms, neither the religious doctrine and its values nor the mentality of the priesthood had been adjusted to modern life. The ignorance and provincialism of the priests had become such an open object of derision that their outdated beliefs and practices greatly embarrassed even those educated Ethiopians who remained faithful to Orthodoxy. The absence of reforms caused such a degradation that "the church lost the reverence and awe it once inspired," especially in the eyes of many Western-educated believers.[16]

The progression of irreligion among Ethiopian students is well reflected in a 1969 unpublished survey done by sociology students and the Department of Sociology and Anthropology of Haile Selassie I University. Titled "Report on a Research on the Social Situation of Haile Selassie I University Students," the survey does not seem completely reliable, although the scholar Siegfried Pausewang was a member of the investigating group. Based on 537 questionnaires filled out by students, there was no apparent check as to the reliability of their answers. Moreover, out of the 537 respondents, 448 were freshmen; thus, the collected data were not very representative of the student body. The report nonetheless shows some interesting statistical data, especially concerning religion. It indicates that more than half of the students claimed to be Orthodox Christians. The rest were divided as follows: "8.5% are Protestants, 5.9% Catholics. 12.2% call themselves atheists. Only 5.2% of all students are Moslems."[17] For a country still immersed in traditionality and with deep attachment to Christianity, 12 percent of atheists is a significant number.

The importance of the progression of atheism stands out even if the majority of students remained faithful to Orthodox Christianity. The existence of a noticeable minority of atheist students in a society so heavily religious indicates a significant erosion of the traditional religion. What is more, radical revolutionaries always constitute a minority; their importance arises not from their number but from the leadership role they play. Add to these arguments the fact that for centuries the Ethiopian Orthodox Church defined the Ethiopian identity. Just as was the case with Russia, the Ethiopian identity was inseparably blended with Orthodox Christianity. In light of the country's long history of stubborn and stunning defense of its religious identity, the emergence of Marxism-Leninism as the dominant ideology of the student movement and among intellectuals constitutes a dramatic rupture.

The explanation for this crucial deviation is, of course, the negative impact of Western education. In the previous chapters we saw how the exposure to Western education had a deep alienating effect on educated Ethiopians, how what Ethiopians had venerated and identified with, had been mercilessly trampled underfoot. The lack of resistance of traditional beliefs to the undermining role of modern rationality created a spiritual vacuum that not only alienated intellectuals from their society but also put them under the exigency of finding a substitute belief. A good Ethiopian analyst of the intelligentsia, Girma Amare, has this to say: "While a great many of the beliefs and values which hitherto gave internal strength to the individual and provided meaning in life are being undermined in the modern schools, no adequate substitutes have been found for them. The modern intellectual is left with no faith and conviction to sustain him in life. He suffers from a psychological void, and nature abhors a void."[18] And as the case of Russia demonstrates, the deeply religious Ethiopians could not be content with academic atheism; rather, they had to recover some of the promises of their religiosity and hence feel the attraction of the communist utopia.

In vain does one try to reduce the infatuation with Marxism-Leninism to the impact of grave social problems rather than to the disaffection with Orthodox Christianity. The truth is that any supposition that Ethiopians could have become Marxists while remaining faithful to their traditional religion is untenable. Even if the majority of students claimed still to be believers, their devotion was shaky, to say the least. Such diluted levels of commitment allowed the ideology of the radical minority to become the dominant ideology of the student movement. The faith of the majority was not strong enough to resent the leadership of avowed opponents of religious beliefs. A good illustration of the weakness of the old belief is found in the recent confession of a former student to the Addis Ababa University Alumni Network. In an unsigned letter titled "The Day I Denied God," he relates his encounter with the radical students of the then Haile Selassie I University. What started as casual conversations soon evolved into serious discussions about religion and the existence of God. At first, the author of the letter confidently defended his religious belief until he progressively realized that he was facing a superior knowledge. In his own words,

> One day I got lost as they started to burble about dialectical materialism and what not. I asked what in the world this materialism was about. Then they shocked my pants out of me by telling me that there is no God. Every way I wanted to argue about the existence of God, they bombarded me with explanation of nature, science, and evolution. They berated me with the philosophy that matter is primary and consciousness is secondary and so on. As the discussion went on, my heart would tell me to stick with my faith while my head would tell me to accept reason. That was one of

the most tormenting moments in my life. After a nerve wrecking and mind boggling conversation, I finally gave in and said "you guys are right—there is no God."[19]

The rapidity of the conversion to atheism discloses the frailty of the traditional belief, namely, its inability to argue against the materialist interpretations of modern science. It clearly shows that a religious commitment banished from modern schools has little chance to counter successfully the detrimental implications drawn from the theory of evolution and other scientific explanations. Also, by defining the process leading to the denial of God in terms of intense struggle and painful torment, the confession reveals the sense of guilt and emptiness that naturally cries for substitute beliefs. As Raymond Aron reminds us, "The seduction of Communism depends not so much on the content of the old belief as on the degree of deracination."[20] If the commitment to the previous religion is maintained, the deracination is less and so is the temptation to espouse radicalism, for "Communism is all the more attractive wherever the throne of God is empty."[21]

A serious consequence of deracination is what Girma calls "moral crisis."[22] Besides despising the priesthood, Ethiopians who went to modern schools and learned English and European history came to consider their own parents as ignorant. This attitude intensified the generational conflict and drastically reduced parental authority. Together with the loss of imperial authority and the church, the reduction of parental authority and guidance created confusion and alienation among many young people. "This moral distress manifested itself in a high incidence of juvenile unruliness, destructiveness, crimes, and suicide. Many joined religious sects, which provided institutionalized mechanisms for releasing tension through shouting, crying, and weeping. Sects hitherto unpopular in Ethiopia, such as the Watchtower [Jehovah's Witnesses], the Bahai, and the Mennonites, attracted increasing numbers of young people desperately searching for meaning in their lives."[23] What else could this unprecedented moral predicament and identity crisis generate but an enhanced sensitivity of young people to revolutionary appeals? Again, according to Girma, "At this time of acute moral crisis, socialism presented itself as one of several religions with its own articles of faith, its priests and prophets, and its messages of eternal salvation. It was the socialism of the pamphleteer and not of the academic; of the emotion and not of intellect."[24]

For a comprehensive approach, the spread of radicalism in Ethiopia is as much connected with the gravity of the country's social problems as it is a consequence of the decline of Orthodox Christianity and the advance of atheism, both stemming from the exposure to Western science and ideologies. Unlike European religions, which had developed ways and means to neutralize the challenge of science, especially through hermeneutical reinterpretations, the Ethiopian Orthodox Church was literally assaulted without having developed any defense mechanism. Because it did not reform itself, because both its doctrine and its priesthood appeared archaic, the impact of Western education was all the more devastating. This decapitated faith needed a surrogate, and Marxism-Leninism became the best candidate by providing a system of belief that also had an enticing program of social change.

Only its ability to serve as a substitute for the discredited Ethiopian church explains the rapidity and magnitude with which Marxism-Leninism fired up young educated Ethiopians. Their conversion was almost natural: it did not require sophisticated arguments. The need to fill the spiritual void was so pressing that even the strong resistance that menace to identity usually provokes became insufficient. In thus playing an important substituting role, in addition to being a theory of fundamental social change, Marxism-Leninism emerged as an irresistible ideology. Its ability to fill the void of religious beliefs was as attractive, if not more so, as its alleged capacity to accelerate development. Putting the finger on the transmutation of religious passion into political action, the well-informed scholar of the Ethiopian student movement Randi Rønning Balsvik writes: "For the majority of students belief in and commitment to socio-economic *change* can be said to have filled the void created by the erosion of their religious roots."[25]

The best evidence of the progression of irreligion among students and of the substituting role of Marxism-Leninism is found in student publications. For instance, *Challenge* editorialized:

> Ethiopian society must be *reorganized in toto*. Thus the first order of business is to prepare systematically to create the revolution that will bring about the reorganization of society on a totally new foundation. . . . Tomorrow after our enemies are swept away, we will promote production and participate actively in scientific experiments, in the flourishing of peoples' arts and cultures. Then Ethiopia will no longer stretch her hands to the "Deities" that have bestowed her with 3000 years of misery.[26]

The editorial is intentionally provocative by being both disrespectful and sarcastic toward Ethiopian traditional beliefs. In mocking the messianic destiny by which Ethiopia traditionally defined itself, the editorial extols the new deal that the revolutionary youth proposed to the Ethiopian people. Whereas the old belief gave the Ethiopian masses nothing but misery, the new deity of socialism guarantees prosperity. Unmistakably, the editorial proposes socialism as a substitute for a belief that has proven utterly deceptive. The superiority of the new deal comes from the fact that it claims to have all that is necessary to achieve what the old belief promised but failed to realize. The status of Ethiopia as the preferred nation of God, transcribed in earthly terms, means nothing else than the achievement of power and prosperity, and Marxism-Leninism can deliver such goals.

Unlike the old religion, the new belief wipes out from Ethiopia all that is obscurantist, backward, and opposed to progress. "The irresistible force which draws so many thinking Ethiopians to Marxist theory consists," the same editorial reminds its readers, "in the fact that the theory is 'in essence critical and revolutionary' (K. Marx)."[27] In sum, as Girma explains, the attraction of Ethiopian students and intellectuals to socialism was that "it promised the creation of an instant utopia; it satisfied the urge for revenge by legitimizing destruction of the past as a method for creating a better future; it supplied emotionally laden terminology to combat opposition and frustrate intellectual argumentation."[28]

An interesting illustration of how the work of substitution operates is found in a poem, titled "The Trinity," written in 1980 by Assefa Gmt, who became famous for penning the "National Anthem of Socialist Ethiopia." In that poem, Assefa replaces the old and discredited Christian Trinity by the new and truly empowering trinity of Marx, Engels, and Lenin. His inspiration says: "The myth of the old book reveals in the New Book."[29] Evidently, Assefa reads Marxism-Leninism with a Christian mentality: though the traditional belief is lost, its lingering nostalgia draws a new trinity from the old one.

The Derg went on to use this attempt to wed the old religion with the new ideology to legitimize its rule through the inference that, in becoming socialist, Ethiopia does no more than remain faithful to the true inspiration of Christianity. One editorial of the governmental newspaper *Addis Zemen* wrote in 1975: "The secret foundation of any good religion is socialism. It teaches about human dignity and love and leads to this great goal."[30] In the past, unfortunately, ruling classes and their leaders used religion to assert their class interest and justify their power. In view of that confiscation, the adoption of socialism means nothing less than the "re-appropriation of the authentic characters of love and peace."[31] As a reappropriation of the original message of Christianity and Islam about human dignity and brotherhood, socialism ceases to be an alien ideology; the only difference with the old beliefs is that socialism attempts to translate their ideal aspirations into a concrete socioeconomic reality.

The Moralization of Political Action

Nowhere is the replacement of religion better illustrated than in the moralization of student activism. In dealing with the Ethiopian church, student publications often accompany condemnation with the allegation that the church has betrayed its mission. For instance, one article in *Struggle* titled "Cursed Be the Church!" reads: "Cursed be the Church which turned a blind eye and a deaf ear to the down-trodden masses. Cursed be it for it has forgotten its duty and lacks moral courage."[32] In other words, since the church has betrayed its own teachings by siding with the rich and the powerful against the people, we students should step in and take up the betrayed mission of the church. In light of the church's abdication, the involvement of students in the political struggle thus turns into a redemptive cause.

Each time *Struggle* asserts the enlightening and leading role of students, it also attempts to respond to the question why students would risk all the dangers of an open confrontation with the government in the name of the interests of the masses instead of tranquilly pursuing their own careers. The moralization of political action is the standard answer to this haunting question. Numerous articles speak of "the duty of university students to speak out, to sacrifice, to struggle for the ultimate welfare of the Ethiopian masses."[33] *Struggle* never appeals to the interest of students as students or to their future carriers as bureaucrats, engineers, and so on. Instead, it speaks of duty with an added emphasis on the notion of sacrifice. The sense of obligation is derived from the presence of a cause transcending the individual interests of students. This cause is none other than society: "The individual cannot exist divorced from society which sustains him by giving him an identity and providing economic security as well. Therefore, it is an undeniable truth that it is the society that is supreme and that the individual has to subordinate himself to the welfare of the society."[34]

Since the student owes everything to society, individualism is wrong and evil. This appeal to duty is used to counter liberalism, which radical students view as the first enemy. Yet, why condemn individualism when history shows that it can be quite effective in undermining imperial powers by inspiring social reforms that promote individual rights and freedom? There is no need to go into the theory of the supremacy of society over individuals in order to activate opposition to imperial rule: not only can common interests against tyranny, oppression, and ascriptive rights mobilize people with different interests, but also this type of mobilization often leads to sustained political associations against the common enemy.

Struggle does not propagate this kind of alliance, mainly because it rejects a bourgeois perspective. An article published in 1966 vigorously attacks opportunism and reformism, which it associates with individualism. It reads:

> The opportunist class . . . has no commitments except to personal gains. Ironically enough, most of its members are of the poorest origin. I consider this class to be the most dangerous and serious enemy of the student movement and the Ethiopian masses at large because it makes up the new emerging middle class that is prospering while advocating peace. The meaning of this peace should be evident because it underlies their whole notion of evolutionary change. It is these people who argue for a reform within a political system.[35]

Reformism is condemned because it is inspired by individualism and, as such, does not uphold the cause of the masses. Interestingly, the article notes that reformism is often the position of students who come from poor families: determined to climb the social ladder, these students consider a university education as an opportunity for personal success. Radical students have to fight these careerists and they do so by turning political activism into an ethical issue. Rather than common interests with other classes, the basis of students' involvement in the political struggle is their duty to society, especially their mission to defend the poor against the powerful. In this way, radical students can denounce careerism as a dereliction of duty in favor of selfish interests.

Why would appeal to duty be more effective than to self-interest? One possible answer to this question is the need to relive the Christian spirit. Given Ethiopia's Christian background, the sense of personal fulfillment is greater when political action invokes duty rather than self-interest. As opposed to self-interest, with its connotations of egoism and pettiness, the call of duty arouses the sense of sacrifice, generosity, and heroism. It is to the power of these noble sentiments that *Struggle* makes its appeal. An existing life of commitment to the cause of the people suddenly illuminates the dull life of students under Haile Selassie. We find here one of the great attractions of Marxism-Leninism: it activates generous sentiments and makes life meaningful under the terrible boredom and senselessness of autocratic rule. These noble sentiments being the very ones that religion nurtured, Marxism-Leninism revives them by proposing a life of revolutionary heroism, that is, a life that overcomes selfish and petty interests.

All the more reason for espousing this new heroism is that the masses have no other representative than students; even the church has deserted them. The system not only exploits the masses; it also incapacitates them to the point of utter defenselessness. Reminding students of their unique responsibility to rescue the helpless, an editorial in *Struggle* writes:

> The individual student has to remember that he owes loyalty not only to himself, his relatives and so on, but also to a huge society which, unfortunately, has been denied its inherent rights of self-expression. In the case of a conflict between his personal values and the general interest of the society, he must be ready to sacrifice his private desires, for in a society like ours, only a man of no conscience can disregard a helpless people in the pursuit of the advancement of personal grandiosity.[36]

Why should students sacrifice their self-interests for the masses? The answer is the Christian compassion for the poor and the helpless. The radicalization of the Ethiopian student movement confirms Hannah Arendt's observation according to which "the passion of compassion has haunted and driven the best men of all revolutions."[37] The passion explains why the fight against individualism, careerism, and hedonism is one of the recurring themes of *Struggle*. The aim of the fight is to awaken the compassion dormant in the students. One editorial admits the attractions of individualism only to say: "As human beings, however, we will reduce ourselves to men whose sole purpose in life is to achieve their instinctual desires, no matter what the cost, no matter who is hurt in the process. Thus, we have a choice— to live alone in a society, or to live together as a society."[38] Does this injunction to give up hedonism so as to devote one's life to the good of society make sense outside a culture influenced by Christian values? Is not *Struggle* presupposing that very culture when it believes that its denunciation of individualism carries convincing arguments?

Far from me to suggest that radical students were actually involved in the task of reviving Christianity in Ethiopia. Their intention was rather to put the noble sentiments of Christianity in the service of the new ideology of Marxism-Leninism. They knew perfectly well that an appeal to sentiments associated with Christianity made Marxism-Leninism even more attractive, just as they knew that the decline of the traditional ideology had created a craving for a new belief. The same editorial in *Struggle* puts the matter clearly:

> If we are to lead this country in the future, then it is essential that we agree upon the pursuit of a common objective, the creation of a common belief, call it an ideology, which we will mend and modify to suit our purposes for the progress of the Ethiopian society. Without such a belief, it will be too late for us to resist or control the feeling of individualism that is already presenting itself to us as a "way of life."[39]

Only the sense of being part of a higher, transcendental cause can justify the sacrifice of individualism. Christianity provided this feeling in the past; now the torch was passing to Marxism-Leninism with its revolutionary commitment to universal equality and freedom. No doubt, the radicals saw individualism as their great enemy. To counter it, they conjured up the Christian themes of sacrifice and compassion and judiciously fastened them to a revolutionary agenda.

Attempts to Reform the Ethiopian Church

What has been said so far must not give the impression that no student came out in defense of the traditional religion. As a matter of fact, articles calling for the defense and renovation of the traditional faith appeared in *Struggle*. Such is the case, for instance, with an article titled "On Revolution in Religion," which appeared in 1968. The article begins with very harsh judgments against the Ethiopian church, of the type "if history calls a spade a spade, it would undoubtedly refer to religious institutions as the most conservative if not reactionary elements the world has ever witnessed."[40] It also vigorously denounces the unity of state and church, arguing that the union forced the Ethiopian church to become an instrument of the imperial autocracy. The church is even accused of partaking in the underdevelopment of Ethiopia, for "the preaching of the doctrine of pacifism and fatalism managed to subdue any opposition and stamina for work."[41] In light of these severe shortcomings, nothing but drastic reforms can save the church. "This is why we believe that religion needs a revolution if it plans to occupy a position of pious respect. Drastic changes have to occur within it if it wishes to remain in the hearts of the masses. Otherwise a policy of retrogression and opposition to progress might endanger its existence in the very near future."[42]

A more assertive position is reflected in an article titled "ReChristianizing Christians?" The article is a forceful defense of the national religion. Noting that Ethiopians adopted Christianity when "all Europeans were in the stage of social development they call barbarism," the article adds: "From the time Christianity came to Ethiopia it had played an important role in the history of this country. The Christian church had preserved the history of the Ethiopians, kept alive the art and literature of our forefathers and at times defended the country against foreign intruders. It had put into the hearts of the Ethiopian people the sacred feeling of freedom and nationalism that kept this country from the rampages of colonialism."[43] The publication of this spirited apology of Ethiopia's Orthodox Christianity in a radical journal comes as a big surprise. The content of the article contrasts with the usual accusations blaming the Ethiopian church for teaching passivity, fatalism, and social stagnation. Orthodox religion is recognized as the root of Ethiopian nationalism and culture and credited with the country's protracted independence.

Why did the radicals allow the publication of this article in a journal they controlled? The need to counter the growing desertion of Ethiopian students to Western religions, such as Protestantism and Catholicism, provides the answer. Specifically, the Pentecostal movement, which took the name Mullu Wengel (Full Gospel), "became the strongest, fastest expanding religious revivalist force in the towns, particularly attracting students from the secondary schools and the university."[44] Rightly, the radicals saw the growing conversion of students to foreign religions as a great obstacle to the spread of Marxism-Leninism. The 1967 resolutions of the student movement condemning "what it called 'missionary activities' within the university 'designed to arrest our political consciousness and obscure our national goal' " underscores the extent to which new religions had become serious competitors to the ideology of Marxism-Leninism.[45] What is more, "when the 'Crocs,' the radical left, lost the USUAA presidential election in December 1968, they blamed the Mullu Wengel, as well as the female students for this."[46] That the radicals themselves perceived a rivalry between their ideology and the foreign religions is another proof of the involvement of concerns of a religious nature behind the revolutionary project of social change. The need to fill the void created by the disenchantment with traditional beliefs explains both the infatuation of students with political activism and their increasing conversion to foreign religions.

To counter the desertion, radicals had no other option but to strike the chord of nationalism. The best way to awaken nationalist feeling was to allude to a conspiracy of foreign missionaries working in tandem with neocolonialists. Various articles in *Struggle* allege an elaborate plan to weaken the national religion so as to replace it by exported beliefs, judged more conducive to the neocolonial project. According to an article already cited, the motto "If you can't colonize his land then try his mind"[47] was behind the attempt to re-Christianize Ethiopians. Missionaries attacked Ethiopia's religion because they knew it had been the bulwark against colonial and neocolonial domination. Stigmatizing students for forgetting this neocolonial project when they converted to Protestantism and other foreign religions, the article writes: "The youngster who adopts western Christianity at the cost of his country's independence is a complete opposite of the true Ethiopian. His nationalist feeling is questionable and his willingness to fight for the betterment of his people and humanity at large is doubted."[48]

The author of course never offers any justification for why Ethiopians who abdicate their religion for Marxism are still called Ethiopian. No less than the converts to Protestantism, Ethiopians who espouse Marxism betrayed their legacy for beliefs imported from the West. If the nationalism of the Ethiopian who becomes a Protestant is questionable, why should it be any different for the Ethiopian who becomes a Marxist? Be that as it may, as a reflection of the radicals' anxiety over the growing defection among the young to Western types of Christianity, the charge of betrayal confirms the existence of a serious rivalry between religion and Marxism-Leninism.

The Case of a Reformist Movement

The need to defend the national religion was not confined to the writing of supportive articles. It actually gave birth to a revivalist movement known as the *Haimanote-Abew* Ethiopian Students' Association (HAESA); the term "haimanote-Abew" means the faith of our fathers. Founded in 1958, the organization comprised activist students like Tadesse Tamrat and Asfaw Damte and had its own publications, *Frontier* and *Sutafe*. The latter was a monthly publication with articles in English and Amharic. The emperor was the patron of the movement; the archbishop, its honorary president; and a cabinet minister, Akale Work Habte-Wold, its president. Besides indicating that the initiation had come from the top, the high level of governmental involvement gives evidence of the importance attached to the movement. In terms of membership, the organization had "in 1970. . . an estimated membership of 7000 with 21 branches throughout the Empire."[49]

The movement reflected the growing awareness among students as well as university, church, and government officials of the increasing desertion of Ethiopian youth to foreign religions and Marxist ideology. The strategy was to counter the movement by encouraging from within reforms that might satisfy young educated Ethiopians. Accordingly, the main concern of the HAESA was to adapt "the church to the contemporary needs while preserving the traditional heritage of the forefathers in a manner meaningful to the younger generation."[50] At first, the effort focused on reforming the liturgy and other outdated customs. Thus, the HAESA advocated the use of Amharic in church services instead of Geez, which was alien to most Ethiopians. It also recommended curtailing the numerous fast and feast days because they were seen as inimical to modern life and economic development. Another important recommendation demanded the exposure of priests to modern education as well as their subjection to higher standards of morality. A publication on the occasion of the 13th Year Seminar reiterated the main goal of the HAESA, which is "to modernize and protect the legacies" of the church.[51]

Already the 1960 *Annual Journal* had made doctrinal modernization one of the objectives of the HAESA. It argued that many among the young "are moving toward atheism because they cannot find a religious teaching commensurate with their intellectual development resulting from advanced scientific and technological education."[52] The analysis admits that Western education has made the Ethiopian youth intellectually too advanced and sophisticated to be content with traditional religious teachings. The dire consequence of the unpreparedness of the Ethiopian church to deal with modern youth is "religious colonization."[53] The spiritual void stemming from the fact that young Ethiopians were no longer adopting the beliefs of their parents had exposed them to mental colonization. The *Annual Journal* readily acknowledged that the issue was none other than the reconciliation of religious beliefs with reason. Unfortunately, the Ethiopian church was totally unprepared for the challenge of modern science and technology. Accordingly, one important purpose of the HAESA was to demonstrate that "reason welcomes rather than opposes faith."[54]

Transcending the initial objective of reforming the church, the HAESA progressively ventured into social questions via discussions on the social role of the church. The evolution was triggered by the decline of the movement, which was neither recruiting new people nor even keeping its old members. There was a growing disenchantment in the face of the HAESA's inability to have an impact on the church and initiate reforms. The survival of the HAESA depended on the extent to which it confronted the important issue of the time, that is, Ethiopia's socioeconomic problems. The movement rejected the view of the radicals according to which modern Ethiopia cannot develop unless it throws away its heritage. The HAESA "maintained that socioeconomic development of Ethiopia could be achieved by skillful hybridization of the indigenous culture with the Western technology."[55] But it also understood that loyalty to the faith of the fathers was becoming increasingly difficult so long as the church did not reform itself radically and begin to champion social reforms. About the social role of the church, one issue of *Sutafe* says: "It is the church which should be pioneer in preaching equality; it is the church which feeds the hungry; it is the church which should stand for justice. . . . When we see the church standing as a social pioneer, then the invisible church becomes visible and only then the teaching of Christ is properly reduplicated."[56] This call for a church that denounces injustice and advocates social reforms was undoubtedly meant to counter the growing influence of Marxism-Leninism and radical students on Ethiopian youth. The threat gave birth to the belief that only the emergence of a socially militant church could stop the desertion of students to foreign religions and to Marxist-Leninist ideology.

The plea for a militant church could not evade the real problem behind the church's resistance to reform: its subordination to the imperial throne. In effect, the resolutions of the 15th Year Annual Conference demanded the reinstatement of the autonomy of the church from the state, arguing that its dependence on the state was the main reason for the social conservatism of the church and the subsequent decline of its influence on young educated Ethiopians. The conference deplored the emperor's power to nominate prominent church officials, including the head of the Ethiopian church. One of the resolutions states: "The Patriarch, archbishops, bishops and the general manager shall be elected by members of the Holy Synod and those of the Council and the accountability of the same shall be to the Holly Synod and the Council."[57] What made the HAESA daring enough to openly challenge the authority of the emperor over the church? The answer lies in the matter of timing: the conference took place the same year as the social revolution that swept the monarchy away.

Reasons for the Failure to Reform

The question arises: Why did government and church officials initiate and officially support the HAESA if they were not going to heed its recommendations? If the purpose of the HAESA was to create a movement that countered the desertion of Ethiopian youth by competing against radical ideologies and Western forms of Christianity, the government and the church were defeating their own initiative by totally rejecting the reformist proposals of the HAESA. As a matter of fact, in the face of growing impatience, HAESA "members were told in no uncertain terms that instead of being merely critical of the Church to show their moral strength through loyalty to what the forefathers handed on."[58] It is not clear how the HAESA was expected to counteract competing ideologies if it could point to no reforms.

It seems to me that the HAESA was based on an initial misunderstanding. The young who became members thought they were authorized to reform and modernize the church. This was wishful thinking on their part as the real objective of the government and the church hierarchy was less to encourage reforms than to generate a movement committed to the defense of the traditional faith. In their eyes, rather than revival and reform, the purpose of the HAESA was to defend the traditional faith by generating a conservative movement among students. The fact that the emperor and the church hierarchy maintained tight control over the HAESA clearly shows that they regarded it as an appendage to the throne rather than an autonomous force of regeneration. The movement is interesting not because of its contributions but because it reflected how strongly many students and even officials believed that the only way to stop the growing conversion of young Ethiopians to foreign religions and Marxism-Leninism was through the reformation of the Ethiopian church. Even though the exercise of imperial control disabled the HAESA, it expressed an authentic concern coming from people committed to the faith who understood that the church will continue to lose ground to Western religions and Marxism-Leninism unless it underwent a serious reformation.

The complete failure of the movement actually presents a challenge, given that so many people were aware of the progressive alienation of the youth and linked that alienation with the conversion to foreign religions and radical ideologies. What can explain the total lack of result of such a wide concern? The inability to reform the church is a necessary but not a sufficient explanation. Other countries show cases of traditional religions resisting and retaining the loyalty of educated elites even when they did not reform themselves. In particular, Islamic countries have better resisted the impact of the West's ideas and radical ideologies. Islam has even inspired a radical form of resistance against Westernization by producing fundamentalist factions. Why, then, was Ethiopia unable to develop the type of nationalist ideology that could go up against Westernization?

Without denying the impact of Haile Selassie's pro-Western stand, the answer must also probe into factors particular to Ethiopia, especially its Orthodox Christian culture. For non-Christian countries, Westernization means the complete loss of identity such that the natural attachment to one's identity impels such countries to defend their legacy even if they are not in tune with modernity. Not so for Ethiopians, who share many beliefs and values with the West through Christianity. For them, the Western way was not so closely tied to a denial of identity, and so seemed less alienating. Especially, young educated Ethiopians considered the adoption of Western ways as a normal and positive evolution.

Contrast Ethiopia's open-ended receptivity with the resistance of Islamic countries, and it becomes clear that Islam resists better because it has developed a tradition of opposition to the West. Followers of Islam do not need to convert to Marxism-Leninism to express their conflict with Western hegemony; simple identification with Islam gives them the needed counteracting ideology. To remain faithful to Islam is to challenge the West; better still, Islam can be so renovated as to propose an alternative form of modernization. Such is the case with the Islamic revolution in Iran: "Shi'ism, as an alternative to Western capitalism and Eastern communism, promised to restore a sense of distinctive identity to individual Iranians and the nation as a whole."[59]

Ethiopia's limitation in developing a similar type of opposition to the West—owing to its Christian tradition—was further reinforced by its other particularity, that it had escaped colonization. Colonized peoples had to reclaim their past heritage both to resist colonization and affirm their right to independence. Thus, Islamic countries glorified Islam and used it as their defining feature in their struggle against colonialism. Likewise, Indians renewed their attachment to Hinduism despite the unfriendliness of some of its beliefs and practices to modern thinking. As a colony, India needed the renovation of Hinduism to defend its identity and resist being assimilated. In black African countries, too, educated Africans, advocating a return to the source, championed revivalist movements.

Because Ethiopia was not colonized, its traditional culture was not summoned to play a similar role of resistance. Consequently, whereas for colonized people modernization included the defense of their traditional identity, for young Ethiopians the eradication of the past became a condition for moving toward modernity. The defense of the traditional personality became all the easier for colonized societies when they found native thinkers with a regenerating ethos. Thus, to the Indian need to preserve identity, Gandhi responded by renewing the traditional belief. Subsequently, most young Indians did not feel the need to espouse utopian ideologies to fill the spiritual void springing from the dismissal of traditional beliefs. Young Ethiopians took the opposite direction because no movement aimed at renovating their traditional identity offered an alternative course.

Talk about identity and its defense force us to deal directly with a particular type of nationalist syndrome. The prevailing view draws the radicalism of students and intellectuals from the colonial humiliation of nationalist feelings, which neocolonial policy and practices further aggravated. Without denying the link between nationalism and radicalism, the next chapter will unravel the metamorphoses of nationalism under the dissolving impact of the Eurocentric imprint.

8

The Sublimation of Desertion

We have established that the cultural deracination fomented by Western education accounts for much of the attractiveness of Marxism-Leninism to Ethiopian students and intellectuals. Because the system of education had undermined traditional values and beliefs, young educated Ethiopians fell for Marxism-Leninism, which was also the dominant ideology in the sixties and early seventies. Nonetheless, the captivating power of Marxism-Leninism would have been reduced without its ability to address the frustration that the persistence of underdevelopment and the hegemony of imperialism had induced.

This chapter analyzes the manner in which betrayal of the traditional legacy and nationalist frustration fed on socialist radicalism. In so doing, it continues the idea of the last chapter, that Marxism became attractive to the extent that it seemed to offer a remedy to the decentering impact of Eurocentrism. Without denying the radicalizing effect of far-reaching socioeconomic challenges, my approach maintains that any explanation of Marxism-Leninism's attraction is only partial if it does not account for the ability of the theory to patch up cultural dislocation by serving as a substitute for devalued beliefs and, as a counteracting ideology against Eurocentrism. A full account of the phenomenon must blend the causes of the disease with the aspirations that the disease induces, all the more so as only the ill-advised nature of such aspirations can explain the longing for an extreme therapy.

Guilt and Atonement

Abandonment of one's religion and traditional values does not come easy. It provokes a sense of betrayal and guilt, especially when a foreign educational system is responsible for the desertion. No guilt would have appeared if the devaluation of traditional beliefs were the result of an internal evolution. In such a case, one would speak of cultural growth and transformation. But when exposure to the alien culture of the West provoked the devaluation of traditional Ethiopian beliefs, the feeling of betrayal was inevitable, since the West was viewed as an adversary.

These feelings of guilt could be overcome if modernized Ethiopians were to adopt a radical theory, the very theory that criticizes Western capitalism and denounces its imperialist practices. Moreover, since Westernized Ethiopians could not avoid the impact of the alien culture, their only choice was to atone for the betrayal by thinking that their desertion was for the better, that it was worthwhile. In other words, as hinted in chapter 5, the need to appease the feeling of guilt spurs the turn to radicalism. For uprooted Ethiopians, the conquest of a prosaic world was not liable to still their guilty consciences. They must go for the highest target, for the best social system. Reform would not appease them; they wanted revolution. Yes, they betrayed, but they did it for revolutionary change, not for cheap, self-serving change. And they vindicated their generosity by specifically upholding the cause of the oppressed and exploited masses. Because Marxism-Leninism held the promise of such a redeeming effect, it was bound to attract Western-educated Ethiopians.

As many scholars have noted, Marxism-Leninism was attractive to Ethiopian students and intellectuals mostly for its sharp and all-around criticism of Western capitalism. The end result of this unsparing critique was that, by becoming Marxist-Leninist, Westernized Ethiopians displayed their rebellion against the West. Not only did their adopted ideology morally defame Western societies, but it was also committed to the complete destruction of the capitalist system itself. While Ethiopians with reformist or liberal views compromised with imperialism, Marxist revolutionaries took the bull by the horns in a deadly fight. Following Ali Mazrui, I called "aggressive dependency" this attitude of using against the West what is essentially a Western product.[1]

Even though the Marxist challenge conserves the viewpoint of the West, Ethiopians could not see the resulting dependency because the anticapitalist inspiration and revolutionary commitment of Marxist discourse seduced them. Identification with what internally challenged the West gave Ethiopian students and intellectuals the feeling of being totally free and faithful to their nationalist sentiment to the highest degree. When the *Manifesto of the Communist Party* states that the bourgeoisie shattered feudalism but only to replace it by a system that knows "no other nexus between man and man than naked self-interest, than callous 'cash payment'" so that the outcome of the replacement of feudalism was "naked, shameless, direct, brutal exploitation," such expressions were no doubt quite agreeable to Ethiopian students and intellectuals.[2] In thus portraying capitalism—the great achievement of the West—as a system that greed and the merciless exploitation of working people made possible, Marxism demystifies Western superiority, even confers some dignity on Ethiopia's poverty. Better still, it allowed the educated elite to hit two birds with one stone: it undermined traditional society while subverting the West. It thus adorned the modernization prospect with the sweet taste of revenge.

Forrest D. Colburn finds highly ironic that the strong anti-Westernism of Ethiopian revolutionaries ended up canonizing Western ideologues to the detriment of national figures. He writes that although Ethiopia was never colonized,

> yet in the aftermath of the Ethiopian Revolution—which ended imperial rule— Addis Ababa's central plaza, renamed Revolutionary Square, was dominated by an enormous billboard bearing the portraits of three Europeans: Marx, Engels, and Lenin. As I strolled past majestic Coptic priests in flowing robes, I wondered if it occurred to them that the Ethiopia which had resisted European encroachment for generations was exalting and following dissident and now discredited Europeans. How could they not notice, I wondered too, that the tallest statue in the city commemorated not one of the many heroes in the Ethiopian pantheon, but a foreigner, a European—Lenin.[3]

No doubt, the canonization of foreigners reveals the depth of the alienation of the educated elite. However, one misses the whole picture if one fails to see what these Europeans meant for young educated Ethiopians. In the eyes of revolutionary Ethiopians, these dissident figures had actually ceased to belong to the West. Ethiopia had become their adopted country, in fact one of the few countries where their views were genuinely put into practice. What these three Europeans said was so inimical to the West that exhibiting their portraits was tantamount to defying and angering the West. The larger the portraits were, the louder the defiance became.

The attitude of Ethiopian students and intellectuals did no more than reproduce the mental itinerary of many African scholars. One explanation for the great inclination of African scholars toward Marxist philosophy in the 1960s and 1970s is Marx's demystification of Western achievements. In revealing the barbarism of capitalism, Marxist philosophy dismisses the colonial discourse that degraded Africans to the level of primitiveness. On the strength of this denunciation, a scholar like Cheikh Anta Diop ascribes the technological backwardness of Africa to the moral superiority of Africans, who, rejecting class exploitation, established an egalitarian social system based on the communal ownership of the means of production. According to Diop, the inability to extract surplus through exploitation is the reason why Africa lagged behind Europe.[4] Even when African scholars resist adhering to Marxist philosophy, they cannot refrain from using Marx's diatribes against capitalism to glorify the precolonial system of African communalism. Such is notably the case of the main thinker of negritude, Léopold Sédar Senghor, when he presents as evidence of African moral superiority the contrast of African communal values with the competitive and acquisitive values of the West.[5]

Generational Conflict and Student Idealism

Together with the denigration of Western achievements, Marxism-Leninism provides an alluring justification for radical dissent against traditional ruling elites. In order to measure the real impact of this justification, we have to go deeper into the psychic temperament of the Ethiopian educated elite, especially into its guilt feelings in a context of intensified generational conflict. We have already alluded to the part played by generational conflict: in undermining traditional values and beliefs, Western education was doing nothing less than reviving the Oedipal conflict. One consequence of the deprecation of traditional norms is the far-reaching "de-authoritization of the elder generation."[6] The traditional society "finds itself challenged by forces emanating from advanced societies. For in such a situation, the generational equilibrium of the traditional society is shattered. The young are ashamed of the old and want to avoid the emasculation which the traditional society inflicts on its members."[7]

Here a note is necessary to ward off the objection that the appeal to oedipal conflict is out of touch with the topic at hand. What would be valid in a context of child-parent relations seems to be arbitrarily extended to a political conflict involving youth-adult relations. Obviously, the interpretation of the revolt of young people in terms of oedipal rivalry no longer maintains that the mother is the object of contention. However, because the old have absolute control over resources and status in a gerontocratic society, conflicts are inevitable, as the preservation of the status quo thwarts the ambition of younger generations. What is more, the complication of gerontocratic societies with de-authorization triggered by Western education turns the normal process of generational succession into a premature and coerced dislodging. The concept of political patricide best describes the phenomenon in that it points to the disturbance of generational succession by a desire seeking an improper dethronement, since what used to be an outcome of a voluntary transfer is thought of as a takeover. This positioning for social leadership through the impeachment of the older generation cannot fail to stir up guilt feelings.

In addition, when young people call for a radical revolution, they know that they invite a society in which the older generation would be not only totally marginalized but also constantly castigated. This culpatory stand aggravates the guilt feeling with the consequence that the accusers welcome lofty ideals as a way of silencing their conscience. The offense of dislodging an established authority, which authority, we know, has its matrix in parental authority, is transfigured into a good action if it is for a noble cause. Indeed,

Sigmund Freud teaches us that the resolution of Oedipal conflict through the surrender of the mother and the formation of the superego establishes the authority of the father, which then becomes the source for the acceptance of all forms of authority, including that of the state. In light of the grounding of authority in the Oedipus drama, the infatuation with radicalism, that is, the excitement for utopian social goals, is not fully intelligible without the involvement of powerful emotions associated with paternal authority.

This study refers to oedipal conflict precisely to show that the attraction to radical ideas implicates an emotional component necessary to account for the ferocity of radicalism. In many instances I was able to verify the strength of the trauma, which was, of course, more intense among students coming from aristocratic or wealthy families because they were actively taking part in the denigration of their own family and class. For example, it transpired in the numerous discussions I had with former activists and leaders of the Ethiopian student movement. One of them even told me that he was not quite able to go along with his new life in the United States until he apologized to his father. Western education served to undermine traditional acceptance of the authority of the father in Ethiopian society. The devaluation of the beliefs and values of the older generation in the modern classroom defies the submission of the younger generation. In challenging everything and wanting to start anew, the revolutionary spirit loudly states that it is fatherless. The best expression of a generational conflict that derails into a radical rebellion is an attitude that willingly embraces discontinuity: severing all ties with the past means an outright defiance of what the father stands for.

One misses the full impact of the phenomenon if the discontinuity is given a merely symbolic meaning. The break alters the relationships that revolutionaries have with their immediate family, especially their parents. Thus, for many Ethiopians, the conversion to Marxism-Leninism explicitly "included the devaluation of familial and affective ties in interpersonal relations in favor of doctrinal fellowship and comradery based on commitment to revolutionary causes."[8] Let us not be fooled by appearances, however. The revolutionary spirit conserves the need for authority figures; they are Marx, Lenin, and Mao, who, as substitute fathers, demand conformity with their revolutionary norms. In turning Ethiopian students into orphans, without however removing the need for authority figures, the devaluation of the father and the complete rejection of tradition were bound to create the disposition to look for new fathers from outside the national culture. This explains why Ethiopian radicalism did not develop a creative impulse: in replacing the natural father with adopted fathers, it maintained the need to adhere rigidly to the principles laid down by them.

Before going further, let us establish distinctly the importance of generational conflict and its impact on the radicalization of students. Lewis S. Feuer remarks that, although generational struggle has been recognized as a universal theme of history, "unlike class struggle, however, the struggle of generations has been little studied and little understood."[9] The underestimation of generational conflict is surprising when we note how deeply student movements have impacted on the history of many countries. Thus, "social revolutions in Russia, China, and Burma sprang from student movements, while governments in Korea, Japan, and the Sudan have fallen in recent years largely because of massive student protest."[10] The fall of the imperial regime in Ethiopia should be added to the list of regimes that student protests undermined. What explains the underestimation of generational conflict is the overwhelming importance that Marxist-influenced scholars attach to class conflict. Yet, class conflict may explain social uprisings, but not the radicalism that pervaded some of these uprisings.

In addition to being a social category consisting of individuals born and living about the same time, generation comprises common responses and attitudes that emanate from certain defining life experiences. That young people form a generation means that they go through similar experiences and crises as a result of which they develop needs and feelings common to their age group. We can therefore speak of generational consciousness in the same way as we speak of class consciousness, with the understanding that, unlike class, generation is not an economic category, but an age-based notion. What unites the young is not their social background or status but the similar ways, characteristic of their age, of evaluating things and responding to challenges. To quote Feuer, "Student movements are founded on *generational consciousness* in the same basic sense in which workers' movements are founded on class consciousness."[11]

The common consciousness among workers arises from the objective and common conditions of exploitation and economic deprivation. Widely experienced economic discontent does not stir the youth movement, since facts show that most of its leaders come from wealthy families. Hence the need to assign generational movements more to cultural crises than to economic discontent: individuals belonging to different economic categories can develop a sense of unity only from the perception that "prevailing official values and symbols appear irrelevant and retrogressive in the face of the need for radical social change."[12] In particular, exposure of students from traditionally oriented communities to Western values and institutions is likely to set the conditions of an acute generational conflict, as the older generation's cultural conservatism prevents such communities from responding appropriately to the challenge of modernity. Under such conditions, the youth become tempted to adopt views and values that defy both parental authority and the existing social order. When generational conflict reaches the level of cultural clash, it sharpens receptivity to revolutionary ideologies.

No account of the presence in social protests of goals going beyond economic grievances is feasible if it excludes the impact of students and intellectuals. The point is that we cannot explain the radicalization of social protests without appealing to the idealism of student movements. For "student movements, unlike those of workingmen, are born of vague, undefined emotions which seek for some issue, some cause, to which to attach themselves. A complex of urges—altruism, idealism, revolt, self-sacrifice and self-destruction—searches the social order for a strategic avenue of expression."[13] A specific feature of student rebellion is that it is never confined to corporate or sectarian demands. On top of devaluing the traditional order, it involves goals that pursue a utopian construction of society. Unlike the economic focus of workers' movements, "a student movement thus tends to take its stand as the pure conscience of the society; it is concerned with ideal issues, not, like an economic movement, with the material, bread-and-butter ones."[14] This idealistic stance implicates a generalized rebellion against authority, a delegitimization of the traditional elite such that its norms are completely repudiated.

That the son rebels against the father by siding with those whom the father oppressed illustrates that generational rebellion rather than mere economic grievances defines student rebellion. Inasmuch as this open disavowal is unnatural, it denotes the eruption of affective impulses, less so the cold calculation of economic interests. One can hardly assign the need to espouse the cause of the oppressed to a rationale of economic nature. As Feuer notes, "The sons are emotionally ready to identify themselves with those whom their fathers oppress. Mao Tse-tung, for instance, recalls how he made common cause as a boy with those peasants whom his harsh father exploited."[15] Undoubtedly, the rejection of reformism and the infatuation with Marxism-Leninism are not fully explicable without consideration of the emotional component of generational conflict.

As we saw in chapter 5, noting the radicalization of many young aristocrats, some authors have characterized the Russian student movement as a generational revolt, the argument being that exposure to Western ideas instigated the revolt. This exposure caused feelings of guilt that sons of well-to-do families tried to assuage by espousing a selfless cause, that is, by changing their revolt into a stand for the defense of the marginalized and the powerless. Hence their receptivity to radical views, such as Marxism and anarchism: accedence to radicalism was how a characteristic sublimation, namely, the commitment to a selfless cause, such as the defense of the poor, excused the revolt against the father. Stated otherwise, the usual association of idealism with youth is not merely a matter of biological attribute; it also may stem from generational revolt. The idealism and extremism of student movements tap into the emotional component of the guilt of patricide: they appease the guilt by sublimating it with lofty goals.

Studies of the radicalization of the Ethiopian student movement rarely, if ever, allude to generational conflict. The predominant view posits the origination of radicalization in harsh economic grievances, such as abject conditions of life, including the fear of unemployment, itself aggravated by a high rate of dropouts. These material factors were all the more conducive to a mounting radicalization as many students came from families experiencing economic hardship. According to this view, so great was the part played by economic hardships that, less than idealism, the need to have allies in the fight against the privileges of the upper class compelled students to support the interests of workers and peasants. Explaining why economic hardship led students to radicalize their demands in support of workers and peasants, John Markakis and Nega Ayele write:

> The abrupt narrowing of its social horizon transformed the educated petty bourgeoisie into a disgruntled and politically dissident class. Its subordinate economic status and dim prospects for the future within the economic structure of the *ancien regime* turned this social group in a radical direction, which led it to make common cause with the workers and peasants. Taking the lead in the attack against the old regime, the educated petty bourgeoisie sector prepared the ground for the popular movement sometime before the crucial year of 1974.[16]

Because students were not numerically strong enough, they needed the support of other classes to impose change. And since they could not ally with the upper classes, they sided with the working people. Though they belonged to the petit bourgeois class, they adopted socialism because of the need to mobilize the masses against the ruling class and the state.

One important point that Markakis and Nega's approach does not explain is that the students did not simply ally with workers. They did more in that they presented themselves as the sole representatives of the working masses. They did not simply say, "Since we have a common enemy, let us join forces"; they identified with working people to the point of becoming their spokespersons. Mere alliance preserves the distinct interests of the partners, and so targets a democratic type of change that allows each class to see its interests defended. Frankly rejecting the idea of alliance, Ethiopian students characterized the attempt to defend petit bourgeois interests as shameful and unworthy. As one editorial in *Challenge* put it, "The choice is clear cut: either [one] is making one's career out of the misery of our people or saying *no* to that and join up their ranks."[17]

The reference to generational revolt helps explain these students' identification with working people. The defense of their own interests would have made the student movement unable to appease the guilt of patricide. Only the prospect of a radical, selfless change was morally high enough to sublimate the guilt, to provide the necessary atonement. Hence the call for the spirit of abnegation by which one denies one's class interest and joins the masses. Coming close to admitting the assuaging impact of lofty causes, one article in *Struggle* says the following: "There is no burden heavier than the load of guilt that comes from the knowledge of not having taken actions or spoken out. Commitment to great causes makes great men."[18] Another important reason not to reduce the student movement to economic conditions is that, as we noted earlier, the most radical students came from well-to-do families. Since such students were neither threatened by unemployment nor experienced revolting conditions of life, their radicalization must have emanated from cultural rather than material causes.

Youth and Gerontocratic Societies

Granted that generational conflict is universal, we still need to know why it has acquired greater intensity in some countries than in others. Various studies suggest that student protests become particularly virulent and widespread in countries where the old generation completely monopolizes power and wealth. Such is typically the case in societies where traditional elites have preserved absolute hegemony by circumscribing the political transformations of modernization. According to Feuer, a student movement "tends to arise in societies which are gerontocratic—that is, where the older generation possesses a disproportionate amount of economic and political power and social status. Where the influences of religion, ideology, and the family are especially designed to strengthen the rule of the old, there a student movement, as an uprising of the young, will be most apt to occur."[19] But Feuer also knows that monopoly of power and wealth is not enough: it must be associated with the clear impression that the older generation has proved incapable of developing the country. In a word, there must be a breakdown of legitimacy of the old ruling elite. To quote Feuer, "A gerontocratic order is not a sufficient condition for the rise of a student movement. Among other factors, there must also be present a feeling that the older generation has failed. We may call this experience the process of the 'de-authoritization' of the old. A student movement will not arise unless there is a sense that the older generation had discredited itself and lost moral standing."[20]

A quick comparative study of student movements establishes the crucial role of failure. Consider the virtual absence of a radical student movement in Japan during the phase of modernization even though a traditional elite monopolized power. Because in the 1920s and 1930s the Japanese leadership inspired pride and confidence both by its successful industrialization and military victories, no "de-authoritization" of the ruling elite occurred. "The prestige of the gerontocracy and military was high during the decade of the thirties. The traditional leadership was evidently taking the Japanese people from one military victory to another," says Feuer.[21] In this condition of successful leadership of the traditional elite, a radical student movement could not develop. Even if revolutionary groups emerged, they were unable to attract many students.

India presents another interesting case. If harsh economic conditions and social exclusion could inevitably cause the spread of revolutionism, India would have been a perfect candidate. Yet, as already indicated, the reality is that India "is notable among Asian countries in having no massive student movement."[22] Not that students failed to protest or remained indifferent; on the contrary, they protested extensively, but without succumbing to radicalism. Though activist groups had emerged, they "recognized sadly that the studentry at large was more interested in sports and movies than in politics."[23] One explanation for the lesser impact of radical ideas on the Indian student body is that "a political de-authoritization of the elder generation had not taken place."[24] Not only was national independence achieved successfully, but also the Congress Party managed to retain the confidence of the majority of students. The confidence owed much to Mahatma Gandhi: his influence dissuaded the younger generation from being attracted to radical ideologies. The legitimacy of the older generation being preserved, the need to overcome guilt by espousing lofty ideals did not arise.

Countries where traditional elites have been removed were also hardly conducive to revolutionism. Such was notably the case with many African countries. Because colonial powers had removed traditional ruling elites, no situations of anger against the failure of the older generation could surface. Though generational conflicts were present, sustained radical student movements did not develop in Africa because of the lack of conditions requiring the "de-authoritization" of traditional ruling elites. The dethronement of traditional elites abolished the need for a lofty form of atonement. The revolt of students was directed more against colonizers and their puppet regimes than against traditional elites.

The great exception here is, of course, Ethiopia, which also had a strongly radicalized generation. The preservation of Ethiopia's independence allowed the traditional elite both to initiate the process of modernization and block its progress, thereby arousing the anger of the younger, educated generation. Conditions specific to Ethiopia have thus particularly aggravated the generational conflict. Whereas the imperial government itself explicitly defined modern education as the training of the future leaders of the country, the older generation proved utterly reluctant to give up power and control. Though the emperor and his entourage insisted parents send their children to modern schools, nothing was done to prepare the transition of power from the older to the educated generation. As decades passed, it became more and more evident that the old elite, going against the great mission of modern education, was limiting the new educated elite to bureaucratic and technical functions, with the consequence that it was excluded from political and economic decision making.

This clinging to power, this refusal to step aside and yield power to those who were entitled by the very norms of the imperial regime, only aggravated the generational conflict. The conflict became explosive as the older generation undertook the systematic blockage of modernization to preserve its hegemony. Speaking of the mission of the Ethiopian student, an article in *Struggle* says: "He has fully understood that he constitutes the reservoir from which future political leaders will be drawn. He has realized that he is the national cadre and tomorrow's leader of the Ethiopian people who will undoubtedly assume their position among the already advanced people of the world."[25] In thus wishing the destruction of the old elite in order to assert the right to fulfill its modernizing mission, the younger generation kindled the guilt feelings leading to its revolutionary idealism.

The path of the Ethiopian student movement is reminiscent of that taken by Chinese students. The resemblance stands out when we ask why reformist alternatives did not attract Chinese students. As John Israel puts it, "The question is *why* Communist slogans had such a wide appeal, *why* Leninism made so much sense to an educated elite, *why* Chiang Kai-shek was so easily cast in the villain's role, and *why* students helped to overthrow a lesser tyranny only to accept a greater one."[26] It is of no use to reiterate the harsh economic conditions of imperial China to account for the radicalization of the educated elite, as economic arguments do not exclude reformism. Instead, psychological factors involving an intensified form of generational conflict give a better insight into the radicalization of educated Chinese. Evidently, the anger and frustration against the traditional ruling elite— which not only failed in the task of modernizing China but even bowed to imperialist forces—aggravated the generational rift to the point of forcing the young generation to wish the complete extirpation of the traditional order. Had the sole issue been the modernization of China, reformism would likely have prevailed. The choice to eliminate the system, what is more, to replace it by a utopian order that sought to empower the very ones whom the traditional system mistreated, betrays both an intense generational conflict and a quest for a remedy against guilt.

Ethiopian students were confronted with similar problems. As in China, Emperor Haile Selassie and the traditional elite did not live up to expectations: in addition to the promised modernization being distressingly slow, the nation had become a satellite of the West, especially of the U.S. government. And as the delegitimized ruling elite was neither admitting its failure nor showing any readiness to hand the country over to those who considered themselves commissioned to lead, change took the form of patricide. The guilt longed for expiation in a selfless commitment, which the ideology of socialism readily provided. The longer the older generation hung on to power, the greater the messianic inspiration of the younger generation became. The depiction of modernization in terms of the powerless masses awaiting their liberators became irresistible. An editorial in *Struggle* states: "The students are not only the violent spokesmen of the oppressed people but also the vanguard in the struggle for democratic rights and against all forms of exploitation."[27]

The Self-Sacrificial Impetus of Political Patricide

In order to highlight better the emotional component that generational conflict imparts to revolutionism, let us briefly review some of the characteristics of the Russian student movement with which, we know, the Ethiopian student movement had close affinities. Admittedly, in terms of idealistic extremism as well as of irrationalism, the Russian student movement represents the prototype of student rebellions. Like other radical student movements, it grew in the social context of "de-authorization" of a traditional ruling elite subsequent to its failure to give Russia a level of development comparable to Western nations. A pronounced tendency to self-sacrifice basically defined the movement. As Feuer says: "The renunciatory, ascetic ethic, this self-punishment, was a sign by which the students demonstrated to their own consciences that theirs was a selfless revolt. It was the way in which they tried to assuage at least partially the guilt which every revolt against the fathers entails."[28] The tendency to self-denial refused all the enjoyments afforded by the social position of modern education. Worse yet, many youngsters, including those who came from rich families, gave up their studies and their careers to serve the people. For these self-sacrificing youths, the sense that the older generation had betrayed its mission meant two things: first, the members of the new generation would look for guidance elsewhere; and second, they will outdo their elders by pursuing higher and selfless causes.

As mentioned already, one of the virtues of explaining revolutionism by recourse to the frustration over the failure of traditional elites is that it clarifies the paradox of the easy radicalization of students coming from upper classes. Shame over the failure of their family and class easily ignited political ambitions; nay, it angered the students to the point of hostility against their own family and class. If such hostility is deep enough, it prepares a fertile ground for the adoption of radical ideologies. That is why such students resent reformist political views: the latter refurbish the traditional system when what they want is to cut the umbilical cord to their family and class. Be it noted that radicalized students from well-to-do families have a great impact on the student body. The rejection of privileges imparts to their political commitment a selfless attribute that has an inspirational effect on other students and gives them great charisma.

Just as with the case of Russian students, the call for self-sacrifice was a recurrent theme of the Ethiopian student movement. Student publications, as stated in the last chapter, reiterated the need to reject individualism and sacrifice class privileges. These calls for self-denial are not quite intelligible outside the need for expiation, given that the lack of bourgeois democratic rights and nationalist indignation over Ethiopia's economic retardation should have been enough to politicize students. The intention of such articles was to divert students from their normal aspirations and talk them into "committing suicide as a class," to use Amilcar Cabral's expression.[29] In this way, they would be fighting and sacrificing not for their own class rights but for the rights and empowerment of lower classes. What else could explain the appeal to self-sacrifice but the need to appease the deeply felt guilt over the desire to dislodge the older generation?

Through the self-sacrificial impetus of guilt alone we can understand the radicalization of Amhara students. Without a massive participation of Amhara students, who, according to various statistical data, represented more than half of the student body, no unified and still less significant student movement would have surfaced. The growing conversion of Amhara students to Marxism-Leninism is a characteristic example of the younger generation longing for values and a social system radically opposed to the older generation. In particular, these Amhara students bitterly denounced the system of land tenure in the south, which was the basis of the Amharas' power, and took on themselves the task of liberating southern peasants from tenancy. In so doing, they knew that they were directly undermining the sociopolitical hegemony of their own ethnic group, and hence their own interests. Bringing change to the southern system of landownership was hardly so vital for modernization that no other political stand was possible. Reformist solutions existed that could have modernized the system without undermining the Amhara elite, and the student movement rejected these solutions, advocating the more radical version of "Land to the Tiller."

These same Amhara students subscribed—after some resistance, it is true—to the idea of Ethiopia being a prison of nationalities and agreed to resolve the national question by granting the right of self-determination to the nations and nationalities under the Amharas' repressive rule. The renunciatory syndrome of Amhara students finds clear expression in the famous article by the activist student Walleligne Mekonnen, who was himself an Amhara from Wollo. He wrote in *Struggle*: "Ethiopia is not really one nation. It is made up of a dozen nationalities with their own languages, ways of dressing, history, social organization and territorial entity. . . . I conclude that in Ethiopia there is the Oromo Nation, the Tigrai Nation, the Amhara Nation, the Gurage Nation, the Sidama Nation, the Wellamo Nation, the Adhere Nation, and however much you may not like it the Somali Nation."[30] What drove Walleligne to write an article that called for nothing less than the dismantling of Ethiopia's state and the fracturing of its unity? Even if terms like "self-determination," "nations," and "nationalities" belong also to the

Leninist lexicon, we need to go deeper than a mere doctrinal conversion to explain their impact on Amhara students. We must appeal to their psychological effect of soothing guilt by inducing a renunciatory mentality. The denunciation of Amhara rule helped separate Amhara students from the evil deeds of their fathers. It offered them the hope of a clear conscience, which they needed to justify their patricidal political stand. Only by feeling morally superior and just could they cope with their psychological trauma, and the best way to assert their ethical stand was to sacrifice what they had cherished or benefited from.

The same self-sacrificial impetus explains the radicalization and ethnicization of Tigrean students. All studies of the Ethiopian student movement agree that Tigrean students were the most intensely and widely radicalized group on the university campus. One explanation limits the cause of this high level of radicalization of Tigrean students to resentment against Amhara rule, but such an account misses the main issue, for one need not have become a Marxist-Leninist to assert and fight for Tigrean interests. Before it came to signify intense hostility against the Amharas, student radicalization expressed a deeper anger of Tigrean students against Tigray's traditional elite itself. Their parents' acceptance of the marginalization of their region made them furious against their own family and class. While traditionally the Tigrean ruling elite had enjoyed autonomy and even competed for imperial power, the generation that lived under Haile Selassie betrayed the legacy and consented to the marginalization of Tigray and the complete dominance of the Showan elite. This abdication and failure made Tigrean students more sensitive to revolutionary ideas than any other ethnic group for the reason that such ideas targeted first of all the dethronement of Tigray's traditional elite. A purely ethnic or nationalist struggle would not have entailed the overthrow of the Tigrean elite; on the contrary, it would have meant the recognition of its legitimacy. To the extent that the desire to overthrow the traditional elite stirred up feelings of guilt, it demanded the appeasing justification of a radical theory of social change.

The combination of ethnonationalism with social radicalism simply continued and amplified Tigrean students' resentment against the Tigrean elite. By fighting to dismantle the Ethiopian state, besides challenging what the older generation had endorsed, the younger generation longed for a new Tigray that would empower the Tigrean peasantry. In thus valuing what their fathers had devalued and shaping it into an instrument of destruction of Amhara hegemony, the younger generation could justify the dethronement of the old Tigrean ruling elite. The road from Marxism-Leninism to ethnonationalism obeys the logic of negation of the negation. While the Marxist-Leninist component gets rid of disappointing traditional elites from Tigray as well as from Amhara, ethnonationalism reasserts Tigray's primacy, thus turning the younger generation into its true representative, as opposed to the elders who are but traitors. But this self-promotion in favor of a narrow, sectarian identity meant the surrender of the cosmopolitan identity accruing from the integrative goal of Tigray's traditional elite. The price for ethnonationalism, that is, for the exaltation of sectarian identity, is the relinquishment of nationalism with a broader basis and higher prospects, such as that represented by Ethiopian nationalism.

Radicalization and ethnicization as a result of resentment against older generations were even truer of students and intellectuals who, like the Eritreans and Oromo nationalists, claimed to belong to colonized peoples. The fact that the older generation accepted Amhara rule and had even helped in its establishment aroused the resentment of the younger generation. While in their radicalism they expressed rebellion against their own traditional elites, in ethnonationalism and the demand for self-determination they targeted the complete cancellation of the shameful conquest. Both were rejections of the aspiration of the older generation to greater integration into the Ethiopian Empire. The desire to destroy the Ethiopian state in the name of self-determination raised the ethnonationalized students to the level of authentic representatives of their ethnic groups. Only the emotional traumatism caused by the antagonizing of the older generation and the resulting generational schism can clarify the obsession with independence to the detriment of the democratization of Ethiopia. Not to long for independence signified agreement with the integrative goal of the older generation. The more the generational conflict intensified, the greater became the need to counter imperial incorporation through the exaltation of a narrower ethno-identity. Clearly, generational conflict was the driving force of ethnonationalism: the sanctification of sectarian identity was as much a rejection of the elders' goal of integration as it was a protest against Amhara hegemony.

Socialism as Patched-up Nationalism

The consensus among scholars assumes that the humiliation of nationalism was the reason Marxism-Leninism enthralled many third world intellectuals. So presented, the explanation appears controversial, given that nationalism presupposes attachment to one's legacies that neither Westernization nor Marxism-Leninism could support. Both are highly critical of traditions and posit modernization squarely in terms of departing from those traditions. How, then, is one to reconcile the apparent reality that third world students and intellectuals became enamored with Marxism-Leninism out of nationalism with the undeniable fact that the main impact of the radical philosophy was to shatter traditions?

Let me illustrate the problem by referring to an article published in *Struggle*. A student by the name of Gezahegn Bekele wrote the following:

"Our past is a past of archaic beliefs and inhuman despotism subjugating the masses; our past is supported by the altar of conservative, defeatist religion; our past is three thousand years of independence that cannot account for a mere five years of development."[31] But the same student went on to criticize the alienation of the younger generation: "Its tastes in music is degenerating and it is adopting western jazz as a model; its views are of an alien nature to the realities in Ethiopia and it conceives of its culture, values, and art to be inferior and less decent than the meaningless foreign culture."[32] That the writer is insensitive to the flagrant contradiction existing between these two statements is baffling. The first statement reflects the denigrating impact of Westernization: compared to Western achievements, the Ethiopian past appears utterly useless and barbaric. From this sweeping devaluation, what else could follow but a decline of nationalist sentiment, if by nationalism we mean attachment to one's characteristics? Paradoxically, however, the second statement stigmatizes Ethiopian youth for adopting Western values and styles to the detriment of the national culture. Why are the youth criticized for abandoning a culture that has been just declared worthless?

The contradiction was real, however incredible this may seem, and my line of argument is to say that one of the attractions of Marxism-Leninism flowed from its ability to suggest a way out. As indicated already, for colonized and humiliated cultures, Marxism is most attractive because the uncovering of the motivation of greed, exploitation, and conquest behind the boasted superiority of the West claims to demystify Western civilization. Diluting the colonial contempt for non-Western civilizations, Marxist discourse describes the West itself as a barbaric civilization. It puts down Western achievements by showing that they are mostly the results of unprecedented greed and untold human suffering. Previously powerless and unable to defend their identity and heritage, third world intellectuals found in Marxism-Leninism basic conceptual and moral tools to debunk Western norms. They thus came to feel they were in possession of a potent philosophy of decolonization that buttressed the rebellion of "the wretched of the earth" against the wealthy and powerful West.

The Marxist devaluation of the West explains why many Ethiopians did not see any incompatibility between Marxism-Leninism and the assertion of nationalism. Aware that Western education was driving them away from tradition, they conceived of Marxism-Leninism as an antidote, in fact as an upgraded form of nationalism. Many young Ethiopians thought that becoming Marxist-Leninist reinvigorated their nationalism. Who could accuse them of lacking in nationalism by succumbing to the West when their Marxism made them so fervently anticapitalist?

This anti-Westernism provided a cover-up for the guilt of betrayal: the rejection of tradition no longer appeared as infidelity, but rather as an expression of real nationalism, a nationalism committed to the defense of working people through the dislodgment of the traditional elite whose alliance with imperialism betrayed the nation. The new ideology would liberate and empower the true, real Ethiopia, namely, the working masses of the country. The discovery of and commitment to working people rather than to traditional institutions and values constituted the empowerment of the real nation: as Marxism asserts, workers are the true makers of history. This valorization of the masses is how the Marxist-Leninist ideology appropriates nationalism: since the working masses make up the real nation, their poverty and mistreatment means the poverty and decline of the nation itself.

Socialism is thus a negation of the negation: Western education alienates, but socialism brings back to nationalism via the embrace of working people and the rejection of capitalism and its allies, the traditional ruling elites. It begins with the refusal of tradition, but it negates that negation by discovering the real Ethiopia, that is, the working people of the country. As such, it is an upgraded nationalism. As Thomas H. Greene notes: "Revolutionary ideology enhances its own legitimacy and threatens the legitimacy of the existing regime insofar as it can claim continuity with the fundamental values and goals of the society. Even leftist revolutionary ideologies frequently cite traditions of the past and argue that revolution is only the necessary means of realizing the society's basic cultural identity and historical purpose. Invariably the choice of traditions is selective."[33] Conversely, native scholars could not defend reformist policies without being accused of wanting in nationalism. When you defend reformism, ipso facto you weaken your nationalist stand, not only because you favor capitalism but also because you side with Western governments, which often support local comprador regimes. While on the one hand the defense of a nationalist platform through the promotion of capitalism appeared difficult, on the other it seemed natural with socialism, since it opposed at once the West and the treacherous local elites.

It is important to understand the extent to which Marxism-Leninism flatters the nationalist feeling of third world intellectuals. Not to emphasize this aspect can obscure the reason Marxism-Leninism seduced so many intellectuals. Colburn, for instance, writes: "Ironically, in an epoch marked by the demise of European colonialism, the minds of those committed to radical change in the poorer countries of the world were captured by a foreign *mentalité* imported after either immediate or circuitous exposure to the European socialist tradition."[34] Colburn is right: it is ironic that educated elites of peripheral countries protested against colonialism and Western domination only to fall under the spell of a revolutionary doctrine fashioned in the West. However, as we saw, the irony disappears if the doctrine is such that it undermines Western capitalism and calls for its demise. Less than its Western origin, Marxism's ability to give weapons against the West is what attracted most third world intellectuals to it. As Noel Parker pointed out,

"Colburn himself seems perversely content to conclude that the common revolutionary beliefs were present [in third world countries] solely by virtue of their transmission from person to person. This reasoning plainly fails to include consciousness 'on its own terms'. . . . Colburn's account [pays] no regard to what the beliefs actually say to those who hold them."[35] What the revolutionary discourse offered to peripheral intellectuals was a renovated nationalism that coupled the resistance against foreign domination with the rejection of tradition that their Western education stigmatized as backward. Hardly could intellectuals resist a Western discourse that also happened to cajole their nationalism.

Through its theory of imperialism as "a parasitic, decaying capitalism," Leninism attempts to shift the historical initiative from the West to Eastern and third world countries.[36] Having reached the stage of imperialism, the West is no longer the driving force of history. Socialist countries and countries that fight imperialism have become the progressive forces of history. We observe here a curious reversal. The colonial ideology had turned native peoples into backward peoples through the notion of a universal history defined according to Western norms. The dialectics inherent in the notion of progressive history reverses the claim, viewing the imperialist goal of the West, in its turn, as the great force of reaction, of blockage against universal progress. The driving force of history is thus no longer capitalism, but forces opposed to capitalism. In catapulting the third world countries from the periphery to the driver's seat of history together with socialist countries, Leninism proved a powerful spur to nationalist feelings.

The Promise of Swift Development

Leninism was all the more bound to have a huge impact on nationalism because it promised rapid socioeconomic development. It did so by a characteristic transformation of socialism into a theory of rapid and even social development. Donald L. Donham judiciously remarks: "The meaning of Marxism in Ethiopia came to be contained not so much in its utopian vision of human liberation—a theme familiar to Western Marxism—but in a story of how a weak and backward collection of nationalities, located outside of Western Europe, attained unity, wealth, and international respect: the allegory of the Russian and, later, the Chinese, revolution."[37] Indeed, had Marxism only meant to Ethiopians the implementation of social justice, it would have had a very limited impact. The Leninist component by which socialism promised a speedy means to get out of poverty and backwardness was the decisive addition.

Capitalism achieves development through the protracted and roundabout way of the market economy, with its ineluctable ups and downs, not to mention the inevitability of satellization by metropolitan capitalism. Not so for socialism, which construes development as a planned process, and hence as a means of achieving accelerated and uniform economic expansion. While the capitalist model of development appeared very slow and even impossible in an international context defined by the dominance of imperialism, the Soviet model offered the opportunity to bypass the problematic stage of capitalism and achieve rapid economic development. In combining the rectification of social injustices with accelerated development, the Soviet model "proved attractive to modernizing intellectuals who were intent on the rapid industrialization of their underdeveloped countries and for whom the capitalist route to industrialization that Marx had envisaged seemed neither available nor desirable."[38]

In addition to being impressed by the swift and extensive economic development first of the Soviet Union and then of China, Ethiopians became specifically attracted to the Soviet model of development because of the many similarities they saw between czarist Russia and Haile Selassie's Ethiopia. As in Russia, the existence of a repressive autocratic regime that not only defended an outdated and particularly reactionary nobility and Orthodox clergy but also instituted the dominance of one ethnic group over other conquered ethnic groups made the Soviet model highly appealing. Given these structural and ideological similarities, it was indeed hard not to assume that similar conditions required similar solutions. Moreover, enthrallment with the successes of the Soviet Union completely veiled the digression of students from their own history by allowing them to entertain the illusion that the Soviet path was simply unleashing the similarly great potential of their own history and culture.

A good testimony of the impact of Leninism on the Ethiopian educated elite is found in the ideological evolution of the late Eshetu Chole, a well-known Ethiopian economist and activist. In an article written in 1968 titled "Toward a Strategy of Development for Ethiopia," which appeared in *Dialogue*, the publication of the Ethiopian University Teachers' Association, Eshetu and his colleague Assefa Bequele underlined that the major hurdle to Ethiopia's development was agriculture. While other sectors of the economy showed some progress, an outdated land tenure system blocked the vast agricultural sector. They advocated an urgent land reform whose most noticeable character was that it did not refer to the necessity of socialism. They also called for better planning and financial policy on the part of the government as well as the elimination of corruption and inefficiency. This reformist or liberal approach reached a fairly optimistic conclusion:

> If the Ethiopian economy can overcome the obstacles we have pointed out, and there is no reason why it cannot, its prospects for growth are certainly bright. But we recognize that this is easier said than done. The energies of the nation and particularly of the leadership should now be devoted to the eradication of such major

hurdles, so that this ancient country may reawaken and face its future with a new sense of confidence.[39]

In an article that appeared two years later, this time in *Challenge*, Eshetu came up with a radically different strategy. He now believed that "socialism is imperative," even though his analysis of the impediments of the Ethiopian economy remained more or less the same.[40]

> Agricultural production is stifled by the feudal nature of production relations in that sector; genuine industrial development is impossible because of the nature of the domestic bourgeois class and the character of international imperialism. *It follows then that any kind of economic development with the prospects of improving the living standards of the masses of Ethiopians is impossible under the current framework of feudalism and imperialism.* It will not do to patch up certain parts of the system without fundamentally altering the structure. In other words, *what is required in Ethiopia now is not reform but revolution, meaning not merely a political revolution but a social revolution.*[41]

How is one to account for this drastic turnaround? In publishing the article in a journal that appeared in America rather than in Ethiopia, Eshetu may well have been expressing his real thoughts now that he was outside the reach of the repressive government. But it is also plausible that the article reflects a real doctrinal evolution on Eshetu's part, essentially imparted by the Leninist exclusion of the feasibility of reformist solutions in the era of imperialism. The arguments by which Eshetu dismisses reformism are entirely Leninist. Because of the association of imperialism with local comprador classes, the transition to capitalism "is no longer available to the native bourgeoisies of underdeveloped countries," he says.[42] Accordingly, a political revolution that only overthrows the traditional elite was seen as insufficient to remove the hurdles; a social revolution aimed at both removing the feudal class and opposing the capitalist road so as to initiate a socialist type of development was needed. Unmistakably, the alleged unfeasibility of the capitalist way, as opposed to the bright prospects of the socialist road to development, put socialism in league with nationalism.

The attraction of Leninism became greater in countries that coupled a long tradition of independence with a nationalist ideology defended by an imperial state. As in the cases of China and Russia, in Ethiopia too an old regime failed to live up to its traditional norms of independence and grandeur. In all such countries, the prospect of lagging behind or losing independence was understandably more difficult to accept than in countries without imperial traditions. Imperial regimes tend to breed a revolutionary youth because their failure frustrates a nationalist sentiment based on a tradition of grandeur. Moreover, the protracted legitimacy and extensive authority that imperial regimes have complicate their removal. Such regimes cannot be simply pushed aside; they must be overthrown, often violently.

Polarizing ideologies rather than reformist approaches seem necessary to challenge their deep-seated authority. Given that the promise of accelerated development appeared to offer a remedy to frustrated nationalists, Leninism could not but captivate the educated youth of Ethiopia.

Nationalism via Internationalism

An objection comes to mind: How does the assumption that Marxism-Leninism cajoles nationalism agree with the equally important commitment of the theory to internationalism? Enshrined in Marx's celebrated declaration "The workingmen have no country," internationalism is certainly not the kind of thought that encourages nationalist fervor.[43] What is more, Lenin's recognition of the right to self-determination of oppressed nationalities was a direct challenge to the very unity of Ethiopia. The danger of the breakup of Ethiopia became so real that a longtime activist, Hagos Gebre Yesus, used the term "national nihilism" to denounce students' endorsement of the right to self-determination.[44] Behind the endorsement, there is nothing but "national self-hatred and nihilism and . . . attachment to ethnicity and separatist politics based on ethnic, religious exclusiveness," he contended.[45] Student publications largely confirmed Hagos's fear. Thus, one editorial in *Struggle* wrote: "A true revolutionary is an internationalist, who has understood the dialectical developments of nature and society and who is above all deeply moved by the injustice humanity is subjected to. Thus, for a revolutionary, there are no regional, linguistic, national or even continental boundaries. The most significant factor is the economic exploitation and subsequent dehumanization of the oppressed classes."[46] We have already alluded to Walleligne's article in which the reality of Ethiopia as a nation is questioned on the ground that it is composed of various conquered and dominated nations. The endorsement of the Marxist-Leninist commitment to internationalism and to the right to self-determination was so categorical that, in the words of Randi Rønning Balsvik, "the feeling was rife that ideology had become more important to the students than the survival of Ethiopia as a state."[47]

Carefully read, student publications reflected a nationalist manifesto rather than national nihilism. The recognition of the right to self-determination was an attempt to preserve the unity of the student movement because it appealed to those students who were going over to ethnonationalism. The latter had become increasingly attractive to students coming from highly aggrieved ethnic groups, such as Eritrean, Tigrean, Oromo, and Gurage students. By revealing in ethnic oppression the dimension of class exploitation, Marxism-Leninism seemed to give a correct analysis of the existing reality, but even more so to offer a solution that fell short of advocating secession. As such, it proposed a pact between revolutionaries coming from oppressed and oppressing groups. Activating the sacrificial ethos on both sides, it demanded of Amhara students that they give up their traditional hegemony in exchange for students of marginalized groups abandoning their separatist goal. The mutual sacrifice sealed a new "nationalist" deal based on the common interests of the working masses.

Herein lies the considerable influence of Leninism on nationalist sentiment: it "offered a narrative of how to weld togetherr . . . disparate ethnic groups into a unitary state defined by the boundaries of a previous conquest—by Russians in the Soviet Union and by Amhara and Tigreans in Ethiopia."[48] Conversely, it was felt that liberalism could not achieve ethnic equality: the maintenance of the class structure will simply preserve the hegemony of the dominant ethnic group. Only the destruction of the class system could pave the way for the autonomy and equal rights of ethnic groups. Once working people from oppressed groups have exercised their right to self-determination, they would unite freely with their class brothers and sisters of conquering ethnicities.

This is exactly what Walleligne had in mind: his diatribes against Amhara domination turn into a calling to "build a genuine national state," which he defines as "a state where Amharas, Tigres, Oromos, Aderes, Somalis, Wollamos, Gurages, etc. are treated equally . . . where no nation dominates another nation be it economically or culturally."[49] But what about the support that Walleligne gave to secessionist movements? Here again, his support was conditional on the secessionist movements being genuinely socialist—the argument being that, with an internationalist outlook, "a socialist movement will never remain secessionist for good."[50] Clearly, the attempt was to strengthen the Ethiopian nation by transcending ethnic attachments through the internationalism of socialist ideology.

The Failure of Ethiopianism

The rise of a rival movement, expressly defining itself as "Ethiopianism," confirms that the safeguarding of Ethiopian nationalism was the concern, especially among many Amhara and Tigrean students. Moderate students initiated the movement to counter the Marxist-Leninist ideology, all the more so as radical students' support of the Eritrean secessionist movement had particularly antagonized nationalist feelings. Observing that the support of secessionism had weakened the influence of the radicals, moderate students saw the nationalist issue as an opportunity to rally the majority of students. An article published in *Struggle* under the title "Ethiopia and Ethiopianism" gives the following definition:

Ethiopianism is the concept that transcends personal, tribal, and regional loyalties. It is the belief held by the Ethiopian who thinks in terms of the people as a whole. . . . To him what matters is not his loyalty to one person, religious or tribal groups, but to the development of the people, as a whole. To him, the leader or the government is but the agent for carrying out the development and reforms needed to lessen the misery of the population.[51]

Written by an Ethiopian Muslim, the article visibly avoids Marxist-Leninist jargon, such as class struggle, revolution, and self-determination; instead, it advocates reformism, as it considers "the accumulation of wealth by a few individuals as undesirable, when there are millions struggling for a decent place in the sun."[52] Reforms pave the way for genuine national integration. They result in the creation of a nation of equal and free individuals through the transcending of linguistic, regional, and religious differences. That Ethiopianism is proposed as a rival ideology is made quite clear by another article in the same issue: "Existence of regionalism and tribalism (primitive sentiments) in Ethiopia are realities that we should accept; but what we should not accept is their perpetuation. But they do not die out by evasion and avoidance. They die out only when they are replaced by a higher and progressive ideology (such as Ethiopianism or Ethiopian Nationalism)."[53]

The moderate students who thought of using the ideology of Ethiopianism to counter the growing influence of Marxism-Leninism did not fully realize the extent to which Marxism-Leninism was an even more powerful seducer of nationalism. For one thing, the promotion of the interests of the oppressed and the exploited as a means of creating a truly united nation appeared more prospective, given the reluctance of the imperial regime to undertake any serious reform. For another, the Leninist proposal alone was likely to enlist the enthusiastic support of oppressed ethnic groups themselves. Above all, Ethiopianism was unlikely to counteract the influence of Marxism-Leninism because its proposals were not enough to undermine the imperial regime and inspire a movement of opposition. In a word, it was not a renovated nationalism: it neither articulated a clear strategy of economic development nor reinterpreted the traditional culture so as to make it conformable with modernization.

Let us reconsider the case of India. Nationalism became an effective and galvanizing ideology because Gandhi was able to reinterpret and revive the traditional culture. Speaking of the regeneration of Hinduism, an Ethiopian scholar rightly remarks: "Gandhi more than anyone gave the new generation intellectuals a 'new philosophy' that had the 'power of a new faith.' "[54] The regeneration is one of the reasons Indians did not summon Marxism-Leninism to resolve India's appalling social conditions. Likewise, Marxism did not seduce Japan because its ruling elite produced an aggressive nationalism. The firm resolution to counter imperialist forces advised the Japanese traditional leadership to rehabilitate and renew the traditional system through the Meiji Restoration. The renovation adapted traditional culture and institutions to the requirements of modernization, thereby retaining and even upgrading traditional nationalist fervor. This context of a renovated nationalism undercut Marxism-Leninism's attractiveness. By contrast, China failed to renew Confucianism with the consequence that it could not activate an aggressive nationalism able both to oppose foreign powers and to inspire serious reforms. As a result, Chinese students and intellectuals increasingly espoused Marxism-Leninism, which filled in for the failures of traditional nationalism.

The case of Ethiopia most closely reproduced the Chinese condition. Marxism-Leninism was a substitute for an unrenovated nationalism, crippled as the traditional nationalism was by the uprooting effect of the educational system and the lack of needed reforms to spur socioeconomic growth. It is therefore not contradictory to assume that the frustration of nationalism is one reason so many young educated Ethiopians turned to Marxism-Leninism in the sixties and early seventies. While in becoming Marxist-Leninists they were going against important features of their legacy, the enchanting promises of socialism made these rejections seem worthwhile, and so negation metamorphosed into an expression of higher fidelity. Accordingly, Marxism-Leninism became the ideology of those driven by "radical nationalism," which became all the more tumultuous as disillusionments over the imperial regime grew.[55] The next chapter will deal directly with these disillusionments in an effort to establish the objective or structural conditions that sustained the radicalization of Ethiopian students and intellectuals.

9

Objective Causes of the Radicalization of Students and Intellectuals

The term "objective causes" refers to socioeconomic and political conditions, and the attempt here is to assess their impact on the radicalization of Ethiopian students and intellectuals. It may surprise some readers that I have waited until the last chapter to explore structural conditions. The dominant view among social scientists, not to speak of Marxist scholars, attributes the primary cause of social discontent and uprisings to socioeconomic conditions and considers cultural motivations as accessories, or worse yet, as mere effects of economic crises. This study has often alluded to the one-sidedness of the structural approach; now is the time to outline the main reasons why the primacy typically given to structural conditions obscures rather than clarifies the phenomenon of political radicalization.

Insufficiency of the Structural Approach

As already indicated, most studies attribute the radicalization of the Ethiopian student movement to economic woes. The general economic stagnation of the country generated, so the studies say, a deep discontent first among the educated elite and students and then among workers and peasants. In order to mobilize a large number of people against the imperial regime, students and intellectuals started to echo the interests of workers and peasants, and so increasingly adopted positions calling for radical social changes. As one Ethiopian author puts it,

> Stagnation in the modern economic sector thus frustrated the illusion of rapid development of capitalist transformation. The possible emergence of the national bourgeoisie was aborted; marginalization of the educated petty-bourgeoisie turned it towards radicalism. Every avenue of promotion within the old system being closed to it, the radicalization of the petty-bourgeoisie was expressed in its identification with the causes of peasants and workers. The petty-bourgeoisie class took the lead in the attack on the old regime.[1]

The problem with this type of explanation is the discrepancy between the political ideology of the educated petite bourgeoisie and the objective conditions. The very backwardness and stagnation of the social system indicated that nothing in the social reality was anywhere near to requiring a socialist transformation. Without throwing away the evolutionary scheme of Marxist philosophy altogether, it should be stressed that socialist ideology cannot be deduced from structural conditions unfit even for capitalism. Moreover, the struggle for bourgeois rights, such as freedom of expression and association, could have been enough both to mobilize workers and peasants and to threaten seriously Haile Selassie's autocratic regime. For instance, the fight for the right to strike would have given workers a better opportunity to improve their conditions of life than the nationalization of the means of production. Likewise, mobilization for the creation of political parties would have shaken the foundations of the autocratic regime. Without the involvement of cultural components, it is just not possible to deduce from the objective conditions any incentive for students and intellectuals to adopt the Marxist-Leninist ideology.

Discontent over economic hardships was undoubtedly high during the last years of Haile Selassie's reign. What is less evident, however, is the association of discontent with radicalization. According to many authors, the lack of economic development created the conviction that capitalism was not the right path to follow. Yet, a more logical conclusion would have been to put the blame, not on capitalism, but on the obstructions to capitalism and on the failure to mobilize people for serious reforms. As we have seen, what led to the discarding of the reformist approach was less the existing reality than the global ideological hegemony of Marxism-Leninism. Besides, the identification of the educated petite bourgeoisie with the interests of workers and peasants does not exclude reformism. If the identification led to the extreme option of a socialist shakeup, then the least demanding and most reasonable option of democratic reforms was even more feasible. Neither workers nor peasants made demands echoing calls for a socialist transformation. Instead, all were interested in democratic reforms as much as the petite bourgeoisie was. The truth is that the proliferation of revolutionary groups among students and intellectuals gave a bad name to reformism.

Of course, revolutionary uprisings, of whatever magnitude, can hardly occur without some deep level of frustration over conditions of life. On this point I fully subscribe to the dominant view, for why would people engage in disruptive activities unless they have good reasons to rebel? Nonetheless, the importance attached to socioeconomic conditions merely confirms the primacy of cultural issues. For economic growth is itself unthinkable without a prior revival of culture by which alone societies convert to modern values and methods. Recall Max Weber's groundbreaking contribution to the study of modernization and economic growth, namely, the demonstration of the concrete link existing between Protestantism and the rise of capitalism. For Weber, the Protestant renovation of Christianity encouraged worldliness through the reading of wealth accumulation as a sign of election. According to many scholars, Weber actually inspired modernization theory, that is, the very school that countered Marxist economic determination by maintaining that "attitudinal and value changes or re-interpretations of ideology are essential prerequisites to creating a modern society and economy."[2]

Let us agree that frustrations over conditions of life are rare in a context of sustained economic growth. The ultimate cause of revolution must then be assigned to cultural demission or dysfunctionality, since the inability to initiate economic takeoff in a given country is the very failure that prepares the ground for revolutionary uprising. Where no cultural renovation in some form has occurred, economic development also tends to be elusive. It is indeed hard to assume that a society can initiate and sustain a process as complex and challenging as economic growth without some form of cultural renovation by which it alters some of its beliefs and values and takes charge of the development process.

A crucial assumption of this study is that revolutionism takes root under conditions of cultural dislocation, which gives advantage to underground, culturally heterodox groups. In thus tying the rise of revolutionism to the lack of economic modernization, the assumption brings out their common underlying cause. By blocking modernization, cultural dysfunctionality also lays the ground for the rise of political radicalism. It does so by generating the need to restructure the system of values and beliefs, and not by being a mere reflection of objective conditions, as Marxist scholars would have it. The need to overcome the dislocation provides an opening for new ideas, especially for those ideas promising rapid modernization. While elite groups undertake the ideological exploration, the same need makes the larger society vulnerable, thereby creating opportunity for radical groups to attract followers.

Value/System Approach to Revolution

To strengthen my analysis, I will appeal to the theory known as the value/system approach to revolution. Going against those theories explaining social revolutions by frustrations over a severe lack of economic development, such as the relative deprivation theory and Marxism, the value/system approach argues that material discontent is not enough to trigger a revolution. Such dissatisfaction may explain demonstrations and protests, but not revolutions, which target the social order. Since revolution primarily means the violent overthrow of the existing social order, social protests reach the revolutionary stage only when the ruling class and the state lose their legitimacy to rule. In the words of Chalmers Johnson, the main proponent of value/system theory,

"The prime characteristic of revolutionary conditions . . . is the 'loss of authority.' "[3]

Given the nature of the social order, coercion alone does not maintain, under normal conditions, social inequalities; they also are undergirded by belief in their necessity and benefit to the entire community, and hence their legitimacy. The belief "stresses that society is a 'moral community,' a collectivity of people who share certain 'definitions of the situation' (called 'values'), which legitimize the inequalities of social organization and cause people to accept them as morally justified."[4] Religious, mythical, and metaphysical beliefs back the moral justification that values provide for social action and stratification. The system of beliefs and values justifying social inequalities is, therefore, constitutive of the social order.

So long as the value system does not come under threat, the state and the ruling class conserve their legitimacy. The conservation of legitimacy rules out the use of violence, and hence the possibility of revolution. In such a situation, people use other means than violence to express their grievances, however frustrated they may be. By contrast, if the system of beliefs justifying both the state's monopoly of violence and social inequalities is undermined, revolution is on the horizon. The liberating impact of the decline of the legitimizing ideology drives people to reclaim their right to use violence and challenge the social order. What this means is clear enough: the stability and the good functioning of a social system depend on the harmony between its value system and the various components of social organization. When the component parts work in harmony, the system achieves equilibrium. But if discrepancy occurs, the system loses its equilibrium and becomes dysfunctional.

If the operations of the political system are notably at odds with dominant values, provided certain facilitating conditions are realized, revolution becomes likely. Thus, the "essential, defining factor of a revolutionary situation is a state of severe disequilibrium in the society."[5] Once disequilibrium materializes resulting in the loss of legitimacy of those who control power, the system is at the mercy of incidents, which can easily degenerate into protests and riots. Among the catalysts or accelerators, we find defeat in war, natural disaster, and economic setback. These incidents are not the primary cause of the revolution; they simply give expression to the deeper disenchantment already undermining the system.

What can cause a social system to fall out of equilibrium and become dysfunctional by generating a tension between the value system and the social order? Johnson suggests that the causes can be either exogenous or endogenous. Endogenous causes refer to internal innovations, as in the case of a technological breakthrough or new cultural movement. The Renaissance, the Reformation, and the Enlightenment are examples of endogenous causes that led to important value changes. This type of change requires the transformation of the social order in accordance with the new beliefs. For instance, a new sense of human dignity can redefine rights, and thus call for a redistribution of wealth and power. Under exogenous causes, we find the demonstration effect arising from cultural or technological borrowings from foreign countries. In particular, Johnson rightly reminds us that "the effect of foreign education and travel on many students from European colonies was primarily to alter their values."[6]

The focus on the value system shows the great importance that the functionalist approach accords to ideological issues. A new religion or a new social ideology can foster a revolutionary situation for the simple reason that it undermines the ideological bonds existing between the masses and the ruling elite. The loss of legitimacy of the ruling elite soon follows the breakdown of ideological consensus and cohesion. Accordingly, what causes revolution is less people's material frustration than the prior breakdown of social consensus. More exactly, material discontent exasperates the breakdown, leading to a social explosion.

How is one to explain the openness to alternative ideologies? One of the effects of the disequilibrium is that the old value system no longer makes sense to the people. Consequently, "people in the society become disoriented, and hence open to conversion to the alternative values proposed by a revolutionary movement."[7] Just as it induces the need for new beliefs among ordinary people, cultural disorientation encourages dissident groups to reinvent values or to be receptive to deviant ideological expressions coming from outside. With their promise to reinstate the social equilibrium, groups advocating the new values are promoted to the leadership of the social protests. Only when social protests fall under the influence of culturally dissident factions do they become radicalized and liable to change into social revolutions.

Without the context of cultural disorientation by which people become open to new beliefs, economic crises by themselves cannot initiate a revolutionary movement. And as we have seen, what happened to Ethiopia's educated elite was exactly a deep cultural disorientation subsequent to its exposure to Western education and the inability of the ruling elite to renovate the traditional value system. The cultural disorientation allowed new beliefs to take hold and facilitated the appearance of culturally dissident groups, who then became influential as the economic crises of the imperial regime deepened. Put otherwise, only when economic plights are combined with cultural dislocation do they produce revolutionary movements. Their specific contribution is to create opportunity for radical groups to assume the leadership of social protests. Without economic crises, such groups remain isolated minorities with no ascendancy over large form of protests. In a context of cultural dislocation already in progress, the eruption of economic crises propels underground groups to positions of political leadership, thus allowing them to present their own cultural idiosyncrasies in terms of a resynchronization of the value system and the social order. With this approach firmly in mind, we can examine the economic hardships that contributed to the radicalization of Ethiopian students.

Discontent over Conditions of Life

To have a good idea of the impacts of economic stagnation and crises, some knowledge of the class composition of the Ethiopian student body is necessary. For economic woes are particularly unbearable to students coming from humble and poor families. Though not fully reliable, existing data show that the majority of students came from a poor family background. According to Randi Rønning Balsvik, "Among the 448 freshmen who entered the university in 1969, 58 percent came from the two lowest groups, 14 percent from the poor category. Two percent came from very rich and 10 percent from the rich families, leaving 26.5 percent in the upper middle category (3.5 percent could not be classified)."[8] We should add that some 20–25 percent of the student population came from a rural background. Also, the number of students from the upper classes was slightly reduced because many were sent abroad for university studies. Even so, close to 40 percent of students were from wealthy and middle-class backgrounds, that is, from social groups that constituted roughly 10 percent of the Ethiopian population, while the majority of the students came from the lowest groups comprising 90 percent of the population.

To draw radicalization from the fact that the majority of students had a background of poverty would be a hasty conclusion. For one thing, as many studies of student movements indicate, the most radical students do not belong to poor families. In the Ethiopian case, those sent abroad were actually more radicalized and had a deeper theoretical knowledge of Marxism than students who never went abroad. For another, poor family background can encourage conservatism as much as radicalization. As already stated, unlike upper- and middle-class students, students belonging to low-income families can tend to develop conservative views because they see university studies as an opportunity for upward mobility within the existing system. As author Donald K. Emmerson puts it,

> Lower social origin leads to leftward politicization because the student is poor, disoriented, frustrated, and identifies more easily with the deprived strata in society, or, on the contrary, that lower social origin leads to conservative or apolitical careerism because the student identifies with higher social strata, whose ranks he has a longed-for chance to enter, because he lacks the economic margin to allow for "time wasted" in politics, and because radical political activity might endanger his career security and the enjoyment of material advantages hitherto denied him.[9]

What is undeniable, however, is that the occurrence of a severe economic crisis can have a particularly mobilizing impact on students from lower social backgrounds. This fact can explain the growing number of Ethiopian students joining the radical opposition, given that the economic crises of the imperial regime deepened in the late sixties and early seventies.

All studies of the Ethiopian student movement underline the appalling conditions of campus life. Students constantly complained about inadequate library, laboratory, and classroom facilities as well as about overcrowded dormitories and deficient food supplies. Numerous reports indicate that students felt that they were underfed, that the services were slow and inefficient, that the time-consuming queues for food were unbearable, and that cleanliness in the cafeteria left much to be desired.[10] This was so true that undernourishment caused food riots at times, as many students, notably those coming from rural areas, did not have additional financial support from their families to make up for nutritional deficiencies.

Conditions deteriorated further as the number of students steadily increased. Because the budget allocated to the university did not increase in proportion to the number of students enrolled, each passing year amplified the deterioration. In the early years of the university, students were actually well treated, even pampered. They "all held government scholarships that included room, board, tuition, textbooks, uniforms, medical care, and laundry and other housekeeping services."[11] These privileged conditions were terminated in 1962 when the government replaced the university boarding system with a stipend of Eth. Birr 50 for food and lodging. Reports assessing the effects of the change speak of dreadful conditions of existence. The houses that students could afford to rent were described as "'wholly unsatisfactory', 'awful', 'deplorable', 'old and dilapidated', and often lacked electricity, adequate toilet and sanitary facilities, and privacy for study."[12] Moreover, the rooms were located "at a considerable distance from the university, making it very difficult for students to participate in activities and use the library in the evening."[13] Worse yet, while rents soon increased, the stipend remained the same, further plunging students into economic distress. Students were allowed to move back onto the campuses in 1965, with the consequence that overcrowdedness reached an all-time high, as "no permanent, decent living quarters had been built for students since the mid-1950s."[14]

These constant causes of discontent are important not so much because they directly caused radicalization but because they provided opportunities for ideologically motivated individuals to agitate and radicalize their fellow students. Studies of various student movements have established that "an agitational campaign against an increase in university fees, ostensibly a campus-based issue, will be led by ideologically committed students."[15] The opportunity for radical students to agitate is all the greater when, as was the case in Ethiopia, students suffer from appalling living conditions. In vehemently denouncing these conditions, radical students appeared as staunch defenders of the interests of students, and not merely as ideologically motivated agitators. This defense of student interests stilled the usual suspicion against political agitators, but even more so allowed radical students to mobilize the student population around concrete and vital issues. That these forms of mobilization then facilitated their rise to the leadership of the movement cannot be disputed.

According to many observers, the fear of unemployment was another radicalizing factor. As already indicated, until the late 1950s the Ethiopian economy was able to employ the educated manpower. But as the number of students increased, the sluggish economy had more and more difficulty in absorbing new influxes of university graduates. The difficulty turned into utter incapacity when economic development drastically slowed in the mid-1960s, creating a serious gap between the supply of educated manpower and the actual needs of the economy. The deterioration was such that "by the mid-1960s, even university graduates were unemployed. In 1966, for example, as many as 136 of these were unable to find work. . . . In 1968, of 937 graduates from the vocational-technical institutes, as many as 636 were unemployed."[16]

The growing number of dropouts further aggravated the problem of unemployment. With the student population steadily growing, the more living conditions and university facilities deteriorated, the higher the number of dropouts became. At the university level, a point was reached "where approximately 40 percent of the students failed to graduate."[17] The problem had become so severe that a 1966 report of an advisory committee stated a clear warning: "We believe that with little or no increase in intake of students, the production of graduates can be doubled if, for the next five years the resources of the university are concentrated on reducing academic failure. A 'drop-out' is not only an unfinished product: he is also a potentially resentful and uncooperative citizen."[18] The problem was not confined to the university; it also included high school students. According to Girma Amare, "The failure rate at the school leaving certificate examination was worse; in 1951–1952, 75.9 percent of those who sat for the examination passed; in 1961–1962, only 22.2 percent; in 1971, only 17.9 percent."[19]

Since even university graduates had difficulty finding employment, college and high school dropouts had nowhere to turn, as many of them could not even return to the villages from which they came. Among these dropouts, many lived by menial jobs while others joined the armed forces. Still more became teachers by enrolling "in one of the many short-term crash programs organized by the Ministry of Education before they were deployed to provincial schools."[20] Analyzing the harmful consequences of dropouts invading the important sectors of education and national defense,

Girma lucidly writes: "The most disgruntled members of the younger generation were given access to the most vital sectors of Ethiopian society: the military and education. By opening these institutions to such groups in order to find a momentary instead of lasting solution to the economic problems, the government took a path which would prove disastrous to it."[21] Not only were these angered dropouts susceptible to radicalization, but they were also able to infiltrate sectors of Ethiopian society most liable to swift politicization. Future events confirm the crucial role of dropouts in the radicalization of the Ethiopian Armed Forces. But keep in mind that, however much these dropouts were disgruntled, their radicalization was an outcome of a more complex process. Their anger can explain their uprising against Haile Selassie's regime but not their commitment to turn everything upside down by becoming Marxist-Leninist zealots.

The Impact of U.S. Policy

According to many authors, the Ethiopian student movement adopted Marxism-Leninism in reaction to U.S. policy toward Ethiopia. These authors argue that the continuous financial, diplomatic, and military support that the U.S. government provided to the imperial regime is the reason the movement turned "antiimperialist and anti-U.S., denouncing the United States as the prime supporter of the imperial regime."[22] In the students' determination to fight the regime, the all-out and unconditional support of the U.S. government gave them no other choice than to oppose both governments by espousing socialist ideology.

So presented, this thesis seems excessive for at least two major reasons. First, as stated earlier, given the autocratic nature of the imperial government, liberal ideology was as unsettling for the regime, if not more so, than was Marxist-Leninist ideology. Second, the support of the United States could have been perfectly denounced through a commitment to liberal values, which would have amounted to asking the American government to be faithful to its own ideals.

Such a criticism does not mean that U.S. involvement did not have a swelling impact, especially in a context of cultural disorientation that, we know, favors the ascendancy of radical students. The fact that Western governments, going against their own beliefs, supported Ethiopian absolutism provided radicalized students with additional arguments. They thus underlined the huge disparity between theory and practice and used the discrepancy to discredit liberalism in the eyes of the majority of students. Liberal values were thus increasingly associated with hypocrisy and duplicity, with the outcome being a generalized suspicion against capitalism. Inversely, the competing ideology of socialism assumed the virtue of uniting theory and practice, all the more so as socialist countries were distinguishing themselves by taking the lead in the crusade against the alliance of Western countries with third world reactionary regimes. The condemnation of the alliance created a link between a nationalist stand and the adoption of socialist ideology, in direct contrast to liberalism, which came to signify acceptance of imperialist hegemony.

The occurrence of a progressive shift among Ethiopian students provides the best evidence that radicalized students' denunciation of U.S. support caused disenchantment with liberal values. Numerous studies show that most Ethiopian students were very sympathetic to the United States and capitalism in the early 1960s. A questionnaire given to seven hundred Ethiopian students in 1960–61 attests that they put the United States at the very top of all nations. "The United States was reportedly admired for maintaining individual freedom, democracy, and a high standard of living, as well as for its aid to other nations," writes Balsvik.[23] The wide admiration for America and the American mode of life continued even as many students, doubting Haile Selassie's reformist will, had concluded that he should be removed.

The astonishing shift of a great number of students and intellectuals from liberalism to socialism points to the growing ascendancy of radicalized groups, who equated the removal of the imperial regime with commitment to socialism. Rightly, Balsvik writes: "Despite favorable attitudes toward the United States, the active few who were also makers of opinion began questioning U.S. virtues, although their opinions were relatively benign until the Vietnam War had raged for some time."[24] Radicalized groups perfectly understood that the mere denunciation of imperial absolutism was not enough to establish their ideological hegemony; they had also to sully capitalism. They did so by denouncing the support that capitalist countries, especially the United States, gave to the hated regime of Haile Selassie. Their campaign bore fruit: the pro-Americanism of the educated elite gradually disappeared. To have an idea of the evolution, consider the situation when in 1960 General Mengistu Neway, the commander of the Imperial Guard, attempted to depose the emperor. To justify the need for change, he invoked liberal values and did not denounce U.S. imperialism. Demonstrating their commitment to a liberal type of change, university students supported his unsuccessful attempt.

What needs to be emphasized here is that the United States' unconditional support of the imperial regime led not only to the denunciation of American involvement in Ethiopian affairs but also to a general disillusionment with liberalism even among formerly enthusiastic proponents. Unraveling the paradox of liberal education producing hardliner Marxist-Leninists, Addis Hiwet correctly notes: "Even if one were generously to assume that US educational policy sought to produce (Jeffersonian) democrats in Ethiopia, 'the support the West was giving to the oppressive Ethiopian regime' and ruthless dictatorships in the chain of the 'free world' subverted and nullified it."[25] The total support given to the imperial regime also subverted what Western education tried to inculcate, in that it allowed radical groups to charge Western values and institutions with duplicity. Indeed, Western governments' support of the imperial regime—while they knew perfectly well how extensive was its oppression and its opposition to Western principles of democracy and freedom—could not but make students receptive to the Marxist-Leninist arguments. These arguments portrayed bourgeois democracy as fake and deceptive and consecrated socialism as the only ideology of honest people. So glaring a contradiction between theory and practice served to prepare the ground for radicalization through the systematic rejection of hypocritical bourgeois democracy.

The negative impact of U.S. foreign policy on the mental makeup of the Ethiopian educated elite tended to tarnish whatever was American. Sandra Rickard gives the following testimony: "When one Ethiopian calls another Ethiopian 'American,' it is a derogatory term. I asked various students what the term means and found that it connotes 'selfishness,' 'a non-caring attitude towards others,' 'a desire to work for one's self,' 'one who is disrespectful to elders, or one who is sloppy in dress.' "[26] This anti-American attitude of students, mostly fed by the support that the U.S. government gave Haile Selassie's regime, is, no doubt, one of the reasons Marxism-Leninism captured the majority of Ethiopian students.

Condemnations of U.S. policy were all the more unavoidable as it had a global provenance. As people in Asia, Latin America, Africa, and the Middle East claimed to be fighting U.S. imperialist policy, this globalism imparted to anti-Americanism a normative character. That Western scholars and teachers joined the movement by denouncing the negative impacts of imperialism on underdeveloped countries reinforced the normativeness of anti-Americanism. Ethiopian students could not but feel the pressure to be in line with the global movement, to add their voice to the general outcry against imperialism, especially as the war in Vietnam dragged on. Combining the domestic and international sources of anti-Americanism, Balsvik writes: "Ethiopian student views about U.S. foreign policy must be seen in the light of worldwide student opposition to what was perceived as U.S. imperialistic and aggressive policy in the underdeveloped world. Equally, it must be seen in terms of Ethiopian student resentment at the deep and intricate involvement of the United States in Ethiopian affairs."[27]

Ethnicity and Radicalization

Some scholars—especially those from dominated ethnic groups—see Ethiopia's ethnic problem as the main driving force behind the radicalization of the student movement. They argue that the movement, which intensified in the early 1960s, took a radical turn later in the decade through adoption of Marxist-Leninist ideology essentially to accommodate the mounting struggles that oppressed ethnic groups, notably the Eritreans, the Tigreans, the Somalis, and the Oromos, waged against Amhara rule. The student movement could not continue its opposition to the imperial regime without addressing the growing demand for the democratization of the Ethiopian state through the dismantling of its imperial structure. For many scholars from oppressed regions, the deep cause of the 1974 Revolution was none other than the need to smash the political and economic structure of Amhara hegemony over other ethnic groups. As scholar Asafa Jalata writes: "The longstanding contradictions between the Ethiopian ruling class, state, and imperialism on one hand, and the colonized nations and the Ethiopian masses on the other hand caused two types of crises in 1974: the revolutionary crisis from below and the crisis of the ruling class and the state at the top."[28]

Believing that liberalism provided the necessary solution, the student movement called at first for a democratic society in which all Ethiopians would have equal rights regardless of their ethnic origin. The great shift occurred when Walleligne Mekonnen's article stated that ethnic groups are actually nations dominated by the Amhara ruling class. As we saw, the article maintained that Ethiopia is not yet a nation, that what is called Ethiopia is simply the imposition of Amhara culture and interests on conquered nations. The use of the concept of dominated nations gave dignity to the resistance against the imperial regime by transforming what so far was belittled as tribalism into national liberation movements. The significant contribution of Walleligne's article lies in the "conceptual change he introduced into the ongoing political and academic discourse by raising the status of non-Amhara peoples in the Ethiopian empire from 'tribes' to nations and nationalities," says Oromo scholar Mekuria Bulcha.[29] Consequently, provided they were socialist, Walleligne supported all the uprisings of oppressed groups, including their right to self-determination. Such movements weakened the regime, but most of all they were liberation movements that fought for the empowerment of working people. Not to support their struggles amounted to allying with the imperial regime and, worse yet, to opposing socialism in the name of a nationalism that reflected nothing more than the dominance of the Amhara ruling elite.

We have already attributed the drastic shift from liberalism to ethnonationalism to what Hagos Gebre Yesus called "national nihilism." Walleligne was an Amhara, and yet going against his own culture and legacy, he did not hesitate to question the status of Ethiopia as a nation. Hardly is it possible to explain this extraordinary self-depreciation without alluding to the prior devaluation of Ethiopian culture and history through the absorption of Eurocentric concepts. Plunged in a severe identity crisis as a result of his Westernized education's marginalizing of Ethiopia, Walleligne could no longer defend this legacy in which he saw nothing but a backward system of cultural and social domination.

Far from ethnic problems accounting for the radicalization of Ethiopian students, the prior commitment to Marxism-Leninism explains the abandonment of the liberal approach. If the issue of ethnic equality progressively appeared unsolvable with a liberal approach, the reason is not so much the inadequacy of liberalism as the need to be consistent with the commands of Marxist-Leninist doctrine. In other words, the students' need for doctrinal consistency, which need authenticated their radical commitment, led them to posit the issue of dominated peoples in terms of dominated nations, even though no historical facts whatsoever supported their new reading. Their overriding concern was the compliance of their approach with Leninism, which required the socialist solution and endorsed the right to self-determination. Anything short of viewing dominated ethnic groups as nations and nationalities would have validated the liberal approach.

A related distortion of the application of Leninism to the Ethiopian context is the interpretation of the southern expansion of Ethiopia as a colonial conquest. The expansion refers to Emperor Menelik's forced incorporation of what are today the southern and eastern parts of Ethiopia. According to some scholars, the doubling of the size of the empire through the incorporation of neighboring peoples at the exact time European powers were vying for colonial possessions in Africa was nothing short of a colonial conquest. This colonial interpretation of the southern expansion does no more than confirm the extent to which Ethiopian history and culture were being depicted through Eurocentric concepts.[30] Once the colonial grid is introduced, the requirement to get rid of the alien ruler is added to oppression and domination and the demand for self-determination overtakes the aspiration for equal rights. The issue is no more the termination of Amhara domination and oppression through democratic changes, but the dismantling of the colonial empire and the accession to independence for ethnonational groups. Rather than calling for a democratic process of national integration, the colonial reading thus aims for nothing less than the political dismantling of Ethiopia.

The history of the Ethiopian student movement shows that a great number of students dragged their feet in endorsing the Leninist solution to ethnic inequality. Aware of the danger of the Leninist idea of self-determination, some students proposed, as indicated in the last chapter, Ethiopianism as a renovated nationalism. Ethiopianism transcended both imperial Ethiopia and ethnic loyalty through the assertion of equal rights and the promotion of national integration; it defined Ethiopia as the integrated unity of free and equal citizens. Moving on the offensive, groups of students that also included activist students denounced the Leninist approach as a promotion of tribalism and national divisions. The offensive proved successful: "The 1967 annual meeting of NUEUS debated the national issue and passed strongly worded resolutions condemning 'sectarian movements in Ethiopia,' labeling supporters of the movements petty bourgeois opportunists and reactionary elements that were encouraged by reactionary Arab forces. . . . The meeting declared Eritrea an indivisible part of Ethiopia."[31] If there was one issue against which the majority resisted the pressure of the radicals, it was the commitment to Ethiopian national unity. Many students were willing to follow the radicals all the way except here. So strong was nationalist sentiment that in the 1968 student union election the candidate of the radicals, Tilahun Gizaw, lost the presidency to Makonnen Bishaw, who represented the moderate view. The radicals explained their defeat by alleging that "students were deceived by professional agitators" who spread rumors suggesting they were in league with secessionist movements.[32]

In light of the deep concern for national unity, how is one to explain the final triumph of Walleligne's position? There was, of course, the important incentive of doctrinal consistency: the more loudly one claimed to be Marxist-Leninist, the harder it became to resist the endorsement of the right to self-determination. The preservation of the unity of students was another cause for the prevalence of the Leninist approach. It was felt that the movement could not maintain its unity unless it took a clear stand against Amhara domination and for the promotion of oppressed peoples. No other way existed to ensure the continued participation of Oromo, Eritrean, Gurage, and Tigrean students in the movement than to concede, in the spirit of genuine equality, the rank of nations and nationalities to dominated ethnic groups. Such recognition was all the more crucial because, of all ethnic groups, Tigrean students were "the most politically active on campus."[33]

No less important were the ideological arguments. Radicals had succeeded in convincing many students that the emphasis of liberalism on individual rights was not the right remedy, unable as it was to structurally undermine Amhara dominance. In the context of the primacy of individual rights, the promotion of individual equality regardless of ethnic belonging is not enough to dismantle an already established dominance. Oppressed ethnics must organize themselves as autonomous groups to conquer and affirm their rights. While the liberal model underscores the rights of the individual, the Leninist formula recognizes group rights. The recognition creates the political reality necessary to tear down the oppressive structure. Above all, the acknowledgment of the right to self-determination is the best way to preserve the unity of Ethiopia for the obvious reason that achievement of real equality would remove the main motive why people want to secede in the first place. Explaining that revolutionaries do not advocate the right to self-determination to promote balkanization, a study published by the Ethiopian Students Union in North America writes: "Revolutionaries strive to create as large a state as possible, for this is to the advantage of the laboring masses; they strive to bring about a rapprochement between nationalities and their further fusion, but they desire to achieve this aim not by violence, but exclusively through free, fraternal union of workers and the toiling masses of all nationalities."[34] Western governments' support of Haile Selassie's regime made easier the repudiation of liberalism as an inadequate solution. And since without genuine equality Ethiopian unity could not be safeguarded, recognition of the right to self-determination appeared as the only correct solution.

The challenge of the Eritrean insurgency further strengthened the commitment of the student movement to the Leninist formula. Even if I do not fully follow Tekeste Negash when he says "it would hardly be an exaggeration to state that it was in response to the Eritrean challenge that the Ethiopian student movement began to develop a strategy for resolving the problems of nation-building," there is no denying that Eritrean students contributed significantly to the ethnicization of student politics in Ethiopia.[35] The ethnicization spread first to Tigrean and then to Oromo students, thus forcing the student movement to find a solution to the national problem. Moreover, the Eritrean armed resistance provoked both admiration and the tendency to emulate. Some factions in the student movement began to advocate the creation of a guerrilla movement to overthrow the imperial regime.

The influence of the Eritrean resistance grew with the emergence from within the insurgency of a Marxist-Leninist guerrilla faction, the Eritrean People's Liberation Front (EPLF). Not only did the Front become "the vanguard of the radical opposition by its doctrine, its organization and its mobilizing power," but also radical students could now support the insurgency in the name both of doctrinal consistency and partnership with a fighting ally.[36] To recognize the EPLF was tantamount to supporting the struggle of the Eritrean working masses. What is more, given the ideological orientation of the Front, the only way to accommodate Eritrea within the unity of Ethiopia was to initiate a socialist revolution and implement the Leninist solution. Since "the formula, disunite to unite, was behind Ethiopian students' attempts to work out a stand on the Eritrean matter," no better way existed to prove the loyalty of the student movement to Marxism-Leninism than to support the Eritrean insurgency.[37]

Radicalizing Impact of Repression

Many scholars ascribe the main reason for the radicalization of Ethiopian students to Haile Selassie's repressive policy. Thus Bahru Zewde writes: "The fact that the emperor made no allowance for even moderate opposition meant that opposition could manifest itself only in a radical form."[38] The history of the relations of the Ethiopian student movement to the government and university officials shows a constant tension interspersed with moments of acute crisis and sometimes bloody confrontations. The reactions of the government and the university administration to student demands and protests exhibit a characteristic pattern. Students come up with demands related to political issues or campus life. The rejection of the demands provokes disturbances, which lead to the prohibition of the student union and publications, and at times to imprisonment of students and closure of the university. After some time, however, the government backs down, reopens the university, releases imprisoned students, and reinstates the student union.

Scholars of student movements are quite familiar with the radicalizing impact of repressive regimes on students. Take the case of Philippine students under President Ferdinand Marcos. When Marcos shut down all democratic institutions and imposed martial law on the Philippines in 1972, the student movement reacted by shifting its initial moderation to radical views. The shift is easily explained: "Repression during martial law eliminated all options for political activity, which in turn led to greater militancy and radicalism among students."[39] Another pertinent case is Nicaragua: radicalization was the response of Nicaraguan students in the 1970s to the repressive policy of the Somoza regime. Their initial moderate stand gradually favored the socialist ideology of the Sandinistas because President Anastasio Somoza's "exclusive rule and centralization of power drastically limited the capacity of the moderate political organizations and thus encouraged radicalism among students."[40] The radicalization of Iranian and Moroccan students had a similar cause: in both cases, repressive government policies made moderate positions unfeasible.

The evolution of the Ethiopian student movement fully confirms the general pattern: in opting for a repressive policy, the imperial government only succeeded in antagonizing students further and pushing them into the hands of radical students. Let there be no misunderstanding: repression does not *create* radical groups; the latter always exist, even in an open and democratic society, as they are related, as we saw in the previous chapters, to movements of ideas subsequent to cultural dislocations. However, repressive regimes give radical groups audience and attraction and end up propelling them to the leadership of discontented students. Repression explains not the emergence of radical groups and ideas but their ability to spread and assume the leadership of student protests. In replying to students' demands with repression, governments do in fact shore up the radicals' arguments as to the futility of expecting change. Where no such regime exists, radical groups tend to remain isolated minority factions, however vocal and organized they may be.

The forceful message of governments' use of repressive methods is their rigid stand against change and their refusal to negotiate. Some such perception of government policy makes the reformist approach utterly irrelevant. This is exactly what happened in Ethiopia: as the government consistently responded to students' most elementary demands with repression and not even once showed its readiness to listen to them, it undermined moderation among students pushing them toward the radical position of Marxist-Leninist groups. The repeated use of repression progressively invited the conclusion that the government must be overthrown, which radicals were quick to present as a vindication of their long-standing position. With the conviction that revolution had become necessary, moderation was perceived as futile, with the consequence that a growing number of students began to cross the line and fill the ranks of activists.

In undermining moderation, repressive governments directly weaken moderate leaders in the eyes of the student population. Since to any demand, however mild it is, such governments respond by repression, the conclusion that moderate leaders do nothing and obtain nothing becomes inevitable. In the end, they themselves join the ranks of the radicals or give up the fight. In thus demonstrating that moderation is powerless, "violent, exclusionary regimes tend to foster unintentionally the hegemony or dominance of their most radical social critics."[41] This outcome reveals the dilemma of repressive regimes. To counter radicalism, governments should grant democratic rights to students. These democratic rights favor moderation, but they also antagonize repressive regimes because they encourage constant student mobilization to protest for reforms. Such regimes are then forced to bar democratic rights and shut down institutions, thereby pushing students to radicalism. For a dictatorial regime, no less than radicalism, moderation is unwanted because it presupposes the granting of democratic rights. However, of the two "evils," dictators prefer radicalism because they think they can cope with it by the use of repression, while the granting of democratic rights deprives them of the means to deal with threatening protests.

The repression of open expression turns politics into a clandestine activity, which gives advantage to radical students. As Girma remarks, "The intensified coercion forced students underground and led to the birth of such movements as the Alligators [Crocodiles], precursors of the various socialist parties that surfaced during the revolution."[42] Apart from demobilizing moderate students, repression brings the student movement under the influence of underground groups whose modus vivendi is secrecy and centralization of decisions to the detriment of open democratic debate. When politics is driven underground, those who have become professional revolutionaries have the upper hand over moderate leaders who have other things to do besides politics. Moreover, where open debate is presumed dangerous, ideas are no longer accepted subsequent to a free examination; instead, students are put in the position of having to take sides without examining arguments. Finally, only two players remain: the government and the radicals, and those who profess moderate views have no other choice but to withdraw or support the radicals even if they do not agree with them. The elimination of the moderate option so drastically polarizes the situation that any opponents of the government can express themselves only by siding with the radicals.

The repeated violence of the government provokes reactions that can only profit the radicals by underlining the imperative of violent response. Once a government has clearly established that it has no other answer to demands for change than repression, the conclusion that it must be overthrown becomes unavoidable. And because of their belief that the use of violence alone can overthrow a repressive regime, most students confront the huge question of justifying the use of violence. The resolution to use violence does not come easily when the majority of students are still faithful to Christian values, as was the case in Ethiopia. When I interviewed Makonnen Bishaw, who became president of the student union after defeating the candidate of the radicals in 1968, he told me that he and many other students decided not to become Marxists because they resented the violence that Marxism considers as an inevitable component of social change, not because they were opposed to socialist ideas. Hence my assumption that one of the attractions of Marxism-Leninism has been for many students the justification of violence, as they felt the regime's repression gave them no other choice than violent opposition to it.

What could be more appropriate to resolve the dilemma of many students over the use of violence than Marx's theory of class struggle? It justified violence in the name of the interests of working people, just as it demystified the throne and the ruling class by depicting their legitimacy as nothing but the imposition of class and ethnic interests through the violent means of the state. This reading of the Ethiopian political system helped to convince many students of the need to overthrow the regime. The same need to justify violence explains the fascination of Ethiopian students for Frantz Fanon. As one former student activist admits, "One of the few simplified leftist publications the radical students had access to in the second half of the sixties was Frantz Fanon's book *The Wretched of the Earth*. His ideas on the role of violence in effecting historical changes gripped radical students whose aspiration and struggle was to bring about social change."[43] Both Fanon and Marx justify violence, not as an eye-for-an-eye response to the violence of the state, but as a means of bringing about a better society. To many angry students, this sublimation of violence came both as liberation and consummation of their disrespect for and disengagement from traditionality. Fanon's view of violence against the colonizer as a liberating therapy became for Ethiopian students a means of definitively severing ties to traditional Ethiopia.

Repression and Utopianism

The prevalence of reconstructive thinking over practicality further illustrates the propensity of political repression to incite radicalism. A prominent precursor of this view is Alexis de Tocqueville. Trying to understand why France under absolutism produced social visionaries, Tocqueville put the blame on the absence of freedom.

> The very situation of these writers prepared them to like general and abstract theories of government and to trust in them blindly. At the almost infinite distance from practice in which they lived, no experience tempered the ardors of their nature; nothing warned them of the obstacles that existing facts might place before even the most desirable reforms; they didn't have any idea of the dangers which always accompany even the most necessary revolutions. They did not have even the least suspicion of them; for the complete absence of political freedom had made the world of action not merely badly known to them, but invisible.[44]

The lack of freedom entailing their exclusion from practical life, these theoreticians gave themselves up to utopian temptations. They became visionaries and developed bold theories of social reconstruction that would turn dangerous because of their impracticality. Obviously, the attempt to implement impractical ideas necessitates the use of destruction and violence. Unable to change things concretely and practically, the thinkers started to dream about society, thereby giving full vent to their imagination rather than their reason. They thus developed abstract and utopian theories, that is, conceptions that were generous but also impractical because imagination supervised their production instead of realism.

In Ethiopia, too, the absence of freedom worked, in conjunction with other factors, toward the flourishing of abstractness and utopianism among Ethiopian students and intellectuals. Frustrations over the lack of political freedom and inexperience with the concrete reality of things conspired to spread the propensity to dream about society and to reconstruct it mentally. Marxism-Leninism splendidly responded to this utopian longing, which was but an outgrowth of the frustration of an educated elite condemned to silence in a society monopolized by an outdated ruling class.

Though many university professors saw the negative effect of the regime's repressive policy on students, they were powerless to do anything about it. For instance, Mesfin Wolde-Mariam strongly defended academic freedom in an article published in 1968 in *Dialogue*, the journal of the Ethiopian University Teachers' Association. He wrote: "A university is a place where people can learn to think fearlessly and objectively. A university is a place where people can express their ideas and thoughts, however unpopular and unfashionable these may be, without let or hindrance."[45] In the article Mesfin underlined, without referring directly to Ethiopia, the importance of academic freedom for university work and mission. He also defended the involvement of the university in politics: "The universities must be deeply involved in public affairs and . . . they should take the initiative and the responsibility of educating the masses politically."[46] He pleaded for academic freedom on the grounds that such a freedom is not dangerous to political regimes. On the contrary, discarding the recourse to violence, it rationalizes political issues and bases politics on persuasion and realism.

Universities should have no place for dogmatism, radicalism, and propaganda. Committed to objectivity, they should draw their ideas from objective assessments of real conditions. They counter extremism and utopian tendencies through the development of the rationalist attitude. Accordingly, when academic freedom is banned, reason, realism, and moderation are barred from the university. Teaching without the freedom to use objective analysis—because of the fear to criticize the imperial regime—only creates the conditions for radicalization and excessive views. In the words of Mesfin, "The main function of the universities will be to speak the truth fearlessly thereby giving politics a rational basis and checking excesses."[47] Clearly then, many Ethiopian professors interpreted the spectacle of Ethiopian students surrendering to doctrines advocating utopian reconstruction and the use of violence as a failure of the university. Because of the lack of academic freedom, the university was failing to educate its own students, to teach them to become rational, realistic, and open to peaceful and democratic debates. The failure had created a situation that Mesfin did not hesitate to call "a nightmare."[48]

Another professor who developed similar arguments is Bisrat Dilnessahu. He defended academic freedom vigorously: the university cannot accomplish the mission of advancing and transmitting knowledge unless the scientist has "every right and protection to reveal the findings of his investigations . . . no matter how disagreeable to the government, and no matter how political the consequences."[49] To bar this right is most dangerous, for if "a state adopts blindly a policy of curtailment of the scientific activities of a university which impinges upon its sphere of interest, it may become impossible to have a rational discourse about a society."[50] In other words, to interdict academic freedom is more dangerous to the state than to recognize it. With academic freedom, teachers and students develop rational views on account of both examining social realities objectively and learning to confront various views in a peaceful manner. The outcome is the development of a sober and realistic view of society, a view that allows debates and the rational and critical appraisal of issues. Short of teaching the rational and critical method, the university "ends up by creating a herd" that easily becomes the target of extremist agitators and propagandists.[51] Contrary to dictators' assumptions, it is not freedom but the lack of it that is the bedrock of radicalism.

The great dilemma of professors was that the vigilant surveillance of the imperial regime forced them either to hide the truth or to praise wrong policies. In a society where they were supposed to spread enlightenment, the pressure to tell falsehoods undermined their professional ethics. As a result, students developed contempt for the professors with the consequence that many students started to listen to the radicals. When university professors have nothing critical to say about a society patently plagued by all sorts of ills, the inevitable outcome is that students lose faith in academia and try to satisfy their urge to understand through other sources, especially underground sources. The impasse was so glaring to many professors that one of them expressed his frustration thus: "Higher institutions in developing countries have special responsibilities and obligations. . . . They are expected to and can play a stronger influencing and enlightening role than their counterparts in the developed countries. To play this role responsibly and constructively, the community of scholars in our universities needs to exercise full freedom both as scholars and as citizens."[52] The complete loss of respect for faculty is clearly in evidence in Ali Mazrui's account of his visit to Haile Selassie I University in 1973. When the host, an Ethiopian professor of political science, stood up to introduce him as the guest speaker, Mazrui reports, "he was immediately shouted down. The students were insisting that the meeting had to be under their sponsorship, or it could not take place at all."[53] The professor had no choice but to capitulate.

Vacillating Repression

One important question comes to mind: if Haile Selassie's regime was so repressive, how could student activism flourish on the campus? To find the answer, we must take a closer look at the pattern of imperial repression. Speaking of the government's response to student protests, we noted a pattern whereby repression was followed by forgiveness. Compared to other countries, especially to the military government that replaced the imperial state, the imperial regime conducted a repressive policy that was not only less stringent but also inconsistent. True, harsh measures were taken: several times the university was closed, the student union disbanded, students were imprisoned, and so forth. But the measures were soon followed by conciliatory gestures that weakened their dissuading impact. A number of observers thus have characterized the repressive response as a vacillating policy. A study by Peter Koehn and Louis D. Hayes has this to say: "In Ethiopia, the mix of student opposition and government vacillation between repression and forgiveness gave rise to confrontation politics of an increasingly violent cast in the later 1960's and early 1970's."[54] Balsvik corroborates their analysis: "Student political activism was able to continue precisely because the regime's response to it was inconsistent, fluctuating between repression, ambivalence and paternalism."[55]

To tell the whole truth, a clear tightening of repression involving violent intimidation and assassination of leaders occurred toward the end of the sixties. The first incidence of this tightened repression was the assassination of a leading figure, Tilahun Gizaw, and the massacre of students during his funeral in 1969. The use of the Imperial Bodyguard and the recourse to massive imprisonment of students were also clear indications of a change of policy in the direction of intensified repression. The radicals felt the change of policy; in consequence, "after the massacre, a number of student leaders left Ethiopia for Europe and North America."[56] Another group attempted to hijack a plane belonging to Ethiopian Airlines. For all these radical students, the student movement had revealed its limitations; it was time to graduate to a different form of struggle.

But by then many students were already radicalized; what is more, even at its height, the repression was not systematic and sustained. Even though the repressive measures increased as students became more and more actively politicized, they never reached a level of ferocity comparable to other repressive governments. For example, in April 1969, when more than five hundred students were arrested and taken to a detainment camp, a student fell from one of the trucks and died. What happened next is indicative of the government's continuous vacillation: "The students held a symbolic funeral, including a march in a long, silent column from the house of their deceased colleague. The police arrived quickly and took another estimated 500 students to a different detainment camp. That evening, however, more than 1000 students were released and traveled back to their campuses in police trucks, chanting political slogans."[57]

What is the reason for the vacillation of the imperial government? This much we know about Haile Selassie: he was extremely jealous of his power and merciless toward those who threatened him. A reluctance to use violence does not, therefore, explain his wavering attitude toward the continuous defiance of students. In addition, a systematic and brutal repression could have seriously crippled student activism: the near total withdrawal of students from politics during the Derg's rule proves this point. Likewise, the bloody repression of the government that overthrew the Derg has discouraged student activism at Addis Ababa University. Given the dissuading impact of governmental violence, what could explain the vacillating repression of Haile Selassie's government?

One reason, many scholars say, is paternalism. Haile Selassie's paternalistic attitude considered student protests as an expression of adolescent immaturity and impatience. Such protests must be punished, but the punishment must aim at disciplining students, just as a father punishes his children. To quote Balsvik, "In accordance with traditional Ethiopian ways of thinking, students were seen as children who had been misled. They ought to be severely punished, then pardoned and finally lifted up."[58] A second reason is that the regime did not see student protests as a real threat. Since the protests were perceived more as a nuisance than as a real danger, they did not arouse the need to adopt a policy of systematic and brutal repression. The imperial government was all the more inclined to think thus because it enjoyed a traditional legitimacy in the eyes of many Ethiopians. The most repressive governments are those that lack wide legitimacy, as the slightest opposition can turn fatal for them.

Still another reason was the international prestige to which Haile Selassie was deeply attached. A brutal repression of university and high school students would have provoked international indignation and sullied his carefully built-up reputation as a benevolent and modernizing monarch. For instance, the numerous closures of the university were hurriedly reversed because they gave bad impression to the international community, notably as the whole world was watching once Addis Ababa had virtually become the "capital of Africa." There is yet another reason: many important sons and daughters of highly placed officials had joined the student protests, some even becoming leaders. The prospect of their sons or daughters being killed in a brutal repression surely softened the resolve of these officials to support the use of extreme methods. Let me relate a personal anecdote. During my time as president of the student association of the French school known as Lycée Guebre Mariam, a friend of mine, who was a university student activist, asked me to mobilize the students to join the ongoing protests at the university. In this way, he explained, the government would have to back down from using brutal repressive methods, as many children of army generals and ministers were studying at the French school.

To sum up, by the time the imperial government decided to harden its repression, many students had already become Marxist-Leninist activists and among them some had left the university with the view of initiating other and more efficient forms of struggle. Among other things, this meant the infiltration of radicals into the various organs of the government, notably the armed forces, educational institutions, and ministries. The infiltration prepared the ground for the major role that the revolutionary spirit, born in the seclusion of university campuses, was to play in shaping the destiny of the country. Subsequent events compelled the student movement to lose the initiative to another unexpected rival, namely, the Derg. How the Derg emerged and took the leadership of a socialist revolution is a different story. Even so, there is no denying that the reconstructive discourse of students and intellectuals had opened a Pandora's box of polarized conflicts and visionary vocations, one outcome of which was the Derg itself.

Conclusion

The main function of culture is to provide the members of a group with shared beliefs and values by means of which they perceive, interpret, and respond to realities and challenges around them. In addition to defining a given community, culture exhibits a systematic character as well as the ability to adapt under the impact of internal and/or external challenges. Culture thus gives the ability to be grounded, to become a center, a force of interpretation such that things are put in perspective and objectified according to inner and self-empowering norms. Because of this ability, incidents and events do not sway members of the group in every direction; on the contrary, they tend to stay centered, like a huge tree, and objectify things and occurrences in a way granting them a taming capacity.

So understood, culture incarnates autonomy, the loss of which produces the pathological condition defined in this study as dislocation. As a phenomenon causing departure or deviation from a normal condition of integration, cultural dislocation means dysfunctionality, which reflects the inability to preserve integrity and activate self-asserting ethos. Dislocation thus primarily affects the interpretative power: in lieu of developing a pragmatic attitude toward external influences, the dislocated culture simply absorbs them without differentiating the harmful from the beneficial. Still less does it integrate these influences: on the contrary, the affected culture turns into a collection of disparate and conflictual beliefs and values reflecting a state of deep disharmony. Speaking of the disruption induced by colonial rule, Aimé Césaire properly uses the term "cultural anarchy" to deplore the replacement of "the primitive cultural unity by heterogeneous culture."[1]

Insofar as culture means identity, contacts between cultures normally mobilize a striving toward cultural preservation. Intrusions from other cultures unfiltered by the interpretative ability imply loss of autonomy, and hence a confusion of identity. In a state of equal relations, cultures in contact effect borrowings that do not threaten the self-preservation of either. However, in a state of inequality, not only does the hegemonic culture's desire to mold the dependent culture overtake self-preservation, but the molding itself aims at the internalization of subordination. The best way to inculcate dependency is to convince members that their (native) culture is not valid or that it is backward or primitive. In this way, members no longer feel the need to defend their culture, and so lose their ability to be grounded and become liable to be pulled by the donor culture in the desired direction. Under such conditions, culture change ceases to involve mere borrowings; it becomes the process of realizing a tabula rasa resulting in the establishment of a hierarchical relationship between donor and recipient cultures.

As we saw, extensive borrowing of cultural traits from a culture construed as superior defines the situation of non-Western peoples exposed to modern, that is, Western, education. A picturesque depiction of the rupture caused by Western education is found in an interview that Getatchew Haile gave to an Ethiopian Web site:

> Today we speak of Ethiopian revolution of the 70s and its consequences, but that revolution and its consequences are nothing compared to the effect of the quiet but fast-moving revolution of introducing the Western educational system. You can say it was a coup of a system, the new system overthrowing the ancient system. The consequence was devastating. We introduced it before we were prepared to receive it. We were unskilled to handle that fire. It burned the nation that ignited it to enlighten it. We were cut off overnight from our past. Children who just graduated from the elementary school suddenly treated those who spent half their lives pursuing their education in the traditional school as ignorant.[2]

All the negative outcomes discussed in various chapters of this study transpire here: alienation, contempt for one's tradition, uprootedness, generational conflict, elitism, all resulting in dire consequences. There is no need to reexamine the consequences; what must be kept in mind is that all are products of cultural dislocation.

The basic fracture stems from the Western construct of world history whose consequence is the portrayal of non-Western cultures as backward. The construct stipulates that emancipation from barbarism and ignorance can only come through indigenous cultures being harnessed to the culture of the West. The scheme of universal history rests on explicit premises, one of which is the proposal making the rupture with non-Western cultures into a sine qua non of modernization. As formulated by G. W. F. Hegel, the scheme assigns the same goals to all cultures, notably the goal of the technological conquest of nature. To the Cartesian assumption that a basic goal of human life is to "render ourselves masters and owners of nature," Hegel added the idea that history realizes this goal through a stage-producing-stage movement.[3] The major consequence of assigning to all human beings common goals that are achieved through a progressive course is that all cultures thus belong to the same historical process, regardless of their particularities. It follows that the variety of human cultures expresses nothing less than "*graduation* in the development," to use Hegel's expression.[4] The culture that shows the highest degree of the mastery of nature becomes the leading culture and the driving force of history. Those cultures that exhibit inabilities to control nature must be defined as existing in backward or retarded stages in the universal process of human development. Arbitrary hierarchization according to Western idiosyncratic characters led to Hegel's definition of Africa as "the Unhistorical, Undeveloped Spirit, still involved in the conditions of mere nature."[5]

With its paradigmatic value, the Hegelian scheme of history is a mental construct rather than an empirical reality. It integrates disparate cultural trends and realities into a successive whole under the hegemony of the West. It selects Western characteristics, such as science and technology, and casts them as universal characteristics, thereby creating the framework for portraying cultures not exhibiting such characteristics as retarded. The decentering and fracturing impact of this theoretical scheme on non-Western cultures reveals its main function: the empowerment of the West. In effect, armed with this ranking theory of history, Europe will soon undertake the conquest of the world, characteristically defining colonization as a civilizing mission.

According to Immanuel Kant, the precursor of constructivism, human knowledge is not the outcome of the mind passively receiving the imprints of objects; it is a construct deploying a mind actively forming the raw material of objects given in perception. The purpose of knowledge is not to reflect reality, but to construct reality in such a way that the human mind is endowed with an objectifying power. In the words of Kant, human reason must approach nature not "in the character of a pupil who listens to everything that the teacher chooses to say, but of an appointed judge who compels the witnesses to answer questions which he has himself formulated."[6] While the ability of knowledge to express things as they are is thus sacrificed, in return the mind gains the power to construct, that is, to transform things into phenomena, which are manipulable notions.

My purpose here is not to dissert on Kant's theory of knowledge, but to indicate that the objectifying nature of Eurocentrism perfectly complies with the Kantian epistemological premise. The Hegelian scheme of history agrees with the goal of knowledge understood as construction, and as such results in the empowerment of the West. Western anthropology is not the learning of other cultures, but the transformation of other cultures into witnesses answering Western questions. The Hegelian theory of history provides the philosophical foundation of the transformation of other cultures into representations of Western culture. The construct does not reflect the intrinsic nature of other cultures; it objectifies them, that is, inserts them into a theoretical framework that both distorts and turns them into manipulable phenomena. When the objectified culture internalizes the framework, it suffers deep dislocations.

In deriving the revolutionary mind primarily from cultural dislocation, this study obviously gives primacy to ideological matters over structural conditions. To put the matter philosophically, in the old philosophical debate between idealism and materialism, it sides with the former. In particular, in emphasizing the empowering role of mental representations, it argues against the reduction of ideas to the status of reflections or emanations of material conditions. When Marx writes that human ideas are "the direct efflux of their material behavior," the definition has little explanatory bearing on the radicalization of Ethiopian students and intellectuals.[7] Neither the backwardness of Ethiopia's economic system nor the little headway made by capitalist relations of production in the country called for a socialist ideology. Rather than being an emanation of material conditions, socialism reached the Ethiopian educated elite through a complex cultural process unleashed by the dislocating impact of Western education. This dislocating impact of cultural contacts gives evidence of the autonomous influence of ideas.

To validate the role of ideas, this study has particularly insisted that socioeconomic problems, however grave they may be, are not enough to explain the birth of the revolutionary mind. Ideational causation by which cultures are decentered is as necessary, if not more so. To the extent that the culture's decentering reveals its loss of self-directedness, it suggests that only cultural renovation can reconstitute the empowering force of fractured cultures. As a recovery of freedom, such a renovation challenges the objectifying intent of Eurocentrism. Nothing is more refractory to objectification than a center of autonomous activity. Hence the approach making the reinterpretation of ideology into a prerequisite to achieving modernization: if modernization is an outcome of empowerment, then it cannot occur without the recentering benefits of renovated beliefs and values. Clearly, both the decentering outcome and the countering ability of renovation attest to the autonomous agency of mental representations.

Now, a normal process of change reconciles novelty with heritage with the consequence that it achieves continuity. As we have seen, the impact of the Western theory of history on young Ethiopians was different; it caused a fundamental rupture with the beliefs and outlook belonging to their family and society. Because the teaching contrasts two societies one of which is taken as a norm, it does not plead for continuity with the Ethiopian legacy but for rupture. History is no longer the framework of continuity moving toward the future through the integration of the new and the old; it is how arrested societies get towed by another history. Some such theory of history asks Ethiopian students to look up to the West; it causes a major cultural fracture resulting in them being cut off from their own people and losing all attachment to their own tradition.

The rupture convinced the Ethiopian intelligentsia to accept Western teachers' and textbooks' explanation of the causes of the social and technological retardation of Ethiopia. Having a clear colonial character, the educational system disseminated a theoretical construct that opposed modernity to tradition, thereby squarely putting the blame for Ethiopia's technological lag on its traditions. Nowhere was the educational system making a provision for an alternative view describing Ethiopian society as an autonomous civilization that pursued goals different from Western countries. The qualification "backward" makes sense only through the assumption that Ethiopia had goals that were similar to the West's, especially as regards the technological conquest of nature. Not only is such an assumption factually indefensible, but it is also based on the idea that Western civilization is universal. As we just saw, this claim reflects a theoretical construct that fraudulently interprets an idiosyncratic pursuit as a universal characteristic.

Far from engaging in the work of cultural renovation, Ethiopia's Westernized elite did not even like the idea of attributing the Ethiopian legacy to a different cultural line, unlike some theoretical developments in Africa, such as the school of negritude.[8] While the Western trend pursued the conquest of nature, negritude posited that African cultures followed the path of harmony and integration. The Ethiopian educated elite utterly refused to dissociate itself culturally from the West, which it considered as an embodiment of universal norms. In the eyes of the Ethiopian educated elite, cultural particularism is nothing but a segregationist view; it implies that universal laws do not govern Africans so that Western realizations stay out of their reach. The more Africans stress their particularity, the further they remove themselves from the European type of achievement, such as in science and technology.

The inability to detect the features of an eccentric trend and development in what is presented as universal history constitutes the most pernicious impact of Western education on non-Western cultures. One detrimental fallout of this inability is the propensity to radicalism, which begins with the conviction that the realizations of non-Western cultures have no value, being but outcomes of frozen traditions. To be sure, the endorsement of Eurocentrism is by itself not enough to foster revolutionary leanings. Without the country's economic failure and the repressive nature of the imperial regime as well as the postponement of necessary reforms, Ethiopia's students and intelligentsia of the sixties and early seventies would not have embraced so enthusiastically Marxist-Leninist doctrine. Still, without the mental orientation springing from the internalization of Eurocentric views, neither would they have been so eager to demolish the defining features of the country. The educational system created a predisposition that the addition of the socioeconomic failures of the regime fully actualized.

On account of failing to synchronize tradition with modernity, the educational system produced a rootless intelligentsia. This rootlessness found political expression when university students, assuming "the role of the only organized opposition, began campaigning for a clear break with the country's history and tradition."⁹ As the goal of creating persons with the ability to interpret, enrich, and adapt the heritage to new needs and changing conditions did not inspire the educational system, the system naturally encouraged the formation of a revolutionary ethos by fostering the desire to discard whatever was not in conformity with Western norms. The rise of radical intellectuals is thus a fallout of countries entering late into the process of modernization: the contrast of their society with those of the West produces a characteristic disenchantment and dissociation that mold them into demolishers. The disenchantment, be it noted, does not support the emergence of a creative mind: being decentered and yoked to the West, such a mind harbors the tendency to imitate the model rather than to deviate.

Another side of this destructive trend was the generation of a crisis of identity and meaning. The rejection of traditional beliefs and values as a result of modern education brought about an ideological void, which in turn activated the longing for substitute beliefs. Consequently, many young Ethiopians joined new religious sects. Analyzing the spread of the Pentecostal movement among educated Ethiopians in the sixties, a recent paper argues that it was the product of a religious crisis resulting from the challenges that secular education posed to the traditional Orthodox Christian faith.¹⁰ An even greater number tried to fill the void by responding to the revolutionary appeal of socialist doctrine.

In producing intellectuals who knew more about Western societies than about Ethiopian realities, the educational system fostered the tendency to project what is true of developed countries onto Ethiopian society, which is then read through a Western lens. This projection of advanced traits on a different society favored idealism and radicalization to the detriment of realism and moderation. As a result, the alien system of education further aggravated the natural idealism of youth by shaping a state of mind prone to extremist leanings. The definition of education as a journey into a superior society can hardly avoid the inculcation of utopianism, any more than it can avoid the idea of an accelerated catching up. When concepts and theories are learned outside their particular and historical contexts, they assume a normative connotation. When such ideas are not inserted into local conditions, they cease to reflect existing realities. They become transcendent, Platonic norms to which reality must be made conformable. Instead of being instruments of analysis and understanding, such ideas turn into mystifying notions.

The distortion of the educational system ironically drove Ethiopian students to reproduce the mistakes of the regime that they so vehemently denounced. The revolutionary theory that they found attractive advocated an authoritarian approach to modernization. Once students and intellectuals had cut themselves off from the people whose traditions they considered as backward, they could not avert the fostering of an elitist attitude. The consequence of the West asserting its power through science and technology was that those Ethiopians with access to Western education came to view themselves as partaking in that power. The task of pulling the society out of backwardness became their calling, all the more so as the monarch failed to live up to his modernizing promises. They visualized an even more centralized and totalitarian leadership because their revolutionary ideas committed them to nothing less than the liberation of the working people. Born of the modernization theory according to which those who assimilate Western culture are entitled to unimpeded authority, elitism is the means by which intellectuals assert their exclusive right to power. No other sector of the society can contest the leadership of the educated elite, which alone holds the key to modernity. That the enormous prestige of modern education—an outcome of the denigration of tradition—created an entitlement to unrestricted power is evidenced by student publications, which reiterated the "vanguard" role of the educated elite.

There is no denying that the lack of national orientation of the educational system greatly encouraged not only the alienation of the educated elite from the traditional elite but also its polarizing tendency. So uprooted an elite could hardly assume the task of unifying the country: subjected to various and contradictory external influences to the detriment of national norms, the educated elite could not produce any consensus about Ethiopia and its future direction. Such was not the case with the traditional system of education. The considerable autonomy of the church from the state in terms of education protected, as we have seen, the integrative and nationalistic function of church schools from political influence and vicissitudes. Church education transcended political rivalries to concentrate on what was permanently Ethiopian, and so was an agent of unity and national cohesion.

Whereas traditional intellectuals (*debteras*) subdued their ethnic and regional attachments to what permanently defined Ethiopia, modern-educated Ethiopians fell back on ethnic and regional ties owing to the loss of their national mission. After the illusory and temporary unity around Marxism-Leninism, which was itself an expression of alienation, nothing was left but to adopt the even more divisive ideology of ethnicization. The great tragedy of modern Ethiopia is, therefore, its failure to produce domestic, homegrown intellectuals who would have conceived of modernization as an upgrading of traditional culture. Such intellectuals could have easily arisen from Ethiopian traditional culture if the system of education had established some form of continuity between traditional and Western education. The choice was made to expel traditional culture and its representatives from modern schooling so as to establish a system of education wholly committed to serving an alien autocratic rule. Is it surprising, then, that Ethiopian intellectuals worked actively toward the dismissal of traditional culture rather than its renewal through purification and reinterpretation? And in so doing, were they not curtailing their ability to achieve consensus, that is, to become a national intelligentsia through the transcending of particularism? Once national norms were put aside, little remained but the promotion of ethnicity. The present infatuation of Ethiopia's educated elite with ethnicity does no more than continue the polarizing tendency inherited from the Marxist-Leninist notion of class struggle.

The undeniable decline of an interpretative power that was quite active in the past validates my analysis. As we have seen, the *Kibre Negast* reveals the interpretative power of the traditional culture; its basic message grants Ethiopia the status of God's favored nation. Surrounded and threatened by pagan and powerful Muslim countries, the survival of Ethiopia as a Christian country seemed to require nothing less than God's special custody. By assigning to the Ethiopian monarch a Solomonic descent, the myth set the scene of God's favor shifting from Israel to Ethiopia because, unlike Ethiopians, the Israelites refused Christianity. In thus enjoying the special protection of God, Ethiopia was assured of its victory. Clearly, the mythical interpretation changes Ethiopia's isolation into a destiny, and thus provides the framework of a teleological history that both centers and makes Ethiopia the goal of universal history.[11]

If the Islamic danger activated the renovation of traditional Ethiopian culture to the point of giving birth to a new myth, a new sense of mission that helped the country survive, the question comes to mind why a similar process did not occur with the new challenge that the West posed. My firm answer is that the endorsement of the Western theory of history, whose main fallout is the construal of Ethiopia as a backward country, stifled the interpretative power. The historical scheme took away from Ethiopia its traditional worth and sense of mission. Let alone being the subject of history, Ethiopia descended to the level of being a mere tutee of the West.

One major implication of the acceptance of backwardness is that modernization was not posed in terms of defending Ethiopia's identity, still less of competing against the West. The latter was not perceived as a threat, an adversary, but as a model, a benevolent tutor. The conception of modernization in terms of competition discards the idea of a passive imitation of the West. Instead, it advocates the use of all resources to win the competition, including the mobilization of those traditional characteristics and peculiarities that bolster the competitive edge of the developing country. When the West is taken as a model, the idea of competition is put aside in favor of reproducing the model. Imitation rules out deviations from the model, which dictates the norms of modernization.

For the imitative paradigm, modernization is the process whereby lagging societies catch up with advanced societies. The operation amounts to fashioning the lagging society in the image of the Western model. Unfortunately, the outcome does not meet the expectation: rather than catching up, the lagging society turns into a peripheral satellite of the model. Since imitation suppresses local initiatives and reduces people to passivity in the thrall of an external mode, its inescapable and adverse outcome is marginalization. Some such conception of modernization activates not the spirit of rivalry but the zeal of the copyist who tries to secure the benefits of the model. Such was Haile Selassie's view of modernization: far from being impregnated with a competitive spirit, his conception of modernization saw the West as both a benevolent ally and a model, especially after he regained his throne in 1941 thanks to the assistance of the British.

If we ask the question why Haile Selassie designed a system of education that was so detrimental to the country, besides his ideological conversion to the Western view of history, we find political reasons associated with the need to establish an autocratic system. We saw how Ethiopia's decline after great advancements was attributed to the rise of regional lords who significantly weakened the country's power. The resulting state of political anarchy and incessant conflicts impeded Ethiopia's progress. This reading suggested one solution, to wit, the establishment of a strong central power. Only under the enlightened leadership of an absolute monarch could Ethiopia get out of its backwardness. To accomplish this task, the modernizing monarch needed a bureaucracy entirely committed to him and emancipated from traditional obligations to the church and the nobility. The need determined the main function of the educational system: the institution of a system of education entirely copied from the West purged the new educated elite from traditional references and commitments to the great benefit of the emperor. Such an uprooted elite signified the integration of Ethiopia into the imperialist world as a dependent partner. The implementation of the directives of core countries called for a denationalized bureaucracy that only an imported system of education could fashion.

The project of fashioning a docile bureaucracy serving a peripheral socioeconomic formation had unintended consequences. The very act of denationalizing the educated elite by cutting its links with traditionality created a rootless intelligentsia that soon succumbed to the sirens of revolutionary appeals. The globalism of Marxist-Leninist doctrine in the sixties and seventies exercised an alluring attraction to an educated elite with a marked extroverted orientation imparted by the educational system. Subsequent events showed that the first victim of the decentering education was the monarchy itself: persuaded of the inanity of Ethiopian traditions, the Ethiopian educated elite could no longer see why some aspects of the legacy, namely, the monarchy, the nobility, and the traditional faith, would become an exception to the tabula rasa rule of modernization.

In initiating and overseeing the implementation of an alienating system of education, Haile Selassie sincerely believed he was forging the instrument necessary to put Ethiopia on the path of sustained modernization under the enlightened leadership of his autocratic rule. What he did not realize was that the instrument he thus forged was bound to turn against him: alienated from native values by its Westernized education, the educated elite could no longer concur with Haile Selassie's legitimizing discourse, any more than it could endorse a modernizing scheme severely handicapped by his autocratic rule. To the extent that this inner contradiction of the imperial system led to Haile Selassie's downfall, it is correct to say that he reaped what he had sown. Unfortunately for the country, the movement that overthrew him went further and removed the lid covering the darkest forces of resentment and revenge fomented by the economic failures and social exclusions of the regime. These unleashed forces soon turned Ethiopian society upside down in the name of socialism and its byproduct, ethnonationalism.

Notes

Introduction

1. Randi Rønning Balsvik, "Haile Selassie's Students: Rise of Social and Political Consciousness" (PhD diss., University of Tromsø, Norway, 1979), 491.

2. V. I. Lenin, "The Three Sources and Three Component Parts of Marxism," *The Lenin Anthology*, ed. Robert C. Tucker (New York: W. W. Norton and Company, 1975), 641.

3. V. I. Lenin, *What Is to Be Done?* (New York: International Publishers, 1929), 32.

4. Ibid., 33.

5. Karl Marx, "Toward a Critique of Hegel's *Philosophy of Right*," in *Selected Writings*, ed. David McLellan (Oxford: Oxford University Press, 1977), 64.

6. Edward B. Taylor, *The Origins of Culture* (New York: Harper Torchbooks, 1958), 1.

7. Department of Sociology and Anthropology, "Report on a Research on the Social Situation of HSIU Students" (unpublished, Haile Selassie I University, 1970), 2.

8. Teshale Tibebu, *The Making of Modern Ethiopia, 1896–1974* (Lawrenceville, NJ: Red Sea Press, 1995), 168.

9. Messay Kebede, *Survival and Modernization—Ethiopia's Enigmatic Present: A Philosophical Discourse* (Lawrenceville, NJ: Red Sea Press, 1999).

Chapter 1

1. Ali A. Mazrui, *Political Values and the Educated Class in Africa* (Berkeley: University of California Press, 1978), 262.

2. Paulos Milkias, *Haile Selassie, Western Education, and Political Revolution in Ethiopia* (New York: Cambria Press, 2006), 209.

3. Seymour Martin Lipset, "University Students and Politics in Underdeveloped Countries," in *Student Politics*, ed. Seymour Martin Lipset (New York: Basic Books, 1967), 5.

4. Ibid., 6.

5. Philip G. Altbach, "Students and Politics," in *Student Politics*, ed. Lipset, 77–78.

6. Ibid., 78.

7. Ibid.

8. Allan Todd, *Revolutions, 1789–1917* (Cambridge: Cambridge University Press, 1998), 2.

9. Aristotle, "Rhetoric," in *The Basic Works of Aristotle*, trans. W. Rhys Roberts (New York: Random House, 1941), 1405.

10. Lewis S. Feuer, *The Conflict of Generations: The Character and Significance of Student Movements* (New York: Basic Books, 1969), 3.

11. Edward Shils, "Dreams of Plenitude, Nightmares of Scarcity," in *Students in Revolt*, ed. Seymour Martin Lipset and Philip G. Altbach (Boston: Houghton Mifflin Company, 1969), 6.

12. Theda Skocpol, *States and Social Revolutions: A Comparative Analysis of France, Russia, and China* (New Work: Cambridge University Press, 1980), 9.

13. Kiflu Tadesse, *The Generation: The History of the Ethiopian People's Revolutionary Party* (Silver Spring, MD: Independent Publishers, 1993), 29.

14. Bahru Zewde, "The Intellectual and the State in Twentieth Century Ethiopia," in *New Trends in Ethiopian Studies: Papers of the 12th International Conference of Ethiopian Studies* (Lawrenceville, NJ: Red Sea Press, 1994), 1:490.

15. Ibid., 489.

16. Ibid., 490.

17. Makonnen Bishaw, e-mail interview by author, September 29, 2004.

18. See Andargachew Asseged, *Beatcher Yeteketche Rejim Guzo* [The Truncated Long Journey] (Addis Ababa: Central Printing Press, 2000), 13–14.

19. Tesfaye Demmellash, "On Marxism and Ethiopian Student Radicalism in North America," *Monthly Review* 35 (1984): 28.

20. Ibid.

21. Ibid.

22. Gebru Mersha, "The Emergence of the Ethiopian 'Left' in the Period 1960–1970 as an Aspect of the Formation of the 'Organic Intellectuals,'" in *The Ethiopian Revolution and Its Impact on the Politics of the Horn of Africa: Proceedings, 2nd International Conference on the Horn of Africa* (New York: New School for Social Research, 1987), 74.

23. Ibid., 79.

24. Ibid., 71.

25. Ibid., 81–83.

26. Addis Hiwet, "A Certain Political Vocation: Reflections on the Ethiopian Intelligentsia," in *Ethiopian Revolution and Its Impact*, 42–43.

27. Ibid., 46.

28. Ibid., 49.

29. Donald L. Donham, *Marxist Modern: An Ethnographic History of the Ethiopian Revolution* (Berkeley: University of California Press, 1999), xix.

30. Melesse Ayalew, "Editorial," *Challenge* 5, no. 1 (1965): 1.

31. Raymond Boudon, "Sources of Student Protest in France," in *The New Pilgrims: Youth Protest in Transition*, ed. Philip G. Altbach and Robert S. Laufer (New York: David McKay Company, 1972), 297.

32. Ibid., 310.

33. John Markakis and Nega Ayele, *Class and Revolution in Ethiopia* (Trenton, NJ: Red Sea Press, 1986), 97.

34. Raymond Aron, "Student Rebellion: Vision of the Future or Echo from the Past?" in *The Seeds of Politics: Youth and Politics in America*, ed. Anthony M. Orum (Englewood Cliffs, NJ: Prentice Hall, 1972), 333.

35. Chalmers Johnson, *Revolutionary Change* (Boston: Little, Brown, and Company, 1966), 85.

36. Kiflu, *The Generation*, 37.

37. Randi Rønning Balsvik, *Haile Sellassie's Students: The Intellectual and Social Background to Revolution, 1952–1977* (East Lansing: Michigan State University, 1985), 118.

38. Mark N. Hagopian, *The Phenomenon of Revolution* (New York: Dodd, Mead and Company, 1974), 299.

39. See Edgar Snow, "Days in Changsha," in *When Men Revolt—and Why*, ed. James Chowning Davies (New York: Free Press, 1971), 77.

40. Ibid.

41. Balsvik, *Haile Sellassie's Students*, 166.

42. Ibid., 172.

43. Ibid., 173.

44. Ibid., 174.

45. Ibid.

46. Kiflu, *The Generation*, 48.

47. Balsvik, *Haile Sellassie's Students*, 126.

48. Ibid., 127.

49. Ibid., 150.

50. Ibid., 149–50.

51. Ibid., 160–61.

52. Misagh Parsa, *States, Ideologies, and Social Revolutions: A Comparative Analysis of Iran, Nicaragua, and the Philippines* (Cambridge: Cambridge University Press, 2000), 11.

53. Balsvik, *Haile Sellassie's Students*, 184.

54. Ghelawdewos Araia, *Ethiopia: The Political Economy of Transition* (Lanham, MD: University Press of America, 1995), 62.

55. Cited in Balsvik, *Haile Sellassie's Students*, 216.

56. See Kiflu, *The Generation*, 46.

57. Makonnen, interview by author.

58. Ibid.

59. Ibid.

60. James H. Billington, *Fire in the Minds of Men: Origins of the Revolutionary Faith* (New York: Basic Books, 1980), 7.

61. Peter Koehn and Louis D. Hayes, "Student Politics in Traditional Monarchies: A Comparative Analysis of Ethiopia and Nepal," *Journal of Asian and African Studies* 13, nos. 1–2 (1978): 33.

62. Ibid.

63. Ibid., 36.

64. Ibid., 38.

65. Ibid., 37.

66. Ibid., 45.

67. Ibid.

Chapter 2

1. Bahru Zewde, *Pioneers of Change in Ethiopia* (Oxford: James Currey, 2002), 99.

2. Richard Flacks, "The Liberated Generation: An Exploration of the Roots of Student Protest," in *Seeds of Politics*, ed. Orum, 361.

3. Margaret Read, "Cultural Contacts in Education," in *Education and Nation-Building in Africa*, ed. L. Gray Cowan, James O'Connell, and David G. Scanlon (New York: Praeger Publishers, 1965), 356.

4. James S. Coleman, *Nigeria: Background to Nationalism* (Berkeley: University of California Press, 1958), 114.

5. Lipset, "University Students and Politics," 3.

6. Ibid., 4.

7. Ibid.

8. Read, "Cultural Contacts in Education," 354.

9. Amadou-Mahtar M'Bow, "Opening Speech," *African Education and Identity*, ed. Abiola Irele (London: Hans Zell Publishers, 1992), 13–14.

10. Mazrui, *Political Values*, 203.

11. E. S. Atieno-Odhiambo, "From African Historiographies to an African Philosophy of History," *Africanizing Knowledge*, ed. Toyin Falola and Christian Jennings (New Brunswick, NJ: Transaction Publishers, 2002), 18.

12. Ibid., 37 (Atieno-Odhiambo cites B. A. Ogot).

13. Mazrui, *Political Values*, 313.

14. Girma Amare, "The Modern Ethiopian Intelligentsia and Its Evolution" (paper prepared for the Interdisciplinary Seminar of the Faculties of Arts and Education of Haile Selassie I University, 1967), 10.

15. Mazrui, *Political Values*, 1.

16. Coleman, *Nigeria*, 170.

17. Mazrui, *Political Values*, 13.

18. Ibid., 368.

19. Ibid., 266.

20. Stanislav Andreski, *The African Predicament: A Study in the Pathology of Modernization* (New York: Atherton Press, 1968), 79.

21. Lipset, "University Students and Politics," 13.

22. For more discussion on the point, see Messay Kebede, *Africa's Quest for a Philosophy of Decolonization* (New York: Rodopi, 1994), 155–76.

23. Tekeste Negash, *The Crisis of Ethiopian Education: Some Implications for Nation-Building* (Uppsala, Sweden: Uppsala University, 1990), 76.

24. Ibid., 69.

25. Asres Yenesew (Aleqa), *Tekami Mikre* [*Useful Advice*] (Addis Ababa: Berhanena Selam Printing Press, 1958), 6 (my translation). Aleqa is a honorific title of the Ethiopian Church; it means chief and designates a highly educated cleric.

26. Ibid.

27. Ibid., 82.

28. Bahru, *Pioneers of Change in Ethiopia*, 23.

29. Ibid., 22–23.

30. Ibid., 33.

31. Ibid., 34.

32. Balsvik, *Haile Sellassie's Students*, 6.

33. Teshome G. Wagaw, *Education in Ethiopia* (Ann Arbor: University of Michigan Press, 1979), 183.

34. Balsvik, *Haile Sellassie's Students*, 4.

35. Ibid., 9.

36. Mulugeta Wodajo, "Postwar Reform in Ethiopian Education," *Comparative Education Review* 2, no. 3 (1959): 24.

37. Sylvia Pankhurst, *Ethiopia: A Cultural History* (Essex, UK: Lalibela House, 1955), 232.

38. Ibid., 234.

39. Paulos Milkias, "Traditional Institutions and Traditional Elites: The Role of Education in the Ethiopian Body-Politic," *African Studies Review* 19, no. 3 (1976): 81.

40. Ibid.

41. Pankhurst, *Ethiopia*, 237.

42. Paulos, "Traditional Institutions and Traditional Elites," 81.

43. Ibid.

44. Ibid., 82.

45. Pankhurst, *Ethiopia*, 245.

46. Mulatu Wubneh and Yohannis Abate, *Ethiopia: Transition and Development in the Horn of Africa* (Boulder, CO: Westview Press, 1988), 1.

47. Royal Chronicle of Abyssinia, *The Glorious Victory of Amda Seyon, King of Ethiopia*, trans. and ed. G. W. B. Huntingford (Oxford: Clarendon Press, 1965), 59.

48. G. W. F. Hegel, *The Philosophy of History* (New York: Dover Publications, 1956), 103.

49. Teshome, *Education in Ethiopia*, 10–11.

50. Addis Alemayehu, *Ye Timirtna Yetemaribet Tirgum* [*The Meaning of Education and School*] (Addis Ababa: Artistic Press, 1956), 107 (my translation).

51. Ibid., 101 (my translation).

52. David G. Scanlon and L. Gray Cowan, preface to *Traditional Ethiopian Church Education* (New York: Teachers College Press, 1970), vi.

53. Mulugeta, "Postwar Reform in Ethiopian Education," 25.

54. Ibid.

55. Ibid., 26.

56. Ibid.

57. Teshome, *Education in Ethiopia*, 12.

58. Ibid., viii.

59. Ibid., 17.

60. Ibid., 21 (Teshome quotes Girma Amare).

61. Addis A., *Ye Timirtna Yetemaribet Tirgum*, 108 (my translation).

Chapter 3

1. Teshome, *Education in Ethiopia*, 186.

2. Forrest D. Colburn, *The Vogue of Revolution in Poor Countries* (Princeton: Princeton University Press, 1994), 21.

3. Anne Cassiers and Jean-Michel Bessette, *Mémoires Ethiopiennes* (Paris: L'Harmattan, 2001), 333 (my translation).

4. Paulos Milkias, "The Political Spectrum of Western Education in Ethiopia," *Journal of African Studies* 9, no. 1 (1982): 25.

5. Teshome, *Education in Ethiopia*, 123.

6. Haile Selassie, *Selected Speeches of His Imperial Majesty Haile Selassie I, 1918 to 1967* (Addis Ababa: Artistic Printers Ltd., 1967), 19–20.

7. Ibid., 20–21.

8. Ibid., 25.

9. Balsvik, "Haile Selassie's Students," 62.

10. Tekeste Negash, *Rethinking Education in Ethiopia* (Uppsala, Sweden: Nordiska Afrikainstitutet, 1996), 31.

11. Ibid., 37.

12. Germa Amare, Abraham Demoz, and Aba Gebre Egziabher Degou, "Education Sector Review: Educational Objectives" (interim draft paper, n.d.), 14.

13. Addis H., "Political Vocation," 45.

14. Addis A., *Ye Timirtna Yetemaribet Tirgum*, 105 (my translation).

15. Ibid., 110.

16. Ibid., 111.

17. Balsvik, *Haile Sellassie's Students*, 66.

18. Kaigo Tokiomi, *Japanese Education: Its Past and Present* (Tokyo: Kokusai Bunka Shinkokai, 1968), 53.

19. Hugh L. Keenleyside and A. F. Thomas, *History of Japanese Education and Present Educational System* (Tokyo: Hokuseido Press, 1937), 98.

20. Tokiomi, *Japanese Education*, 54.

21. Mazrui, *Political Values*, 32–33.

22. Stanley Burstein, *Ancient African Civilizations: Kush and Axum* (Princeton: Markus Wiener Publishers, 1998), 14.

23. Guebre-Heywet Baykedagne, *L'empereur Menelik et L'Ethiopie* (Addis Ababa and Paris: Maison des Etudes Ethiopiennes, Institut National des Langues et Civilisations Orientales, 1993), 16 (my translation).

24. Bahru, *Pioneers of Change in Ethiopia*, 120.

25. Kebede Mikael, *Ethiopia and Western Civilization*, trans. Marcel Hassid (1949), i.

26. Major J. I. Eadie, *An Amharic Reader* (Cambridge: Cambridge University Press, 1924), 99.

27. Ibid., 229.

28. Paulos, "Western Education in Ethiopia," 26.

29. Cassiers and Bessette, *Mémoires Éthiopiennes*, 334 (my translation).

30. Keenleyside and Thomas, *History of Japanese Education*, 74.

31. Mazrui, *Political Values*, 320.

32. Teshome quotes Haile Selassie, *Education in Ethiopia*, 26.

33. Ibid., 35.

34. Soedjatmoko, *Development in the Non-Western World* (Tokyo: University of Tokyo Press, 1982), xiii.

35. Girma Amare, "Education and Society in Prerevolutionary Ethiopia," *Northeast African Studies* 6, nos. 1–2 (1984): 64.

36. Haile Selassie, *Selected Speeches*, 35.

37. Paulos, "Western Education in Ethiopia," 26.

38. Ibid.

39. Girma, "Education and Society," 68.

Chapter 4

1. Cited in Rickard, "Ethiopian Student and Ethiopia's Transition," 47.

2. Tekeste, *Crisis of Ethiopian Education*, 8.

3. "Editorial: Our Principles and Tasks in the Ethiopian Revolution," *Challenge* 12, no. 1 (1972): 7.

4. For more discussion on negritude, see Messay, *Africa's Quest.*

5. Léopold Sédar Senghor, *Prose and Poetry*, trans. John Reed and Clive Wake (London: Heinemann, 1976), 73.

6. Gene Ellis, "The Feudal Paradigm as a Hindrance to Understanding Ethiopia," *Journal of Modern African Studies* 14, no. 2 (1976): 276.

7. Hagos Gebre Yesus, "The Bankruptcy of the Ethiopian 'Left' Meisone-EPRP, a Two Headed Hydra: A Commentary on the Ideology and Politics of National Nihilism," in *Ethiopian Revolution and Its Impact*, 115.

8. "Editorial," *Struggle* 5, no. 2 (1969): 1.

9. "The National Question and Revolution in Ethiopia," *Challenge* 14, no. 1 (1975): 56–57.

10. Addis H., "Political Vocation," 49.

11. Ibid.

12. Ibid., 50–51.

13. Gezahegn Bekele, "The New Generation," *Struggle* 3, no. 1 (1968): 5, 13.

14. Ibid., 13.

15. Balsvik, *Haile Sellassie's Students*, 232.

16. Hagopian, *Phenomenon of Revolution*, 107.

17. Ibid., 112.

18. Mark N. Katz, *Reflections on Revolutions* (New York: St. Martin's Press, 1999), 26.

19. Bahru, "The Intellectual and the State," 487–88.

20. Karl Mannheim, "The Problem of Generations," in *The New Pilgrims*, ed. Altbach and Laufer, 129.

21. V. I. Lenin, *Imperialism: The Highest Stage of Capitalism* (New York: International Publishers, 1972), 14.

22. Robert A. Scalapino, "Prelude to Marxism: The Chinese Student Movement in Japan, 1900–1910," in *Approaches to Modern Chinese History* (Berkeley: University of California Press, 1967), 211.

23. Skocpol, *States and Social Revolutions*, 4.

24. Colburn, *Vogue of Revolution*, 14.

25. Ibid.

26. Ibid., 98.

27. Ibid., 21–22.

28. Ibid., 16.

29. Noel Parker, *Revolutions and History: An Essay in Interpretation* (Malden, MA: Blackwell Publishers, 1999), 149.

Chapter 5

1. David C. McClelland, "The Achievement Motive in Economic Growth," in *Development and Underdevelopment*, ed. Mitchell A. Seligson and John T. Passé-Smith (Boulder, CO: Lynne Reinner Publishers, 1998), 171.

2. Edward W. Blyden, *Christianity, Islam, and the Negro Race* (Edinburgh: Edinburgh University Press, 1967), 76.

3. Ibid.

4. Richard Greenfield, *Ethiopia: A New Political History* (London: Pall Mall Press, 1965), 340.

5. Ibid., 341.

6. Gebru, "Emergence of the Ethiopian 'Left,'" 81–83.

7. Mao Tse-tung, "The Role of the Chinese Communist Party in the National War," in *Selected Works* (New York: International Publishers, 1954), 2:260.

8. Hagopian, *Phenomenon of Revolution*, 277.

9. James Cotton, "The Chinese Revolution and the Chinese Tradition of Political Thought," in *Revolutionary Theory and Political Reality*, ed. Noel O'Sullivan (New York: St. Martin's Press, 1983), 125.

10. Beseat Kifle Selassie, "Class Struggle or Jockeying for Position? A Review of Ethiopian Student Movements from 1900 to 1975," in *The Role of African Student Movements in the Political and Social Evolution of Africa from 1900 to 1975* (Paris: UNESCO Publishing, 1994), 173.

11. B. Kotchy, "The Cultural Dimensions of FEANF," in *Role of African Student Movements*, 101.

12. Tekeste, *Crisis of Ethiopian Education*, 54.

13. Donham, *Marxist Modern*, 25.

14. Ibid., 29.

15. Mulatu Wubneh and Yohannis Abate, *Ethiopia*, 36.

16. Marina Ottaway and David Ottaway, *Ethiopia: Empire in Revolution* (New York: Africana Publishing Company, 1978), 24.

17. Cited in Ottaway and Ottaway, *Ethiopia*, 194.

18. "Editorial: The Spirit of Solidarity," *Challenge* 6, no. 1 (1966): 1.

19. Ibid., 2.

20. Tesfaye, "Marxism and Ethiopian Student Radicalism," 36.

21. Samuel P. Huntington, *Political Order in Changing Societies* (New Haven: Yale University Press, 1968), 371–72.

22. Feuer, *Conflict of Generations*, 4.

23. Ibid., 5.

24. Donald Rothchild and Michael Foley, "Ideology and Policy in Afro-Marxist Regimes: The Effort to Cope with Domestic and International Constraints," in *Afro-Marxist Regimes: Ideology and Public Policy*, ed. Edmond J. Keller and Donald Rothchild (Boulder, CO: Lynne Rienner Publishers, 1987), 288.

25. Walter Carlsnaes, *The Concept of Ideology and Political Analysis* (Westport, CT: Greenwood Press, 1981), 112.

26. Plato, *The Republic*, trans. Desmond Lee (London: Penguin Books, 1987), 263.

27. Lenin, *What Is to Be Done?*, 57.

28. Carlsnaes, *Ideology and Political Analysis*, 99.

29. John H. Kautsky, *Marxism and Leninism, Not Marxism-Leninism* (Westport, CT: Greenwood Press, 1994), 28.

30. Ibid., 55.

31. Scalapino, "Prelude to Marxism," 212.

32. Ibid., 211.

33. Rothchild and Foley, "Ideology and Policy," 288.

34. Ibid.

35. Rene Lefort, *Ethiopia: An Heretical Revolution?* trans. A. M. Berrett (London: Zed Press, 1981), 253.

36. Edward Shils, "The Intellectuals in the Political Development of the New States," *World Politics* 12, no. 3 (1960): 358.

37. Mohandas K. Gandhi, "A Rejoinder from M. K. Gandhi," in *Social and Religious Reform: The Hindus of British India*, ed. Amiya P. Sen (New Delhi: Oxford University Press, 2003), 200.

38. E. V. Ramasami Periyar, "Social Reform or Social Revolution?" in *Social and Religious Reform*, 71.

Chapter 6

1. Gérard Chaliand, *Revolution in the Third World* (New York: Penguin Books, 1977), 103.

2. Ibid.

3. Jeff Goodwin, *No Other Way Out: States and Revolutionary Movements, 1945–1991* (New York: Cambridge University Press, 2001), 9.

4. Ibid.

5. S. N. Eisenstadt, *Revolution and the Transformation of Societies: A Comparative Study of Civilizations* (New York: Free Press, 1978), xv.

6. Ibid., 2.

7. Ibid., 47.

8. Ibid., 202.

9. Hamid Enayat, "Revolution in Iran 1979: Religion as Political Ideology," in *Revolutionary Theory and Political Reality*, ed. Noel O'Sullivan (New York: St. Martin's Press, 1983), 200.

10. Ibid., 201.

11. Eisenstadt, *Revolution and Transformation of Societies*, 148.

12. Johnson, *Revolutionary Change*, 85.

13. Karl Marx, "Toward a Critique of Hegel's *Philosophy of Right*," in *Selected Writings*, ed. David McLellan (Oxford: Oxford University Press, 1977), 64.

14. Richard C. Salter, "Time, Authority, and Ethics in the Khmer Rouge: Elements of the Millennial Vision in Year Zero," in *Millennialism, Persecution, and Violence*, ed. Catherine Wessinger (New York: Syracuse University Press, 2000), 285.

15. Ibid.

16. Eisenstadt, *Revolution and Transformation of Societies*, 203–4.

17. Ibid., 261.

18. Ibid., 262.

19. Ibid., 117.

20. Ibid., 94.

21. Barrington Moore Jr., *Social Origins of Dictatorship and Democracy: Land and Peasant in the Making of the Modern World* (Boston: Beacon Press, 1966), 335.

22. Philip G. Altbach, "The International Student Movement," *Journal of Contemporary History* 5, no. 1 (1970): 165.

23. Eisenstadt, *Revolution and Transformation of Societies*, 128.

24. Frederic Wakeman Jr., *History and Will: Philosophical Perspectives of Mao Tse-tung's Thought* (Berkeley: University of California Press, 1973), 101.

25. Ibid., 102.

26. Ibid.

27. Cited in ibid., 99.

28. Merid Wolde Aregay, "Literary Origins of Ethiopian Millenarianism," in *Proceedings of the Ninth International Congress of Ethiopian Studies* (Moscow: Nauka Publishers, 1986), 5:164.

29. Patrick Gilkes, *The Dying Lion* (London: Julian Friedmann Publishers, 1975), 17.

30. Fred Halliday and Maxine Molyneux, *The Ethiopian Revolution* (London: Verso Editions and NLB, 1981), 14.

31. Eisenstadt, *Revolution and Transformation of Societies*, 332.

32. Cheikh Anta Diop, *The Cultural Unity of Negro Africa* (Paris: Presence Africaine, 1982), 182.

33. Tesfaye, "Marxism and Ethiopian Student Radicalism," 34.

34. For an extensive discussion on the notion of *idil*, see Messay, *Survival and Modernization—Ethiopia's Enigmatic Present*, 179–242.

35. Ibid., 50.

36. Kebede Mikael, *Ye Kine Azmara* [The Harvest of Poetry] (Addis Ababa: Berhanena Selam Press, 1956), 47–48 (my translation).

37. Heraclitus, "Fragments," in *The Presocratics*, ed. Philip Wheelwright (New York: Odyssey Press, 1966), 78.

38. Ibid., 71.

Chapter 7

1. Hannah Arendt, *On Revolution* (New York: Viking Press, 1963), 18.

2. Nicholas Berdyaev, *The Russian Revolution*, trans. D. B. (London: Sheed and Ward, 1931), 3.

3. Ibid., 10.

4. Ibid., 40.

5. Hagopian, *Phenomenon of Revolution*, 175.

6. Berdyaev, *Russian Revolution*, 10.

7. James H. Billington, *Fire in the Minds of Men: Origins of the Revolutionary Faith* (New York: Basic Books, 1980), 204.

8. Raymond Aron, *The Opium of the Intellectuals*, trans. Terence Kilmartin (New York: W. W. Norton and Company, 1962), 215.

9. Alexis de Tocqueville, *The Old Regime and the Revolution*, trans. Alan S. Kahan (Chicago: University of Chicago Press, 1998), 96.

10. Ibid.

11. Ibid.

12. Ibid., 206.

13. Ibid., 208.

14. Ibid., 101.

15. Ibid., 208.

16. Girma, "Education and Society," 76.

17. Siegfried Pausewang, "Report on a Research on the Social Situation of HSIU Students" (working paper, Department of Sociology and Anthropology, Haile Selassie I University, 1970), 3.

18. Girma, "Ethiopian Intelligentsia and Its Evolution," 12.

19. Unsigned letter, "The Day I Denied God, May 1, 2008, http://groups.yahoo.com/group/Addis-Ababa-university-alumi.com (May 6, 2008).

20. Aron, *Opium of the Intellectuals*, 257.

21. Ibid.

22. Girma, "Education and Society," 76.

23. Ibid., 77.

24. Ibid.

25. Balsvik, "Haile Selassie's Students," 491.

26. "Editorial: The National Democratic Revolution in Ethiopia," *Challenge* 12, no. 1 (1972): 7–8.

27. Ibid., 1.

28. Girma, "Education and Society," 78.

29. Cited in Colburn, *Vogue of Revolution*, 101.

30. "Editorial: Askedmo Ethiopiawinet Neber" [Ethiopianness Was First], *Addis Zemen*, March 16, 1975 (my translation).

31. Ibid.

32. Admasu Gebre Michael, "Cursed Be the Church!" *Struggle* 3, no. 1 (1968): 5.

33. "Editorial," *Struggle* 2, no. 2 (1968): 1.

34. Ibid.

35. Temesgen Haile, "A Deeper Look into Our Composition," *Struggle* (1966): 4.

36. "Editorial: Struggle for Progress," *Struggle*, no. 2 (1966): 1.

37. Arendt, *On Revolution*, 65.

38. "Struggle for Progress," 1.

39. Ibid.

40. Yohannes Berhane, "On Revolution in Religion," *Struggle* 2, no. 2 (1968): 4.

41. Ibid.

42. Ibid.

43. Germa Gebre Selassie, "ReChristianizing Christians?" *Struggle*, no. 2 (1967): 12.

44. Balsvik, *Haile Sellassie's Students*, 242.

45. Balsvik, "Haile Selassie's Students," 487.

46. Ibid.

47. Germa, "ReChristianizing Christians?" 12.

48. Ibid.

49. Haile M. Larebo, "Quest for Change: Haymanote-Abew Ethiopian Students' Association and the Ethiopian Orthodox Church, 1959–1974," in *Ethiopia in Broader Perspective: Papers of the 13th International Conference of Ethiopian Studies*, ed. Katsuyoshi Fukui, Eisei Kurimoto, and Masayoshi Shigeta (Kyoto: Shokado Book Sellers, 1997), 1:327.

50. Ibid., 328.

51. *Haimanote-Abew* Ethiopian Students' Association, "13th Year Seminar" (Addis Ababa, April 22–25, 1971), 4 (my translation).

52. Girma W. Aregay and Inde Mariam Tsega, "Yekolej Temarioch Ametawi Metsehet" [Annual Journal of *Haimanote-Abew* Ethiopian Students' Association], July 1960, 7 (my translation).

53. Ibid.

54. Ibid., 20 (my translation).

55. Haile, "Quest for Change," 331.

56. "Editorial: The Church the Social Pioneer," *Sutafe* 2, no. 2, n.d.: 1.

57. *Haimanote-Abew* Ethiopian Students' Association, "Resolutions: 15th Year Annual Conference" (Addis Ababa, April 16–20, 1974), 6.

58. Haile, "Quest for Change," 334.

59. Tim McDaniel, *Autocracy, Modernization, and Revolution in Russia and Iran* (Princeton: Princeton University Press, 1991), 216.

Chapter 8

1. Mazrui, *Political Values*, 370. See chapter 2 above.

2. Karl Marx and Friedrich Engels, "Manifesto of the Communist Party," *Basic Writings on Politics and Philosophy* (New York: Anchor Books, 1959), 9–10.

3. Colburn, *Vogue of Revolution*, 97.

4. See Messay, *Africa's Quest*, 108–9.

5. See ibid., 58.

6. Feuer, *Conflict of Generations*, 173.

7. Ibid.

8. Tesfaye, "Marxism and Ethiopian Student Radicalism," 33.

9. Feuer, *Conflict of Generations*, 10.

10. Ibid.

11. Ibid., 30.

12. Milton Mankoff and Richard Flacks, "The Changing Social Base of the American Student Movement," in *The New Pilgrims*, ed. Altbach and Laufer, 55–56.

13. Feuer, *Conflict of Generations*, p, 10.

14. Ibid., 20.

15. Ibid., 97.

16. Markakis and Nega, *Class and Revolution in Ethiopia*, 53–54.

17. "Editorial: The National Democratic Revolution in Ethiopia," *Challenge* 12, no. 1 (1972): 8.

18. Admasu, "Cursed Be the Church!" 5.

19. Feuer, *Conflict of Generations*, 12.

20. Ibid.

21. Ibid., 199.

22. Ibid., 218.

23. Ibid.

24. Ibid.

25. "We Look Forward," *Struggle* 2, no. 2 (1967): 11.

26. John Israel, "Reflections on the Modern Chinese Student Movement," in *Students in Revolt*, ed. Lipset and Altbach, 322.

27. "Editorial: Call for a Democratic Front," *Struggle* 2, no. 2 (1967): 1.

28. Feuer, *Conflict of Generations*, 91.

29. Amilcar Cabral, *Revolution in Guinea*, trans. and ed. Richard Handyside (New York: Monthly Review Press, 1972), 110.

30. Walleligne Mekonnen, "On the Question of Nationalities in Ethiopia," *Struggle* 5, no. 2 (1969): 4.

31. Gezahegn Bekele, "The New Generation," *Struggle* 3, no. 1 (1968): 13.

32. Ibid.

33. Thomas H. Greene, *Comparative Revolutionary Movements: Search for Theory and Justice* (Englewood Cliffs, NJ: Prentice Hall, 1990), 85.

34. Colburn, *Vogue of Revolution*, 5–6.

35. Parker, *Revolutions and History*, 150.

36. Lenin, *Imperialism*, 102.

37. Donham, *Marxist Modern*, 123.

38. Kautsky, *Marxism and Leninism, Not Marxism-Leninism*, 39.

39. Assefa Bequele and Eshetu Chole, "Toward a Strategy for Ethiopia," *Dialogue* 1, no. 2 (1968): 60.

40. Eshetu Chole, "The Mode of Production in Ethiopia and the Realities Thereof," *Challenge* 11, no. 3 (1971): 13.

41. Ibid. 17.

42. Ibid.

43. Marx and Engels, "Manifesto of the Communist Party," 26.

44. Hagos, "Bankruptcy of the Ethiopian 'Left,' " 113.

45. Ibid., 115.

46. "Editorial: Purge of Feudal Legacy," *Struggle* 5, no. 2 (1969): 1.

47. Balsvik, *Haile Sellassie's Students*, 266.

48. Donham, *Marxist Modern*, 130.

49. Walleligne, "Question of Nationalities in Ethiopia," 5.

50. Ibid., 7.

51. Abdul Mejid Hussein, "Ethiopia and Ethiopianism," *Struggle* 3, no. 1 (1968): 9.

52. Ibid.

53. Iob Tadesse, *Struggle* 3, no. 1 (1968): 15.

54. Girma, "Ethiopian Intelligentsia and Its Evolution," 12.

55. Andargachew Tsege, *Netsanet Yemayawk Netsa Awtchi* [A Liberator with No Knowledge of Freedom] (n.p., 1997), 19 (my translation).

Chapter 9

1. Fentahun Tiruneh, *The Ethiopian Students: Their Struggle to Articulate the Ethiopian Revolution* (Chicago: Nyala Type, 1990), 40.

2. Norman Long, *An Introduction to the Sociology of Rural Development* (London: Tavistock Publications, 1977), 59. For further discussion on this point, see Messay Kebede, "The Philosophical Platform of Modernity," *Meaning and Development* (Amsterdam: Rodopi, 1994).

3. Johnson, *Revolutionary Change*, 31.

4. Ibid., 19.

5. Jack A. Goldstone, "Theories of Revolution: The Third Generation," *World Politics* 32, no. 3 (1980): 428.

6. Johnson, *Revolutionary Change*, 65.

7. Skocpol, *States and Social Revolutions*, 12.

8. Balsvik, *Haile Sellassie's Students*, 46.

9. Donald K. Emmerson, "Conclusion," in *Students and Politics in Developing Nations*, ed. Donald K. Emmerson (New York: Praeger Publishers, 1968), 396.

10. Balsvik, *Haile Sellassie's Students*, 35.

11. Ibid., 31.

12. Ibid., 32.

13. Ibid.

14. Ibid., 34.

15. Altbach, "Students and Politics," 81.

16. Girma, "Education and Society," 73.

17. Balsvik, *Haile Sellassie's Students*, 31.

18. Ibid.

19. Girma, "Education and Society," 73.

20. Ibid., 74.

21. Ibid.

22. Mulatu Wubneh and Yohannis Abate, *Ethiopia*, 37.

23. Balsvik, *Haile Sellassie's Students*, 198.

24. Ibid., 199.

25. Addis H., "Political Vocation," 48–49.

26. Rickard, "Ethiopian Student and Ethiopia's Transition," 66.

27. Balsvik, *Haile Sellassie's Students*, 201.

28. Asafa Jalata, *Oromia and Ethiopia: State Formation and Ethnonational Conflict, 1868–1992* (Boulder, CO: Lynne Rienner Publishers, 1993), 115.

29. Mekuria Bulcha, "Modern Education and Social Movements in the Development of Political Consciousness: The Case of the Oromo," *African Sociological Review* 1, no. 1 (1997): 48.

30. For more on the southern expansion, see Messay, *Survival and Modernization— Ethiopia's Enigmatic Present.*

31. Kiflu, *The Generation*, 53.

32. "Elections in the University," *Struggle* 3, no. 1 (1968): 4.

33. Rickard, "Ethiopian Student and Ethiopia's Transition," 76.

34. Ethiopian Students Union in North America, "The National Question and Revolution in Ethiopia," *Challenge* 14, no. 1 (1975): 30.

35. Tekeste, *Rethinking Education in Ethiopia*, 79.

36. Lefort, *Ethiopia: An Heretical Revolution?*, 42.

37. Balsvik, *Haile Sellassie's Students*, 284.

38. Bahru Zewde, "Hayla-Sellase: From Progressive to Reactionary," in *Ethiopia in Change*, ed. Abebe Zegeye and Siegfried Pausewang (London: British Academic Press, 1994), 41.

39. Parsa, *States, Ideologies, and Social Revolutions*, 116.

40. Ibid., 107.

41. Goodwin, *No Other Way Out*, 48.

42. Girma, "Education and Society," 78.

43. Gebru, "Emergence of the Ethiopian 'Left,'" 82.

44. Tocqueville, *Old Regime and the Revolution*, 197.

45. Mesfin Wolde-Mariam, "The Role of Universities in Underdeveloped Countries," *Dialogue* 1, no. 2 (1968): 4.

46. Ibid., 13.

47. Ibid.

48. Ibid., 16.

49. Bisrat Dilnessahu, "The University and Knowledge versus Value and the Normative Order," *Dialogue* 1, no. 2 (1968): 22.

50. Ibid., 26.

51. Ibid., 27.

52. Abebe Ambatchew, "Academic Freedom in a University of a Developing Country," *Dialogue* 1, no. 1 (1968): 28.

53. Mazrui, *Political Values*, 262.

54. Koehn and Hayes, "Student Politics in Traditional Monarchies," 42.

55. Randi Rønning Balsvik, "An Important Root of the Ethiopian Revolution: The Student Movement," in *Ethiopia in Change: Peasantry, Nationalism, and Democracy*, 90.

56. Ghelawdewos, *Ethiopia*, 66.

57. Legesse Lemma, "The Ethiopian Student Movement, 1960–1974: A Challenge to the Monarchy and Imperialism in Ethiopia," *Northeast African Studies* 1, no. 1 (1979): 35.

58. Balsvik, "Root of the Ethiopian Revolution," 90.

Conclusion

1. Aimé Césaire, "The Man of Culture and His Responsibilities," *Présence Africaine* 24–25 (1959): 129–30.

2. *Senamirmir*, "Interview with Dr. Getatchew Haile," http://www.senamirmir.com/interviews/theme/5-2001/gh/cup.html (accessed April 18, 2008).

3. Rene Descartes, "Discourse on the Method," in *Descartes: Philosophical Writings*, ed. Elizabeth Anscombe and Peter Thomas Geach (Indianapolis: Bobbs-Merrill Educational Publishing, 1971), 46.

4. G. W. F. Hegel, *The Philosophy of History*, trans. J. Sibree (New York: Dover Publications, 1956), 56.

5. Ibid., 99.

6. Immanuel Kant, *Critique of Pure Reason*, trans. Norman Kemp Smith (New York: St. Martin's Press, 1965), 20.

7. Karl Marx and Friedrich Engels, *The German Ideology* (New York: International Publishers, 1965), 14.

8. For more discussion, see Messay, *Africa's Quest*.

9. Tekeste, *Crisis of Ethiopian Education*, 8.

10. Tibebe Eshete, "Education, Modernity, and Revival Movements: Making Sense of the Pentecostal Movement in Ethiopia" (paper presented at the Workshop on Education and Social Change in Ethiopia, Dayton, Ohio, May 13–14, 2006), 1.

11. For further reading on this point, see Messay, *Survival and Modernization—Ethiopia's Enigmatic Present*, 76–87.

Glossary

Aksumite civilization: Ancient and powerful civilization that flourished in northern Ethiopia and whose capital was the town of Aksum

Amhara: Ethnic group primarily located in the central highlands of Ethiopia. The Amhara, who make up approximately 30 percent of the population, speak Amharic and dominated the country's political and economic life until the fall of the Derg in 1991.

Amharic: Official language of Ethiopia

Challenge: Journal of the Ethiopian Students Union of North America

debtera: Scholar of the traditional system who was also teacher

Derg: Term meaning committee or council, it is the popular designation for the Provisional Military Administrative Council (PMAC), which ruled Ethiopia from 1974 to 1991. The Derg overthrew the monarchy and implemented a radical program of socialist transformation. Originally composed of 120 members, none of its members was above the rank of major.

Dialogue: Journal of Ethiopian University Teachers' Association

Geez: Ancient tongue of the kingdom of Aksum and the main language of the Ethiopian Church

Gurage: Ethnic group living in southwest Ethiopia

Kibre Negast: Book compiled early in the fourteenth century and considered to be Ethiopia's most important literary work. Translated as the "Glory of the Kings," it relates, among other things, the Solomonic descent of Ethiopian kings.

Oromo: Ethnic group located in eastern and southern Ethiopia, considered to be the largest in the country. They were conquered and incorporated into the Ethiopian Empire by Menelik II (r. 1889–1913).

Showa: Locale in the southern part of Amhara region that has produced the most influential elite of modern Ethiopia. Both Emperors Menelik II and Haile Selassie I were from Showa.

Sidama: Ethnic group living in southern Ethiopia

Struggle: Journal of the University Students' Union of Addis Ababa

Tigreans: Ethnic group living in northern Ethiopia where the ancient Aksumite kingdom flourished. Tigreans and Amharas share the same culture and have a long history of political rivalry.

Wellamo: Ethnic group located in southern Ethiopia

Bibliography

Abdul Mejid Hussein. "Ethiopia and Ethiopianism." *Struggle* 3, no. 1 (1968): 9–11.

Abebe Ambatchew. "Academic Freedom in a University of a Developing Country." *Dialogue* 1, no. 1 (1968): 28–36.

Addis Alemayehu. *Ye Timirtna Yetemaribet Tirgum* [The Meaning of Education and School]. Addis Ababa: Artistic Press, 1956.

Addis Hiwet. "A Certain Political Vocation: Reflections on the Ethiopian Intelligentsia." In *The Ethiopian Revolution and Its Impact on the Politics of the Horn of Africa: Proceedings of the 2nd International Conference on the Horn of Africa*, 41–64. New York: New School for Social Research, 1987.

Addis Zemen. "Askedmo Ethiopiawinet Neber" [Ethiopianness Was First]. March 16, 1975.

Admasu Gebre Michael. "Cursed Be the Church!" *Struggle* 3, no. 1 (1968): 5.

Altbach, Philip G. "The International Student Movement." *Journal of Contemporary History* 5, no. 1 (1970): 156–74.

———. "Students and Politics." In *Student Politics*, edited by Seymour M. Lipset, 74–93. New York: Basic Books, 1967.

Andargachew Asseged. *Beatcher Yeteketche Rejim Guzo* [The Truncated Long Journey]. Addis Ababa: Central Printing Press, 2000.

Andargachew Tscge. *Netsanet Yemayawk Netsa Awtchi.* [A Liberator with No Knowledge of Freedom]. N.p., 1997.

Andreski, Stanislav. *The African Predicament: A Study in the Pathology of Modernization.* New York: Atherton Press, 1968.

Arendt, Hannah. *On Revolution.* New York: Viking Press, 1963.

Aristotle. "Rhetoric." In *The Basic Works of Aristotle*. Translated by W. Rhys Roberts, 1318–1451. New York: Random House, 1941.

Aron, Raymond. *The Opium of the Intellectuals.* Translated by Terence Kilmartin. New York: W. W. Norton and Company, 1962.

———. "Student Rebellion: Vision of the Future or Echo from the Past?" In *The Seeds of Politics: Youth and Politics in America*, edited by Anthony M. Orum, 327–44. Englewood Cliffs, NJ: Prentice Hall, 1972.

Asafa Jalata. *Oromia and Ethiopia: State Formation and Ethnonational Conflict, 1868–1992.* Boulder, CO: Lynne Rienner Publishers, 1993.

Asres Yenesew (Aleqa). *Tekami Mikre* [*Useful Advice*] Addis Ababa: Berhanena Selam Printing Press, 1956.

Assefa Bequele and Eshetu Chole. "Toward a Strategy for Ethiopia." *Dialogue* 1, no. 2 (1968): 56–60.

Atieno-Odhiambo, E. S. "From African Historiographies to an African Philosophy of History." In *Africanizing Knowledge*, edited by Toyin Falola and Christian Jennings, 13–42. New Brunswick, NJ: Transaction Publishers, 2002.

Bahru Zewde. "Hayla-Sellase: From Progressive to Reactionary." In *Ethiopia in Change*, edited by Abebe Zegeye and Siegfried Pausewang, 31–44. London: British Academic Press, 1994.

———. "The Intellectual and the State in Twentieth Century Ethiopia." In *New Trends in Ethiopian Studies: Papers of the 12th International Conference of Ethiopian Studies*, edited by Harold G. Marcus, 1:483–96. Lawrenceville, NJ: Red Sea Press, 1994.

———. *Pioneers of Change in Ethiopia*. Oxford: James Currey, 2002.

Balsvik, Randi Rønning. "Haile Selassie's Students: Rise of Social and Political Consciousness." PhD diss., University of Tromsø, Norway, 1979.

———. *Haile Sellassie's Students: The Intellectuals and Social Background to Revolution, 1952–1977*. East Lansing: Michigan State University, 1985.

———. "An Important Root of the Ethiopian Revolution: The Student Movement." In *Ethiopia in Change*, edited by Abebe Zegeye and Siegfried Pausewang, 77–94. London: British Academic Press, 1994.

Berdyaev, Nicholas. *The Russian Revolution*. Translated by D. B. London: Sheed and Ward, 1931.

Beseat Kifle Selassie. "Class Struggle or Jockeying for Position? A Review of Ethiopian Student Movements from 1900 to 1975." In *The Role of African Student Movements in the Political and Social Evolution of Africa from 1900 to 1975*, 157–74. Paris: UNESCO Publishing, 1994.

Billington, James H. *Fire in the Minds of Men: Origins of the Revolutionary Faith*. New York: Basic Books, 1980.

Bisrat Dilnessahu. "The University and Knowledge versus Value and the Normative Order." *Dialogue* 1, no. 2 (1968): 17–26.

Blyden, Edward W. *Christianity, Islam, and the Negro Race*. Edinburgh: Edinburgh University Press, 1967.

Boudon, Raymond. "Sources of Student Protest in France." In *The New Pilgrims: Youth Protest in Transition*, edited by Philip G. Altbach and Robert S. Laufer, 297–310. New York: David McKay Company, 1972.

Burstein, Stanley. *Ancient African Civilizations: Kush and Axum*. Princeton: Markus Wiener Publishers, 1998.

Cabral, Amilcar. *Revolution in Guinea*. Translated and edited by Richard Handyside. New York: Monthly Review Press, 1972.

Carlsnaes, Walter. *The Concept of Ideology and Political Analysis*. Westport, CT: Greenwood Press, 1981.

Cassiers, Anne, and Jean-Michel Bessette. *Mémoires Ethiopiennes*. Paris: L'Harmattan, 2001.

Césaire, Aimé. "The Man of Culture and His Responsibilities." *Présence Africaine* 24–25 (1959): 123–32

Chaliand, Gérard. *Revolution in the Third World*. New York: Penguin Books, 1977.

Challenge. "Editorial: The Spirit of Solidarity." vol. 6, no. 1 (1966): 1–3

———. "The National Democratic Revolution in Ethiopia." *Challenge* 12, no. 1 (1972): 1–9.

Colburn, Forrest D. *The Vogue of Revolution in Poor Countries*. Princeton: Princeton University Press, 1994.

Coleman, James S. *Nigeria: Background to Nationalism.* Berkeley: University of California Press, 1958.

Cotton, James. "The Chinese Revolution and the Chinese Tradition of Political Thought." In *Revolutionary Theory and Political Reality*, edited by Noel O' Sullivan, 118–36. New York: St. Martin's Press, 1983.

"The Day I Denied God." Online posting. May 6, 2008. http://groups.yahoo.com/group/Addis-Ababa-university-alumni.com

Descartes, Rene. "Discourse on the Method." In *Descartes: Philosophical Writings*, edited by Elizabeth Anscombe and Peter Thomas Geach, 7–57. Indianapolis: Bobbs-Merrill Educational Publishing, 1971.

Diop, Cheikh Anta. *The Cultural Unity of Negro Africa.* Paris: Presence Africaine, 1982.

Donham, Donald L. *Marxist Modern: An Ethnographic History of the Ethiopian Revolution.* Berkeley: University of California Press, 1999.

Eadie, J. I., Major. *An Amharic Reader.* Cambridge: Cambridge University Press, 1924.

Eisenstadt, S. N. *Revolution and the Transformation of Societies: A Comparative Study of Civilizations.* New York: Free Press, 1978.

Ellis, Gene. "The Feudal Paradigm as a Hindrance to Understanding Ethiopia." *Journal of Modern African Studies* 14, no. 2 (1976): 275–95.

Emmerson, Donald K. "Conclusion." In *Students and Politics in Developing Nations*, edited by Donald K. Emmerson, 390–426. New York: Praeger Publishers, 1968.

Enayat, Hamid. "Revolution in Iran 1979: Religion as Political Ideology." In *Revolutionary Theory and Political Reality*, edited by Noel O'Sullivan, 191–206. New York: St. Martin's Press, 1983.

Eshetu Chole. "The Mode of Production in Ethiopia and the Realities Thereof." *Challenge* 11, no. 3 (1971): 3–19.

Ethiopian Students Union in North America. "The National Question and Revolution in Ethiopia." *Challenge* 14, no. 1 (1975): 6–65.

Fentahun Tiruneh. *The Ethiopian Students: Their Struggle to Articulate the Ethiopian Revolution.* Chicago: Nyala Type, 1990.

Feuer, Lewis S. *The Conflict of Generations: The Character and Significance of Student Movements.* New York: Basic Books, 1969.

Flacks, Richard. "The Liberated Generation: An Exploration of the Roots of Student Protest." In *The Seeds of Politics: Youth and Politics in America*, edited by Anthony M. Orum, 353–64. Englewood Cliffs, NJ: Prentice Hall, 1972.

Gandhi, Mohandas K. "A Rejoinder from M. K. Gandhi." In *Social and Religious Reform: The Hindus of British India*, edited by Amiya P. Sen, 199–201. New Delhi: Oxford University Press, 2003.

Gebru Mersha. "The Emergence of the Ethiopian 'Left' in the Period 1960–1970 as an Aspect of the Formation of the 'Organic Intellectuals.'" In *The Ethiopian Revolution and Its Impact on the Politics on the Horn of Africa: Proceedings of the 2nd International Conference on the Horn of Africa*, 71–84. New York: New School for Social Research, 1987.

Germa Amare, Abraham Demoz, and Aba Gebre Egziabher Degou. "Education Sector Review: Educational Objectives." Interim draft paper, Addis Ababa, n.d.

Germa Gebre Selassie. "ReChristianizing Christians?" *Struggle* 2, no. 2 (1967).

Gezahegn Bekele. "The New Generation." *Struggle* 3, no. 1 (1968): 13.

Ghelawdewos Araia. *Ethiopia: The Political Economy of Transition.* Lanham, MD: University Press of America, 1995.

Gilkes, Patrick. *The Dying Lion.* London: Julian Friedmann Publishers, 1975.

Girma Amare. "Education and Society in Prerevolutionary Ethiopia." *Northeast African Studies* 6, nos. 1–2 (1984): 61–79.

———. "The Modern Ethiopian Intelligentsia and Its Evolution." Paper prepared for the Interdisciplinary Seminar of the Faculties of Arts and Education of Haile Selassie I University, 1967.

Girma W. Aregay and Inde Mariam Tsega. "Yekolej Temarioch Ametawi Metsehet" [Annual Journal of Haimanote-Abew Ethiopian Students' Association], July 1960, 7.

Goldstone, Jack A. "Theories of Revolution: The Third Generation." *World Politics* 32, no. 3 (1980): 425–53.

Goodwin, Jeff. *No Other Way Out: States and Revolutionary Movements, 1945–1991.* New York: Cambridge University Press, 2001.

Greene, Thomas H. *Comparative Revolutionary Movements: Search for Theory and Justice.* Englewood Cliffs, NJ: Prentice Hall, 1990.

Greenfield, Richard. *Ethiopia: A New Political History.* London: Pall Mall Press, 1965.

Guebre-Heywet Baykedagne. *L'empereur Menelik et L'Ethiopie.* Addis Abeba and Paris, Maison des Etudes Ethiopiennes, Institut National des Langues et Civilisations Orientales, 1993.

Hagopian, Mark N. *The Phenomenon of Revolution.* New York: Dodd, Mead and Company, 1974.

Hagos Gebre Yesus. "The Bankruptcy of the Ethiopian 'Left' Meisone-EPRP, a Two Headed Hydra: A Commentary on the Ideology and Politics of National Nihilism." In *The Ethiopian Revolution and Its Impact on the Politics on the Horn of Africa: Proceedings of the 2nd International Conference on the Horn of Africa*, 113–19. New York: New School for Social Research, 1987.

Haile M. Larebo. "Quest for Change: Haymanote-Abew Ethiopian Students' Association and the Ethiopian Orthodox Church, 1959–1974." In *Ethiopia in Broader Perspective: Papers of the 13th International Conference of Ethiopian Studies,* edited by Katsuyoshi Fukui, Eisei Kurimoto, and Masayoshi Shigeta, 1:326—37. Kyoto: Shokado Book Sellers, 1997.

Haile Selassie. *Selected Speeches of His Imperial Majesty Haile Selassie I, 1918 to 1967.* Addis Ababa: Artistic Printers Ltd., 1967.

Haimanote-Abew Ethiopian Students' Association. "Resolutions: 15th Year Annual Conference," Addis Ababa, Ethiopia, April 16–20, 1974.

———. "13th Year Seminar" (1971): 4

Halliday, Fred, and Maxine Molyneux. *The Ethiopian Revolution.* London: Verso Editions and NLB, 1981.

Hegel, G. W. F. *The Philosophy of History.* Translated by J. Sibree. New York: Dover Publications, 1956.

Heraclitus. "Fragments." In *The Presocratics*, edited by Philip Wheelwright, 95–98. New York: Odyssey Press, 1966.

Huntington, Samuel P. *Political Order in Changing Societies.* New Haven: Yale University Press, 1968.

Iob Tadesse. "Editorial," *Struggle* 3, no. 1 (1968): 15.

Israel, John. "Reflections on the Modern Chinese Student Movement." In *Students in Revolt*, edited by Seymour Martin Lipset and Philip G. Altbach, 310–33. Boston: Houghton Mifflin Company, 1969.

Johnson, Chalmers. *Revolutionary Change*. Boston: Little, Brown, and Company, 1966.

Kant, Immanuel. *Critique of Pure Reason*. Translated by Norman Kemp Smith. New York: St. Martin's Press, 1965.

Katz, Mark N. *Reflections on Revolutions*. New York: St. Martin's Press, 1999.

Kautsky, John H. *Marxism and Leninism, Not Marxism-Leninism*. Westport, CT: Greenwood Press, 1994.

Kebede Mikael. *Ethiopia and Western Civilization*. Translated by Marcel Hassid. N.p., 1949.

———. *Ye Kine Azmara* [The Harvest of Poetry]. Addis Ababa: Berhanena Selam Press, 1956.

Keenleyside, Hugh L., and A. F. Thomas. *History of Japanese Education and Present Educational System*. Tokyo: Hokuseido Press, 1937.

Kiflu Tadesse. *The Generation: The History of the Ethiopian People's Revolutionary Party*. Silver Spring, MD: Independent Publishers, 1993.

Koehn, Peter, and Louis D. Hayes. "Student Politics in Traditional Monarchies: A Comparative Analysis of Ethiopia and Nepal." *Journal of Asian and African Studies* 13, nos. 1–2 (1978): 33–49.

Kotchy, B. "The Cultural Dimensions of FEANF." In *The Role of African Student Movements in the Political and Social Evolution of Africa from 1900 to 1975*, 95—108. Paris: UNESCO Publishing, 1994.

Lefort, Rene. *Ethiopia: An Heretical Revolution?* Translated by A. M. Berrett. London: Zed Press, 1981.

Legesse Lemma. "The Ethiopian Student Movement, 1960–1974: A Challenge to the Monarchy and Imperialism in Ethiopia." *Northeast African Studies* 1, no. 1 (1979): 31–46.

Lenin, V. I. *Imperialism: The Highest Stage of Capitalism*. New York: International Publishers, 1972.

———. "The Three Sources and Three Component Parts of Marxism." In *The Lenin Anthology*, edited by Robert C. Tucker, 640–44. New York: W. W. Norton and Company, 1975.

———. *What Is to Be Done?* New York: International Publishers, 1929.

Lipset, Seymour Martin. "University Students and Politics in Underdeveloped Countries." In *Student Politics*, edited by Seymour M. Lipset, 3–53. New York: Basic Books, 1967.

Long, Norman. *An Introduction to the Sociology of Rural Development*. London: Tavistock Publications, 1977.

Makonnen Bishaw. E-mail interview by author, September 29, 2004.

Mankoff, Milton, and Richard Flacks. "The Changing Social Base of the American Student Movement." In *The New Pilgrims: Youth Protest in Transition*, edited by Philip G. Altbach and Robert S. Laufer, 46–62. New York: David McKay Company, 1972.

Mannheim, Karl. "The Problem of Generations." In *The New Pilgrims: Youth Protest in Transition*, edited by Philip G. Altbach and Robert S. Laufer, 101–38. New York: David McKay Company, 1972.

Mao Tse-tung. "The Role of the Chinese Communist Party in the National War." In *Selected Works*, 2:244–61. New York: International Publishers, 1954.

Markakis, John, and Nega Ayele. *Class and Revolution in Ethiopia.* Trenton, NJ: Red Sea Press, 1986.

Marx, Karl. "Toward a Critique of Hegel's *Philosophy of Right.*" In *Selected Writings*, edited by David McLellan, 63–74. Oxford: Oxford University Press, 1977.

Marx, Karl, and Friedrich Engels. *The German Ideology*, edited by R. Pascal. New York: International Publishers, 1965.

———. "Manifesto of the Communist Party." In *Basic Writings on Politics and Philosophy*, edited by Lewis S. Feuer, 1–41. New York: Anchor Books, 1959.

Mazrui, Ali A. *Political Values and the Educated Class in Africa.* Berkeley: University of California Press, 1978.

M'Bow, Amadou-Mahtar. "Opening Speech." In *African Education and Identity*, edited by Abiola Irele, 11–15. London: Hans Zell Publishers, 1992.

McClelland, David C. "The Achievement Motive in Economic Growth." In *Development and Underdevelopment*, edited by Mitchell A. Seligson and John T. Passé-Smith, 141–57. Boulder, CO: Lynne Rienner Publishers, 1998.

McDaniel, Tim. *Autocracy, Modernization, and Revolution in Russia and Iran.* Princeton: Princeton University Press, 1991.

Mekuria Bulcha. "Modern Education and Social Movements in the Development of Political Consciousness: The Case of the Oromo." *African Sociological Review* 1, no. 1 (1997): 30–65.

Melesse Ayalew. "Editorial." *Challenge* 5, no. 1 (1965): 1–3.

Merid Wolde Aregay. "Literary Origins of Ethiopian Millenarianism." In *Proceedings of the Ninth International Congress of Ethiopian Studies*, 5:161—73. Moscow: Nauka Publishers, 1986.

Mesfin Wolde-Mariam. "The Role of Universities in Underdeveloped Countries." *Dialogue* 1, no. 2 (1968): 3–16.

Messay Kebede. *Africa's Quest for a Philosophy of Decolonization.* New York: Rodopi, 2004.

———. *Meaning and Development.* Amsterdam: Rodopi, 1994.

———. *Survival and Modernization—Ethiopia's Enigmatic Present: A Philosophical Discourse.* Lawrenceville, NJ: Red Sea Press, 1999.

Moore, Barrington, Jr. *Social Origins of Dictatorship and Democracy: Land and Peasant in the Making of the Modern World.* Boston: Beacon Press, 1966.

Mulatu Wubneh and Yohannis Abate. *Ethiopia: Transition and Development in the Horn of Africa.* Boulder, CO: Westview Press, 1988.

Mulugeta Wodajo. "Postwar Reform in Ethiopian Education." *Comparative Education Review* 2, no. 3 (1959): 24–30.

Ottaway, Marina, and David Ottaway. *Ethiopia: Empire in Revolution.* New York: Africana Publishing Company, 1978.

Pankhurst, Sylvia. *Ethiopia: A Cultural History.* Essex, UK: Lalibela House, 1955.

Parker, Noel. *Revolutions and History: An Essay in Interpretation.* Malden, MA: Blackwell Publishers, 1999.

Parsa, Misagh. *States, Ideologies, and Social Revolutions: A Comparative Analysis of Iran, Nicaragua, and the Philippines.* Cambridge: Cambridge University Press, 2000.

Paulos Milkias. *Haile Selassie, Western Education, and Political Revolution in Ethiopia.* New York: Cambria Press, 2006.

———. "The Political Spectrum of Western Education in Ethiopia." *Journal of African Studies* 9, no. 1 (1982): 22–29.

———. "Traditional Institutions and Traditional Elites: The Role of Education in the Ethiopian Body-Politic." *African Studies Review* 19, no. 3 (1976): 70–93.

Pausewang, Siegfried. "Report on a Research on the Social Situation of HSIU Students." Working paper, Department of Sociology and Anthropology, Haile Selassie I University, 1970.

Periyar Ramasami, E. V. "Social Reform or Social Revolution?" In *Social and Religious Reform*, edited by Amiya P. Sen, 69–72. New Delhi: Oxford University Press, 2003.

Plato. *The Republic.* Translated by Desmond Lee. London: Penguin Books, 1987.

Read, Margaret. "Cultural Contacts in Education." In *Education and Nation-Building in Africa*, edited by L. Gray Cowan, James O'Connell, and David G. Scanlon, 351–62. New York: Praeger Publishers, 1965.

Rickard, Sandra. "The Ethiopian Student and Ethiopia's Transition into the Twentieth Century." Paper submitted in partial fulfillment of the requirements of the Student Project for Amity among Nations, University of Minnesota, 1967.

Rothchild, Donald, and Michael Foley. "Ideology and Policy in Afro-Marxist Regimes: The Effort to Cope with Domestic and International Constraints." *Afro-Marxist Regimes: Ideology and Public Policy*, edited by Edmond J. Keller and Donald Rothchild, 281–321. Boulder, CO: Lynne Rienner Publishers, 1987.

Royal Chronicle of Abyssinia. *The Glorious Victory of Amda Seyon, King of Ethiopia.* Translated and edited by G. W. B. Huntingford. Oxford: Clarendon Press, 1965.

Salter, Richard C. "Time, Authority, and Ethics in the Khmer Rouge: Elements of the Millennial Vision in Year Zero." *Millennialism, Persecution, and Violence*, edited by Catherine Wessinger, 281–98. New York: Syracuse University Press, 2000.

Scalapino, Robert A. "Prelude to Marxism: The Chinese Student Movement in Japan, 1900–1910." In *Approaches to Modern Chinese History*, edited by Albert Feuerwerker, Rhoads Murphey, Mary C. Wright, 190–215. Berkeley: University of California Press, 1967.

Scanlon, David G., and L. Gray Cowan. Preface to *Traditional Ethiopian Church Education*, v–ix. New York: Teachers College Press, 1970.

Senamirmir. "Interview with Dr. Getatchew Haile." http://www.senamirmir.com/interviews/theme/5-2001/gh/cup.html (accessed April 18, 2008).

Senghor, Léopold Sédar. *Prose and Poetry.* Translated by John Reed and Clive Wake. London: Heinemann, 1976.

Shils, Edward. "Dreams of Plenitude, Nightmares of Scarcity." In *Students in Revolt*, edited by Seymour Martin Lipset and Philip G. Altbach, 1–31. Boston: Houghton Mifflin Company, 1969.

———. "The Intellectuals in the Political Development of the New States." *World Politics* 12, no. 3 (1960): 329–68.

Skocpol, Theda. *States and Social Revolutions: A Comparative Analysis of France, Russia, and China.* New York: Cambridge University Press, 1980.

Snow, Edgar. "Days in Changsha." In *When Men Revolt—and Why*, edited by James Chowning Davies, 73–78. New York: Free Press, 1971.

Soedjatmoko. *Development in the Non-Western World.* Tokyo: University of Tokyo Press, 1982.

Struggle. "Call for a Democratic Front," vol. 2, no. 2 (1967): 1–2.

———. "Editorial," vol. 2, no. 2 (1968): 1.

———. "Elections in the University," vol. 3, no. 1 (1968): 4.

———. "Purge of Feudal Legacy," vol. 5, no. 2 (1969): 1.

Struggle. "Struggle for Progress," no. 2 (1966): 1.

———. "We Look Forward," vol. 2, no. 2 (1967): 11.

Sutafe. "The Church the Social Pioneer," vol. 2, no. 2 (n.d.): 1.

Taylor, Edward B. *The Origins of Culture.* New York: Harper Torchbooks, 1958.

Tekeste Negash. *The Crisis of Ethiopian Education: Some Implications for Nation-Building.* Uppsala, Sweden: Uppsala University, 1990.

———. *Rethinking Education in Ethiopia.* Uppsala, Sweden: Nordiska Afrikainstitutet, 1996.

Temesgen Haile. "A Deeper Look into Our Composition." *Struggle* (1966): 4.

Tesfaye Demmellash. "On Marxism and Ethiopian Student Radicalism in North America." *Monthly Review* 35, no. 9 (1984): 25–37.

Teshale Tibebu. *The Making of Modern Ethiopia, 1896–1974.* Lawrenceville, NJ: Red Sea Press, 1995.

Teshome G. Wagaw. *Education in Ethiopia.* Ann Arbor: University of Michigan Press, 1979.

Tocqueville, Alexis de. *The Old Regime and the Revolution.* Translated by Alan S. Kahan. Chicago: University of Chicago Press, 1998.

Todd, Allan. *Revolutions, 1789–1917.* Cambridge: Cambridge University Press, 1998.

Tokiomi, Kaigo. *Japanese Education: Its Past and Present.* Tokyo: Kokusai Bunka Shinkokai, 1968.

Wakeman, Frederic, Jr. *History and Will: Philosophical Perspectives of Mao Tse-tung's Thought.* Berkeley: University of California Press, 1973.

Walleligne Mekonen. "On the Question of Nationalities in Ethiopia." *Struggle* 5, no.2 (1969): 4–7.

Yohannes Berhane. "On Revolution in Religion." *Struggle* 2, no. 2 (1968): 4.

Index

superiority, 42, 92, 129, 141, 142, 155. *See also* West
survival, 4, 24, 40, 51, 52, 89, 110, 111, 136, 160, 194
Sutafe, 135, 137
Sweden, 27
system: capitalist, 141; caste, 12, 101, 109; educational, 3, 4, 19, 21, 33, 34, 38, 42, 46, 48, 49, 53, 54, 55, 56, 57, 59, 60, 61, 62, 68, 71, 75, 85, 90, 140, 163, 191, 192, 193, 195, 196; social, 10, 11, 12, 21, 52, 60, 73, 87, 94, 105, 108, 111, 112, 119, 141, 142, 152, 165, 167, 169; value, 23, 167, 168–69. *See also* education; society
systemness, 5

Tadesse Tamrat, 135
Tafari Makonnen Lyceum, 66
Tarike-Negest, 50
Taylor, Edward B., 5
teachers, 22, 47, 48, 52, 91, 171, 183, 189; foreign, 48; Western, 47, 70, 174, 190. *See also* school
technology, 39, 40, 53, 61, 66, 72, 73, 91, 98, 101, 136, 137, 189, 191, 193
Tekeste Negash, 46, 59, 178
tenancy, 27, 152
tenants, 27
Tesfaye Demmellash, 16–17, 92, 113
Teshome Wagaw, 48, 53–54
Testaments, Old and New, 50
textbooks, 48, 49, 50, 56, 57, 61, 70, 170, 190
theocracy, 111
theology, 50
theoreticians, 96, 122, 182
theorists, modernization, 39, 85
theories, 15, 17, 31, 32, 68, 69, 72, 79, 86, 87, 95, 96, 99, 107, 113, 128, 129, 130, 131, 140, 141, 153, 157, 160, 181, 189, 190, 192, 194; modernization, 84, 85, 90, 100, 166, 193; relative deprivation, 12, 166; social, 31, 96; value/system, 166; and practice, 44–45, 172, 174. *See also* Marxism-Leninism
therapy, 4, 15, 140, 181
Third World, 66, 111
thought, school of, 12, 166, 191
Tigray, 6, 15, 115, 153–54
Tigreans, 161, 175
Tilahun Gizaw, 15, 26, 177, 185

Tilly, Charles, 12
time, Ethiopian, 116–18
Tocqueville, Alexis de, 123–25, 182
Tokiomi, Kaigo, 61
traditionalism, 1
traditionality, 84, 126, 181, 195
traditions, 12, 16, 20, 43, 45, 49, 50, 54, 60, 62, 65, 66, 67, 69, 70, 74, 86, 92, 93, 101, 103, 107, 112, 115, 124, 139, 144, 155, 156, 157, 159, 188, 190, 193; and modernity, 44, 65, 71, 72, 84, 99, 191–92
transformation, 5, 24, 38, 120, 125, 140, 157, 164, 165, 168, 189
transition, 45, 64, 84, 98, 102, 119, 149, 159
trauma, 144, 153
traumatism, 154
tribalism, 162, 175, 176
tribes, 175
tutelage, 98
tutors, 64, 66, 96, 97, 99, 194
tutorship, 98–99
tyranny, 92, 105, 131, 150

underdevelopment, 44, 78, 134, 140
unemployment, 14, 22, 147, 148, 171
UNESCO, 55
union, labor, 9; citywide, 25–26
United States, 11, 49, 56, 69, 78, 80, 123, 144, 172–74
unity, Ethiopian, 52, 60, 60, 74, 152, 160, 176, 177, 178, 193; and struggle of opposites, 116, 118; student, 26, 113, 160, 177, 193. *See also* church; state
universalism, 76
universality, 71, 73, 78
universalization, 73
universities, 9, 11, 29, 30, 39–40, 56, 58, 80, 136, 170, 179, 182, 183, 184; African, 40; American, 13, 56, 80; Western, 81, 82, 84
University Women's Club, 29
untouchability, 101
uprootedness, 6, 44, 45, 61, 70, 74, 75, 103, 188
U.S., 172, 173. *See also* government; policy; United States
USUAA, 16, 26, 30, 74, 134
Utah, 56
utopia, 104, 112, 114, 122, 125, 127, 130

Rochester Studies in
African History and the Diaspora

During the 1960s and early 1970s, a majority of Ethiopian students and intellectuals adopted a Marxist-Leninist ideology with fanatic fervor. The leading force in an uprising against the imperial regime of Emperor Haile Selassie, they played a decisive role in the rise of a Leninist military regime. In this original study, Messay Kebede examines the sociopolitical and cultural factors that contributed to the radicalization of the educated elite in Ethiopia, and how this phenomenon contributed to the country's uninterrupted political crises and economic setbacks since the Revolution of 1974.

Offering a unique, insider's perspective garnered from his direct participation in the student movement, the author emphasizes the role of the Western education system in the progressive radicalization of students and assesses the impact of Western education on traditional cultures. The most comprehensive study of the role of students in modern Ethiopian political history to date, *Radicalism and Cultural Dislocation in Ethiopia, 1960–1974* opens the door for discussion and debate on the issue of African modernization and the effects of cultural colonization.

Messay Kebede is professor in the Department of Philosophy at the University of Dayton and is author of *Survival and Modernization—Ethiopia's Enigmatic Present: A Philosophical Discourse* (1999).

"In this engaging and necessary book, Messay Kebede boldly argues that Ethiopian intellectuals failed disastrously in their revolutionary métier for lack of originality, creativity, and authenticity. It is a stirring interpretation bound to delight and infuriate, but even those who disagree with its point of view will find much that is informative and illuminating. Extensive in analysis and unsparing in clarity, this is a work of impressive range and depth. It is hard to think of a more significant contribution on this highly controversial subject."

—Gebru Tareke, Professor of History,
Hobart and William Smith Colleges

"No one concerned with the fate of contemporary Ethiopia and indeed of the nature of modern revolutionary ideologies will want to miss this eye-opening account. Marshaling a trove of little-known data and a circumspect selection of theoretic insights, Messay Kebede offers an instant benchmark in the contemporary history of this troubled nation in his artfully crafted work."

—Donald N. Levine, Peter B. Ritzma Professor of Sociology,
University of Chicago, and author of *Greater Ethiopia*